Native America from Prehistory to First Contact

Other titles in ABC-CLIO's

TURNING POINTS—ACTUAL AND ALTERNATE HISTORIES

series

Colonial America from Settlement to the Revolution
Manifest Destiny and the Expansion of America
A House Divided during the Civil War Era
America in Revolt during the 1960s and 1970s
The Reagan Era

Books in the Turning Points—Actual and Alternate Histories series ask the question, What would have happened if . . . ? In a unique editorial format, each book examines a specific period in American history, presents the real, or actual, history, and then offers an alternate history—speculations from historical experts on what might have happened had the course of history turned.

If a particular event had turned out differently, history from that turning point forward could be affected. Important outcomes frequently hinge on an individual decision, an accidental encounter, a turn in the weather, the spread of a disease, or a missed piece of information. Such events stimulate our imagination, accentuating the role of luck, chance, and individual decision or character at particular moments in time. The examination of such key turning points is one of the reasons that the study of history is so fascinating.

For the student, examining alternate histories springing from turning points and exploring, What would have happened if . . . ? gives insight into many of the questions at the heart of our civilization today.

Native America
from Prehistory to First Contact

Rodney P. Carlisle and J. Geoffrey Golson, *Editors*

A B C  C L I O

Santa Barbara, California
Denver, Colorado
Oxford, England

Library of Congress Cataloging-in-Publication Data
Native America from prehistory to first contact / Rodney P. Carlisle and J. Geoffrey Golson, editors.
    p. cm. — (Turning points—actual and alternate histories)
    Includes bibliographical references and index.
    ISBN 1-85109-829-1 (hardcover : alk. paper) — ISBN 1-85109-830-5 (ebook)
1. Paleo-Indians—North America. 2. Indians of North America—First contact with Europeans. 3. Indians of North America—History. I. Carlisle, Rodney P. II. Golson, J. Geoffrey. III. Series: Turning points in history (Santa Barbara, Calif.)

E77.9.N37 2006
970.01—dc22   2006017673

11 10 09 08 07   10 9 8 7 6 5 4 3 2 1

ISBN 13: 978-1-85109-829-3   (ebook) 978-1-85109-830-9
ISBN 10: 1-85109-829-1   (ebook) 1-85109-830-5

Production Editor: Kristine Swift
Editorial Assistant: Alisha Martinez
Production Manager: Don Schmidt
Media Production Coordinator: Ellen Brenna Dougherty
Media Resources Manager: Caroline Price
File Manager: Paula Gerard
Text design: Devenish Design

This book is also available on the World Wide Web as an eBook. Visit http://www.abc-clio.com for details.

ABC-CLIO, Inc.
130 Cremona Drive, P.O. Box 1911
Santa Barbara, California 93116-1911

This book is printed on acid-free paper ∞

Manufactured in the United States of America

Contents

7 First Contacts 123

TURNING POINT

European diseases took a heavy toll on Native Americans. What if the situation had been reversed and European explorers were decimated by diseases from Native Americans?

8 First Settlements 143

TURNING POINT

The first settlements by whites often failed from an inability to adapt to the new environment. What if settlers adopted Native lifestyles and the first settlements were peaceful and successful?

Appendix
Native American Myths, Narratives, and Songs 161

Contributors

Chapter 1 • Peopling North America
Al Carroll, Ph.D.
St. Phillip's College

Chapter 2 • Pacific Northwest Culture
Deborah Clark
Independent Scholar

Chapter 3 • California and Intermountain
Culture
Mel White
Independent Scholar

Chapter 4 • The Plains Culture
Francis Flavin, Ph.D.
University of Texas, Dallas

Chapter 5 • The Southwest Culture
Richard W. Dawson, Ph.D.
China Agricultural University

Chapter 6 • The Woodlands Culture
Tyler W. Boulware, Ph.D.
West Virginia University

Chapter 7 • First Contacts
John F. Murphy, Jr.
American Military University

Chapter 8 • First Settlements
Robert Stacy
Independent Scholar

Appendix • Native American Myths, Narratives,
and Songs
Kathleen L. Nichols
Pittsburg State University

Chronology
Phil Konstantin
Independent Scholar

I . . . regard the chief utility of all historical and sociological investigations to be to admonish us of the alternative possibilities of history.

—Oscar Jaszi, *The Dissolution of the Habsburg Monarchy*

There is nothing new about counterfactual inference. Historians have been doing it for at least two thousand years.

—Philip Tetlock and Aaron Belkin, *Counterfactual Thought Experiments in World Politics Monarchy*

The question, What would have happened if . . . ? is asked all the time as historians, students, and readers of history examine past events. If some event had turned out differently, the whole course of history from that particular turning point forward could have been affected, we are often reminded. Important outcomes frequently hinge on an individual decision, an accidental encounter, a turn in the weather, the spread of a disease, or a missed piece of information. Such events stimulate our imagination, accentuating the role of luck, chance, and individual decision or character at particular moments in time. The examination of such key hinge points is one of the reasons that the study of history is so fascinating.

"Alternate history" has become a fictional genre, similar to science fiction, in that it proposes other worlds, spun off from the one we live in, derived from some key hinge point in the past. Harry Turtledove, among others, has produced novels along these lines. Turtledove has written a widely sold sequence of books that follow an alternate past from a "counterfactual" Confederate victory at the battle of Antietam, resulting in the rise of the Confederate States of America as a separate nation, with consequences well into the twentieth century.

Alternate or counterfactual history is more than a form of imaginative speculation or engaging entertainment, however. Historians are able to highlight the significance of an event they examine by pointing to the consequences of the event. When many significant consequences flow from a single event, the alternate history question is implicit—the consequences would have been different, and a strange and different history would have flowed from that time forward if the specific event in question had turned out differently. Those events that would have made the most dramatic or drastic alternate set of consequences are clearly among the most important; thus key battles in wars are often studied in great detail, but not only for their own sake. The importance of such battles as Gettysburg and Antietam is not simply military. Instead, those battles and others are significant because such deep consequences flowed from their outcomes. The same could be said of General Erich Ludendorff's offensive in 1918—had it been successful, the Allies might have been defeated in World War I, and the map of Europe and the rest of the twentieth century would have been very different than the way they actually turned out. Similarly, if for some reason the nuclear weapons used at Hiroshima and Nagasaki in 1945 had failed, the outcome of World War II could have been very different, perhaps with a greater role for Russia in the dissolution of the Japanese Empire. Others have argued that had the bombs not been used, Japan would have been defeated quite promptly even without them.

Every key event raises similar issues. What might the world have been like if Christopher Columbus and his sailors had failed to return from their voyage in 1492? What if Hernán Cortéz and Francisco Pizarro had been soundly defeated in their attempts to defeat the Aztecs and the Inca Empire? What if John Wilkes Booth had failed in his assassination attempt against Abraham Lincoln? What sort of world would we live in if any of the other famous victims of assassination had survived, such as John F. Kennedy, Martin Luther King, Jr., or Malcolm X?

For the student, examining alternate histories springing from multiple turning points and exploring what would have happened if . . . , gives insight into many of the questions at the heart of history. What was the role of specific individuals, and how did their exercise of free will and choice at a moment in time affect later events? On the other hand, to what extent are the actions of individuals irrelevant to the larger outcomes? That is, in any particular period of history, were certain underlying forces at work that would have led to the same result, no matter what the individual did? Do underlying structures and deeper causes, such as economic conditions, technological progress, climate, natural resources, and diseases, force events into a mold that individuals have always been powerless to alter? Do certain ideas have such importance that they would spread, even if particular advocates had never lived to voice them?

The classic contest of free will and determinism is constantly at work in history, and an examination of pivotal turning points is key to understanding the balance between deep determining forces and the role of individuals. Frequently, it seems, no matter what individuals tried to do to affect the course of events, the events flowed onward in their same course; in other cases, however, a single small mistake or different personal decision seems to have affected events and altered the course of history. Close study of specific events and how they might have otherwise turned out can illuminate this challenging and recurrent issue.

Of course, when reviewing what would have happened if . . . , it is important to realize exactly what in fact really did happen. So in every chapter presented in this series, we are careful to explain first what actually happened, before turning to a possible alternative set of events that could have happened, and the consequences through later history that might have flowed from an alternate development at a particular turning point. By looking at a wide variety of such alternatives, we see how much of history is contingent, and we gain greater insight into its specific events and developments.

Alternate histories would have flowed, had there been different outcomes of a great variety of events, many of them far less famous than the outstanding battles, and the lives and deaths of explorers, conquerors, statesmen, and political leaders. Seemingly obscure or little-recognized events in the past, such as legislative decisions, court cases, small military engagements, and even the lives of obscure minor officials, preachers, writers, and private citizens, frequently played a crucial part in shaping the flow of events. It is clear that if any of the great leaders of the world had died as infants, the events in which they participated would have been altered; but we tend to forget that millions of minor players and less famous people take actions in their daily lives in events such as battles, elections, legislative and judicial decisions, sermons, speeches, and published statements that have sometimes altered the course of history.

Alternate histories are known as "counterfactuals," that is, events that did not in fact happen. Some counterfactuals are more plausible than others. A few historians have argued that all counterfactuals are absurd and should not be studied or considered. However, any historical work that goes beyond simply presenting a narrative or chronological list of what happened, and begins to explore causes through the use of such terms as "influenced," "precipitated," or "led to," is in fact implying some counterfactual sequences. A historian, in describing one event as having consequences, is by implication suggesting the counterfactual that if the event had not occurred, the consequences would have been different.

If history is to be more than a chronicle or simple listing of what happened and is to present "lessons" about statecraft, society, technology development, diplomacy, the flow of ideas, military affairs, and economic policy, it must explore how causes led to consequences. Only by the study of such relationships can future leaders, military officers, business people and bankers, legislators and judges, and, perhaps most important, voters in democratic nations gain any knowledge of how to conduct their affairs. To derive the lessons of history, one has to ask what the important causes were, the important hinge events that made a difference. And once that question is asked, counterfactuals are implied. Thus the defenders of the approach suggest that counterfactual reasoning is a prerequisite to learning lessons from history. Even many historians who resolutely avoid talking about "what might have been" are implying that what in fact happened was important because the alternative, counterfactual event did *not* happen.

Two scholars who have studied counterfactuals in depth, Philip E. Tetlock and Aaron Belkin, in an edited collection of articles, *Counterfactual Thought Experiments in World Politics* (Princeton University Press, 1996), have concluded that counterfactual reasoning can serve several quite different purposes in the study of history. They define these types of counterfactual work:

1. Case-study counterfactuals that "highlight moments of indeterminacy" in history by showing how things might have turned out differently at such hinge points because of individual free choices. These studies tend to focus on the uniqueness of specific events.

2. "Nomothetic" counterfactuals that focus on underlying deterministic laws or processes, examining key events to show how likely or unlikely it was for events to have turned out differently. The purpose of this type of study is to test how powerful an underlying law or process is by imagining alternative situations or decisions.

3. A combination of types one and two above, blending the test of theory or underlying law approach with the unique event approach.

4. "Mental stimulation" counterfactuals that highlight underlying assumptions most people have by showing how causes that most people believe are inconsequential could have major effects, and other causes that most people believe are very important might have little or no effect in changing the course of history.

The reader will recognize aspects of each of these different models in the accounts that follow. Moreover, the reader can find the contrasts between actual history and alternate history quite puzzling and thought provoking, as they are intended to be. As readers study the cases, they may want to keep asking questions such as these:

What was the key hinge point on which the author focused?

Is the altered key event a plausible change—something that could easily have happened?

Was the change "minimal" in the sense that only one or a few turning point events had to turn out differently than they in fact did?

Did the alternate outcome seem to develop in a realistic way; that is, does the alternate sequence of events seem to be one that would be likely once the precipitating change took place?

How plausible is the alternate long-term outcome or consequence that the author suggested?

Was the changed key event a matter of an individual person's choice, an accident, or a change in some broader social or technological development?

Does the counterfactual story help us make judgments about the actual quality of leadership displayed in fact at the time? That is, did key actors in real history act more or less wisely than they did in the counterfactual account?

Does the outcome of the episode suggest that, despite the role of chance and individual choice, certain powerful forces shaped history in similar directions, in both the factual and counterfactual account?

Does the account make me think differently about what was important in history?

Does the counterfactual story challenge any assumptions I had before I read it?

Remember, however, that what really happened is the object of historical study. We examine the counterfactual, alternate histories to get a better understanding of the forces and people that were at work in what really did occur. These counterfactual stories will make you think about history in ways that you have never encountered before; but when you have explored them, you should be able to go back to the real events with fresh questions in mind.

Introduction to the Native America Volume

In this volume of the series, we see how counterfactual and alternative history can shed light on what really happened by looking closely at the history of the Native American peoples of North America. Through the chapters presented here, the reader will think more deeply about the influence of disease on history, about the roots and persistence of racism, about the annihilation of peoples, and about the rich strengths of Native American cultures. Sometimes it is too easy to take certain assumptions about the past for granted. By looking deeply into the events in Native American history, we can begin to challenge some of those assumptions and realize some of the deeper causes at work that shaped our past.

Before studying the subject in much depth, most people might assume they know the answers to these questions:

How and when did the Native American peoples come to North America?

Why did Europeans want to take over the lands of the New World?

What factors or reasons made European dominance of the Native American peoples likely?

Why did some Native American peoples adapt easily to the coming of European culture and tradition while others fought back, some to the point of annihilation?

Why did Native American peoples engage in so much warfare among themselves?

Why did so much of Native American religion and culture disappear?

Why did so many Native Americans rely on hunting wild animals for meat rather than raising domestic animals?

Why did the Plains Natives fight against the U.S. Army after the American Civil War?

The authors who developed the chapters for this volume grounded each study on a solid knowledge of the actual history of Native Americans, gained through the study of diverse fields of archaeology, anthropology, social history, and the document-based history of recent centuries. Each has provided a list of solid historical and social science reference works that give further information. Often, very recent research, reflected in websites and new publications listed, sheds new light on some of these issues.

Through the chapters that follow, we gain deeper insight into the questions suggested above as well as others. Each of the chapters asks how things might have turned out differently. In some cases, the turning point in history depended on the action of a few individuals. In other cases, the turning point came with a broader development, like the accidental development of a disease mutation that struck either people or certain animals. Other broad developments that would represent turning points include the accidental discovery of a technical process, such as making bronze or developing improved agricultural and irrigation methods. In other cases, the crucial turning point came with a broader social development, such as the spread of the Iroquois federation. If things had gone a little differently at some of these turning points, we realize, the history not only of North

America, but of the whole Western world could have been very different from the reality in which we live.

In actual history, the United States emerged as a powerful nation that began to influence world affairs in profound ways in the nineteenth and twentieth centuries. But in a number of the alternate worlds we think about in this volume, the United States does not emerge in quite the same way, or at all. Thinking about how the history of Native Americans might have been different if things had gone differently at a particular turning point makes us think more deeply about some of aspects of the history of the United States and of Western civilization. Can you imagine how the twentieth century might have unfolded if the United States had been smaller, if it had been made up of a more racially diverse population, or if it had never existed in the first place? As you think about such issues, you have to start raising questions and finding out information about broader aspects of U.S. history. So, while this work starts with and presents issues about Native American history, it soon leads us into the study of many other subjects.

WARNING!

You are probably used to reading a book of history to find out what happened. We offer this book with a major warning. In this volume, the reader will see and be led to think deeply about what actually happened, and that part of history is always designated ACTUAL HISTORY. However, the last part of each chapter presents a history that never happened, and that is presented as the ALTERNATE HISTORY.

> To be sure that it is clear that the ALTERNATE HISTORY is an account of what would have happened differently if a TURNING POINT had turned out differently than it really did, the ALTERNATE HISTORY is always presented against a gray background, like these lines. The ALTERNATE HISTORY is what might have happened, what could have happened, and perhaps what would have happened, if the TURNING POINT had gone a little differently. Think about this ALTERNATE HISTORY, and why it would have been different. But don't think that it represents the way things actually happened!

Each chapter is also accompanied by informative sidebars and a few discussion questions that take off from the ACTUAL HISTORY and the ALTERNATE HISTORY that allow readers to think through and argue the different sides of the issues that are raised here.

We also want to warn readers that some may be surprised to discover that history, when viewed in this light, suddenly becomes so fascinating they may never want to stop learning about it!

Rodney Carlisle

TURNING POINT

Some theories say North America was first settled by people migrating across a land bridge from Siberia to Alaska. What if Native groups did not cross, or crossed in fewer numbers?

INTRODUCTION

No issue has caused more debate in American and world history than the origins of Native Americans in the western hemisphere. European invaders had their whole worldview challenged by the existence of some 100 million inhabitants in a land they did not expect to find. The Bible made no mention of the Americas or its Native peoples. Many Europeans insisted that Native Americans must be the Lost Tribes of Israel, or even more fancifully, from the lost civilizations of Atlantis or Mu. When scientists first joined the debate, they too chimed in with a (perhaps unconscious) cultural bias coming from a Christian worldview, an insistence that Native Americans must have come from somewhere else.

The Book of Genesis insisted all humanity came from the Tigris and Euphrates river valleys. Science, even today, has moved that place of origin only a little farther south to East Africa. Recently, many scientists have begun to listen to the voices of Native Americans insisting that they are indigenous to these continents, truly the First Nations in the Americas. These are not just issues that concern Native peoples. Tied into the debates are legal standings over Native sovereignty, land rights, possession of Native remains and sacred artifacts, who gets to decide for or speak for Native Americans, and the rules of evidence for science and history.

Could others have been here too? Early European racists insisted that indigenous peoples were too primitive or unsophisticated to build such great structures as the pyramids in Mexico and at Cahokia in present-day Illinois, the great earthen mounds that cover the Mississippi and Ohio valleys, or the Nazca lines in South America. Many historians and scientists believed in heliocentric diffusion, that all human cultures come from a single origin. Not by coincidence, most of these European or white scientists insisted that the origin of all human cultures must have been ancient Greece, or perhaps Sumeria. Many white Americans in earlier times insisted that Native American cultures came from ancient Israel, Rome, or the lands of the Vikings, the Welsh, or the Irish.

KEY CONCEPT   Cohokia Mounds

One of the examples of early Native American culture, Cohokia Mounds, puzzles scientists because it is an engineering marvel thought beyond the skills of Native peoples. Today a World Heritage site run by the U.S. Park Service, Cahokia Mounds State Historic Site, is located in Illinois on the Mississippi River across from St. Louis, Missouri. This area was first inhabited by Natives of the Woodland culture about 700 C.E. By about 900, the Cahokia site was the regional center for the Mississippian culture with satellite settlements around it. After about 400 years, the population began to decline and the site was abandoned by 1500.

In the late 1600s, the Cahokia Indians came to the area, giving the place its current name. However, it is the building accomplishments of the earlier Indians that make this site significant. They constructed more than one hundred earthen mounds, eighty-seven of which have been documented. It is estimated that these industrious people moved fifty million cubic feet of earth in woven baskets to create this network of mounds. Monk's Mound, for example, covers an area of fourteen acres and rises in four terraces to a height of one hundred feet. Atop this would have been a massive building another fifty feet high. As the largest prehistoric earthen construction in the Americas, Monk's Mound is a testament to the sophisticated engineering skills of these people.

Some scientists and historians had a very big stake in claiming that Native peoples must have been completely isolated, cut off from the rest of the world as though a force field surrounded the Americas once the Bering Strait land bridge closed. Claiming this isolation made the Americas sound more like the pristine wilderness many wanted to believe it was, and it also fit with images of Native Americans as primitive children of nature untouched by other civilizations.

Some people today still use both arguments to restrict Native rights, as in the debate over the return of Paha Sapa, the Black Hills sacred to the Lakota people. Senator Bill Bradley proposed returning part of the Black Hills but found enormous opposition from local white racists in North and South Dakota, who insisted the Lakota were just one more group of recent immigrants. A European pagan group, called Asatru, tried to take possession of an archaeological find called Kennewick Man, based on their contention he was "Caucasian." Actually his alleged "white" features were the fanciful creation of an artist doing a facial reconstruction, who later admitted his mistake and apologized. This did not stop archaeologists, angry over the challenges to their profession from Native activists, from backing the claim that Kennewick Man was "white." Two bizarre racist New Age cults called the Washitaws and the Nuwaubians claim full possession of the Americas, declaring that all black Africans are the true native Americans. Their black supremacist ideology believes that "casino Indians" recognized by the government are just light-skinned imposters who intermarried with whites.

Almost absent from all these debates were the voices of indigenous peoples saying, "Yes, we have always been here in this land, and yes, we also had many visitors from other lands who traded and intermingled

KEY CONCEPT   Bering Land Bridge and Continental Glaciation

Grasping the magnitude of Ice Age glaciation is possible today only on Earth's two extant polar ice sheets in Greenland and Antarctica. During the final Ice Age push, vast sheets of ice up to nearly two miles thick burdened much of America. Because the amount of water in Earth's hydrosphere is constant, the great ice sheets' hoarding of global waters caused sea levels to fall significantly. As a result, land masses grew dramatically where continental shelves slope gradually, as they do in the Bering Strait.

Continental shelves are the shallow submarine plains that border many continents and typically end in steep slopes to an oceanic abyss. Where a wide continental shelf slopes gradually, a small drop in sea level can increase shoreline areas greatly.

During the time of the Bering land bridge, a sea level drop of approximately 300 feet during the Wisconsinan glacial period revealed a relatively flat, low-lying stretch of continental plain linking North America to Asia.

"Bridge" is really a misnomer, for the land mass ranged up to 1,000 miles wide. Just when humans first traversed the land bridge is subject to less agreement. The Pleistocene epoch began 1.6 million years ago and ended only 10,000 years ago after a final onslaught of ice known as the late Wisconsinan glaciation. It is theoretically possible for people to have entered North America from Asia at repeated intervals between 40,000 and 13,000 years ago.

Sea level now rises an average of one foot per century because global warming is melting the great polar ice masses of the Arctic and Antarctic. The greenhouse effect and loss of stratospheric ozone may have increased the rate of global warming recently. Many clues to this intriguing puzzle about how and when humans first peopled the Americas undoubtedly lie underwater now.

---

with us." Today, scientific evidence often agrees with both assertions of Native people.

What this chapter does is ask: Suppose the Bering Strait land bridge had never opened up? Who, then, would take possession of the Americas? It will surely surprise some readers that the Bering Strait Theory was not the one and only possibility—Native peoples still could have made it to the Americas. Closing the land bridge only reduces the numbers of some groups, and weights the population of the Americas in favor of the two groups of Indians we know without a doubt had boats and used them to travel widely: Athapascans and Inuit. With fewer Indians, particularly in South America and the Caribbean, other populations that likely traveled to the Americas and intermingled with Native peoples become more distinct and populous. The main focus of this chapter is on North America as populated by Athapascans and Inuit.

Prehistoric pictographs carved into sand rocks in Adamana, Arizona. (D. Griffiths/National Archives)

TURNING POINT

The eastern edge of Siberia, sometime around 10,000 B.C.E.:

The tribe came to the water's edge. The trail had come to an end, and there was near freezing water as far as the eye could see. The new obstacle changed their plans only slightly. They began to build their boats in preparation for the crossing. They knew there was land not too far away, as their keepers of tradition told them. Many of their people on the other side of the Bering Strait traveled back and forth by boat frequently. Some of the people on the other side of the strait were relatives, and travel across the short stretch of water was routine to trade and to find marriage partners.

Like the ripples from throwing a rock in the pond, Athapascans and Inuits spread outward by crossing the strait from Siberia to Alaska. Other Native peoples may also have been able to travel across the Bering Strait, but perhaps not as many. Athapascans and Inuits, we know without a doubt, traveled by boat around the Arctic Circle and the Pacific coast of North America. In this scenario, it is the Athapascans in particular who take possession of, or predominate, in North America and possibly parts of South America.

Fish drying in an Inuit village show the centuries-old methods and traditions of Inuit culture. (Leonard Lee Rue III/National Archives)

ACTUAL HISTORY

What historians, archaeologists, and anthropologists know and believe about the origins of Native people in the Americas is finally catching up to what virtually all Native people have said about their own beginnings: that today's Native Americans were always in this hemisphere as far back as anyone can meaningfully trace. Their ancestors likely arrived before *Homo sapiens* existed.

The Bering Strait Theory is being questioned more and more. For the first time, a majority of professionals in history, archaeology, and anthropology think it likely that the ancestors of most Native peoples did not cross over solely by the Bering Strait land bridge, but instead came here in multiple migrations, mostly traveling by boat. Most experts in the field also now believe the migrations happened much earlier than the time frame suggested by the Bering Strait Theory—at the very least 30,000 or 40,000 years back, perhaps stretching as far back as hundreds of thousands of years ago. A majority of researchers are also considering the possibility that the migrations came from multiple directions, not simply by boat over the

A Warm Spring Tribe member, of Athapascan stock, reflects the traits and legacy left by the original Athapascans. (National Archives)

Bering Strait and by foot over the land bridge, but also by sea travel from Polynesia, with possibly even a few coming from Europe. Dr. Albert Goodyear, associate director of the South Carolina Institute of Archaeology, quoted in the *U.S. News and World Report* article "Rediscovering America: The New World May Be 20,000 Years Older Than Experts Thought" (October 12, 1998), describes the new attitude in the social sciences studying Native origins: "Just five years ago, nothing was possible in American prehistory, because of dogma. Now everything is possible, the veil has been lifted."

These expansions of human beings into the Americas were part of the same waves of migration that first spread *Homo sapiens'* ancestors from Africa to across Asia and Europe. We know from archaeological evidence that boats were being used in Asia at least 50,000 years ago. Linguistic evidence also points to at least a 30,000-year presence in the Americas necessary for the incredibly large number of Native languages to have developed. Genetic evidence suggests that Native people arrived in the Americas a minimum of 15,000 and possibly more than 30,000 years ago, far too long ago for them to have waited to bridge the Bering Strait because of lowering sea levels. Perhaps the most intriguing recent discovery we have is from University of Hawaii geneticist Rebecca Cann, who found evidence of Polynesian DNA among at least five different Native tribes: the Cayapa of Ecuador, the Mapuche, Huilleche, and Atacameno of Chile, and the Nuu-Chal-Nulth on the Pacific coast of Canada.

IN CONTEXT   Beringia

The term *Beringia* comes from the name of Vitus Bering, a Danish explorer for the Russian czar in the eighteenth century. The Bering-Chirikov expedition explored the waters of the North Pacific between Asia and North America. The Bering Strait, which lies between Alaska and Northeast Russia, and Bering Island, in the Commander Islands, are named after him.

In the late 1920s and early 1930s, P. Sushkin and E. Hulten began to use the word *Beringia* as a geographic description. Today, we use the term to describe a vast area between the Kolyma River in the Russian Far East to the Mackenzie River in the Northwest Territories of Canada. It is a region of worldwide significance for cultural and natural resources. This area also provides an unparalleled opportunity for a comprehensive study of the Earth—its unusually intact landforms and biological remains may reveal the character of past climates and the ebb and flow of Earth forces at the continents' edge. Biological research leads to the understanding of the natural history of the region and distribution of flora and fauna. As one of the world's great ancient crossroads, Beringia may hold solutions to puzzles about who the first people were to come to North America, how and when they traveled, and how they survived under such harsh climatic conditions.

Archeological evidence, human remains, or evidence of human activity such as charcoal and tools, once considered the trump card in the arguments of Bering Strait Theory supporters, is increasingly favoring pre-Bering Strait land bridge origins for Native peoples. Archaeological sites such as Pedro Furada, Meadowcroft, and more than a dozen others testify to the existence of humans in the Americas before the Bering Strait land bridge was created.

None of the evidence from scientists is nearly so overwhelming as the agreement among thousands of oral traditions among Native Americans. Virtually none of these accounts mention crossing the Bering Strait on foot. The one major exception, the Wallum Olum or Red Record of the Lenni Lenape (Delawares) does describe crossing the land bridge. However, it describes a *return* journey, and its beginning insists that the Lenni Lenape are from the Americas. (Because of the account's alleged antiquity, 1500 B.C.E. or earlier, it is highly controversial. Some social scientists consider it fraudulent.)

Instead, most Native oral traditions, when they speak of a journey in their origin stories, talk of coming to the Americas by boat. Some speak of coming from another world, which can also be interpreted metaphysically as meaning another plane of existence, or perhaps meaning simply that the world changed dramatically at some point in their history. Perhaps the most fascinating accounts come from tribes in the Pacific Northwest, who say their ancestors were animals. One way of interpreting their origin stories is that the Pacific Northwest tribes are describing human evolution from other species.

Many Native oral traditions also speak of visitors and traders from overseas. When Christopher Columbus and his explorers first encountered the indigenous people of the Caribbean, the Tainos, the explorers described people with darker skin and kinky hair with whom they frequently traded; among the trade items was guanine, an alloy made in Africa. The Tainos used many of the same words found in West African languages, including *guanine*. The now-extinct Beothuk tribe in Newfoundland that fought the

IN CONTEXT *Beringia (Continued)*

It is currently believed that the ocean levels rose and fell several times in the past. During extended cold periods, tremendous volumes of water are deposited on land in the form of ice and snow, which can cause a corresponding drop in sea level. The last Ice Age occurred around 12,000 years ago. During this period, the shallow seas now separating Asia from North America near the present day Bering Strait dropped about 300 feet and created a 1,000-mile-wide grassland steppe, linking Asia and North America with the so-called Bering land bridge. Across this vast steppe, plants and animals traveled in both directions, and humans, it has been theorized, entered the Americas.

The U.S. National Park Service administers the Shared Beringian Heritage Program and is actively working for the establishment of a Beringian Heritage International Park. The park service's area of primary focus for research and cultural development is Central Beringia, that area adjoining the Bering Strait between 64 and 70 degrees north latitude and 160 and 180 degrees west longitude. In addition to promoting the conservation and enjoyment of the natural and physical features of the region, the program supports the understanding and celebration of the common shared heritage between the United States and Russia in that part of the world.

Vikings were fairer in hair and skin tone than other tribes and came by boat from the east according to the accounts of other nearby tribes. While a few of these newer arrivals such as the Beothuk remained distinct and separate, more often they became part of the societies of Native peoples already here.

Prehistoric Native American markings discovered on a slate cliff near Juneau, Alaska. (National Archives)

ANOTHER VIEW Polynesian Settlement of South America

If the Bering Strait had never closed, the two most likely groups outside of Native Americans to settle the Americas based on scientific evidence and accounts from oral traditions and ancient histories, it is argued, are Polynesians and Afro-Phoenicians. The Polynesians, according to scientists, originally came from either the coast of China and Taiwan, or from islands near New Guinea. Linguistic, genetic, and archaeological evidence suggests that they migrated across an amazingly wide area of the earth by boat. Polynesians traveled as far west from their homelands as Madagascar near the East African coast, as far east as the Pacific coast of South America, as far south as New Zealand, and as far north as what is today British Columbia in western Canada. Polynesians were some of the best sailors and navigators in history, as well as formidable warriors and military tacticians who often fought the British to a standstill.

Imagine the scene in Tahiti, around the year 1000 C.E.:

Polynesian men and women gathered provisions for the latest long journey in their outrigger canoes. Some of their canoes were more than ninety feet long, sturdy, with intricate carvings and capable of sailing over one hundred miles a day with crews of more than twenty men. Their people had traveled to South America and been trapped on the way back at Rapa Nui (Easter Island). Some of them and those who would follow became part of the peoples of South America. Some would travel even farther north along the coast.

In Aotearoa, what the British and others would come to call New Zealand, the Polynesian Maori population grew to perhaps one million people. In some parts of the islands, the population became as dense as in the Netherlands, almost as dense as in Bangladesh. And they had another huge advantage. Within a century of their first contact with European diseases, the population had recovered, returning to the same number of people there had been before their encounter with the illnesses. With far fewer or perhaps even no Native Americans in South America, there is no reason the Polynesians could not have filled the continent. Francisco Pizarro and the other Spaniards would instead have faced something very different from the Incas.

In South America, the Polynesians would have met, intermarried, and traded with, and perhaps fought with Athapascan Native Americans. With different technology and warfare traditions that fall somewhere between Europeans and Native peoples in the degree to which they practiced

For both critics and defenders of the Bering Strait Theory, what happens next in the history of the Americas is far less controversial: Native peoples take possession of the Americas. Virtually no corner of the two continents and the adjacent islands goes unpopulated. Environments as diverse as ice-covered frozen tundra, jungles, swamps, rainforests, deserts, plains, forested woodlands, and high mountain plateaus become sacred homelands to an amazing variety of tribal peoples. What is now the continental United States is the ancestral home to more than 500 Indian nations. California alone is home to more than 60 tribes, averaging 30,000 to 40,000 people each before the European invasion. In terms of political organization, most Indian nations were not modern nation-states, but then neither were most of the kingdoms and dukedoms of Europe in 1492. Archaeologist Julian Granberry argues that there were seventeen Native political units that likely would have developed into modern nation-states had there been no European invasion.

ANOTHER VIEW   *Polynesian Settlement of South America (Continued)*

total warfare, Polynesian Americans would have had more success fighting Europeans and less susceptibility to their diseases. Pizarro would also have faced a number of Polynesian tribes compared to, in real history, a highly centralized Incan Empire that was exhausted from a civil war between two rivals for the throne.

Imagine the Polynesians' first contact with Europeans in the northern region of South America in 1531:

Pizarro had been leading his men for weeks now, determined to succeed where the Italian, Cristobal Colon (Columbus), had ended his days in disgrace. True, some plantations had been set up on islands like Dominica, but the imported African slaves too easily escaped and sought refuge among the peoples of Hispaniola and other islands. Pizarro deliberately avoided such peoples on the coast. Perhaps there would be easier conquest farther inland.

He did indeed find different peoples. These tribes had full face tattoos they called mokos, and they fought with carved wooden staffs the length of a man's body they called taiaha. Battle after battle, Pizarro found himself losing more and more men. These people were battle strategists to match El Cid himself. Pizarro found himself in one trap after another, led into ambushes where he was hemmed in by wooden palisades and forced to fight in close combat where the taiaha proved far superior to the clumsy cutlasses

wielded by Spaniards in bulky armor. And he had found no gold, no silver, nothing to make up for his losses. Discouraged and with most of his men dead, he went back to Panama, never to return.

Pizarro's abandoning the invasion of South America would fit well with the Spanish pattern of conquest. In actual history, when Spanish forces invaded a region and found strong opposition and no wealth to keep them there, they tended either to abandon efforts to conquer the region or to establish somewhat isolated outposts. In Florida, for example, the Spanish had dozens of missions but otherwise little of a colonial presence outside of the city of St. Augustine. And in the Mississippi Valley and the Great Plains, invaders like Hernando De Soto and Francisco Coronado wrought devastation but not permanent conquest.

In what became Latin America in real history, how would it look if the Spanish and Portuguese invaders had faced Polynesians in multiple tribes who resisted disease better, instead of initially an Incan empire vulnerable because of a civil war? It would still have been a region partly conquered and colonized, but not nearly so completely as it was. Parts of the coasts of Central America, eastern Mexico, and the north coast of South America might have fallen to the Spaniards. The Portuguese also could have gotten a foothold on the north coast of what is now Brazil, but they would have had a much harder time farther south, where there likely would have been more Polynesians.

What is also not controversial are the facts of what happened to Native peoples. Many social scientists say the European invasion of the Americas was the worst genocide carried out in all of human history. Some Native tribes, like the Beothuk, the same people who drove off the Vikings, were wiped out to the last person. Most Native nations lost more than 90 percent of their people. Confronted with both better weapons technology and traditions of warfare far more violent and extreme than anything ever seen in the Americas, most Native tribes were ill-equipped to fight off the invaders. Warfare in most Native cultures was much closer to raiding than to the full-scale, total warfare for political conquest as practiced in Europe. Even those organizations the Europeans erroneously called empires, such as that of the Aztecs, were closer to political confederacies, with subject peoples giving tribute more than submitting to absolute control. But among the tactics of the European invaders were the massacre of noncombatants and biological

KEY CONCEPT Poverty Point Culture

North American Native American peoples built numerous large settlements long before they had any sustained European contact. In addition to the large stone and adobe towns of Mesa Verde, Chaco Canyon, Acoma, and others in the Colorado-New Mexico area, less well-known large communities could be found in the Mississippi Valley.

From 1500 to 1000 B.C.E. a culture known as Poverty Point spread throughout parts of Louisiana, Arkansas, and Mississippi. Independent groups throughout this region shared several cultural traits but may have spoken different languages. The groups in the region traded goods

and lived in small villages, in areas that clustered around larger settlements. Apparently the center of the culture was at the Poverty Point site, located in northern Louisiana, with trade routes stretching up the Mississippi Valley as far as the Great Lakes and through the region along the Gulf of Mexico coast.

Although exact figures cannot be established, several thousand people lived in the settlement at Poverty Point, centered around at least five large earth mounds. Dwellings were built atop a series of six concentric semicircles of raised ridges facing a central plaza that was apparently the ceremonial

warfare, including deliberate starvation and the spread of disease. At least 75 million Indians died. Some estimates are as high as 112 million victims, more than nine times as many as were killed by Adolf Hitler's Third Reich and almost three times as many as died in the purges of Josef Stalin or Mao Zedong.

Petroglyphs on a rock outcropping near Juneau, Alaska. Squares with a cross above are symbolic of Native graves. (W.N. Parke/National Archives)

KEY CONCEPT   *Poverty Point Culture (Continued)*

and perhaps administrative center of the settle-ment. Whether the culture developed independ-ently from the cultures in Mesoamerica, like those at Tenochtitlan and Monte Alban, or represented a diffusion of cultural ideas is still debated. Other mysteries remain. Although there is no evidence of agricultural practices in the period, it seems unlikely that such a large community could have been sustained simply through hunting and gath-ering and long-distance river trade. Furthermore, the culture at Poverty Point and its surrounding region lasted several hundred years, suggesting an organized system of hierarchal and powerful leadership rather than a smaller band structure led by elders or selected chiefs.

This city and others like the Mississippian set-tlements at Cahokia in Illinois and the Eastern Woodlands site at Moundville, Alabama, had thousands of residents and many more in outlying communities apparently subject to the central jurisdiction of the larger cities, or at least under the influence of the center. Archaeologists speculate as to whether such communities established dynastic rule by families of chiefs or had other forms of government.

For much of the recent past, some historians tried to lay the blame for the loss of most Native lives on disease spread accidentally. But such denial ignores the use of deliberate starvation tactics by the invaders that dramat-ically increased the susceptibility of Native peoples to disease. Without these starvation tactics, Native peoples would have died from disease at rates closer to the number of European deaths from the Black Plague—one-quarter to one-third instead of over 90 percent of the population. A desire to lay the blame on accidental spread of disease was one reason that sup-porters of the Bering Strait Theory insisted on portraying the Americas as completely isolated once the land bridge closed. Nevertheless, Indians were somewhat more vulnerable to disease for two reasons: Europeans had more contact with, and thus more immunity to, diseases spread by domes-ticated animals. Europeans in the fifteenth and sixteenth centuries also practiced very poor hygiene, sometimes bathing only once a year, customs that were quite different from those of every other group that may have had contact with Native peoples before Columbus.

The result of this warfare, both physical and biological, was dispposses-sion of most land in the Americas from Native people into the hands of the invaders and their descendants. In the United States, the Native land base was reduced by 92 percent. Just 8 percent of all American territory is now theoretically protected Indian reservations, and even there, most of the land is sold to, leased to, or otherwise under the control of out-siders. As for Latin America, only Brazil, Costa Rica, and Panama have sys-tems of protected reserves for Native peoples.

Yet side by side with this aggression against Native peoples came an influence by Native peoples on the way Europeans and their descendants think of themselves and live their lives. The wealth from the Americas helped fueled the rise of capitalism. The gold and silver, and new lands and people under their control, made Spain the premier power in the world. Once the mines were depleted and the Native people laboring in them were largely killed off by brutal conditions, Spain went into a long, slow decline.

Wealth from plantations represented the next large transfer of wealth from America to Europe, this time provided largely by the work of African slaves. Sugar cane, cotton, and tobacco crops helped make Great Britain and France world powers. The fur trade with Native hunters was especially lucrative for France, at one time providing more than one-third of the entire revenue of its economy.

Some historians believe the growth of European empires in the Americas created modern racism. Whereas cultural conflict and prejudice were common throughout human history, the creation of categories of superior and inferior people based on perceived innate physical differences was something entirely new. This is exactly what the scientist and humanist Juan de Sepulveda did when he argued in a famous debate with Father Bartolome de las Casas that Native people were not human beings. (Some scholars believe that justification for African plantation slavery also played a major part in the creation of racism, whereas others point to precedents in how the English oppressed the Irish or how the Spanish warred against Canary Islanders.)

The example of Native people also played a role in the developments in European intellectual thought. Philosophers Jean Jacques Rousseau, Baron Charles de Montesquieu, John Locke, Adam Smith, Thomas More, and even Karl Marx all studied how Native peoples ran their societies when formulating their ideas. Both Montesquieu and Locke would, in turn, influence the Founding Fathers of the new United States. Another way Native peoples would indirectly influence American government was through the constitution of the Six Nations of the Iroquois, the Law of the Great Peace. Benjamin Franklin studied the Law of the Great Peace and proposed the Albany Plan, influencing the writing of the Articles of Confederation, which, in turn, influenced the U.S. Constitution. Some scholars, such as Oren Lyons, go so far as to claim that the example of the Six Nations of the Iroquois influenced the United Nations.

Another influence on Europeans and their descendants was Native-cultivated crops and medicinal plants. Up to three-quarters of the world's agricultural crops were originally developed by Native Americans, along with numerous medicinal cures such as quinine. Some other technologies such as freeze-dried foods, the hammock, the kayak, snowshoes, apartment buildings (first developed by the Pueblo peoples), asphalt on roads, and even the internet (one of its five inventors was a Muskogee) came in whole or in part from Natives Americans. It is no exaggeration to say that without Native peoples' influence, Western culture would be dramatically different.

ALTERNATE HISTORY

Before we discuss how the Americas look with mostly Inuit, Athapascan, Polynesian, and Afro-Phoenician people, are there any other groups that could credibly have come to populate the Western Hemisphere? Most stories of the Irish, Welsh, Romans, or other Europeans, even if we accept the little evidence they have to back them up, would have amounted to brief visits by a small number of people or perhaps tiny isolated colonies, not migrations of groups large enough to permanently occupy a substantial area. Even a fairly small number of Vikings came to North America. Their village in Newfoundland was little more than a winter camp with fewer than one hundred people. Though conflict with Native peoples played a role, the Viking settlement of North America failed largely because of lack of items to trade with other Vikings in Iceland and Scandinavia.

Spanish accounts do mention shipwrecked "junks" off the coast of California. Chinese sailors told the Spanish they had been coming to the west coast of the Americas to trade "for centuries." Within the nineteenth and twentieth centuries alone, more than sixty Japanese vessels, sailing near their home islands, have been pulled off course and shipwrecked in North America. Conceivably, any Asian sailors lost on the American coasts in ancient times could have sailed back. Still heavily debated is the archaeological evidence showing pottery and other artifacts found in Mexico and South America that seem to be similar to Japanese and Chinese crafts. If Japanese or Chinese vessels came to the Americas before Columbus but within historical times, with a smaller Native population there is the possibility of Asian colonies being founded on the Pacific Coast of North or South America.

Chinese culture emphasized that China was the Middle Kingdom, that all other lands were secondary in importance to this land. This cultural trait is one reason the Chinese emperors never sought to colonize or conquer outside of Asia, aside from sending out one famous fleet in the fifteenth century. Japan also chose to isolate itself for much of its history. If anyone from these two lands had tried to colonize the Americas, the settlers would likely have been political refugees or criminals. Any Europeans facing conflict with Asian colonies of refugees or criminals would have been facing those who believed and practiced radical equality, far different from beliefs held in the Chinese and Japanese empires. Even so, we are still talking about what would have been fairly isolated outposts, not waves of migration large enough to make a major difference in the history of two continents.

What would the Americas look like with fewer Native people, or with different groups of Native people? Even assuming the Bering Strait Theory supporters are absolutely right, the Americas would still have had Aleuts and Inuit people (Eskimos) in the Arctic Circle. Europeans and their descendants have known about Inuit routine migration, trade, and intermarriage across the Bering Strait by boat since Europeans first invaded Alaska in the eighteenth century. The closing of the land bridge did nothing to halt their entry into the Americas. Perhaps, as with other Native groups, lack of the land bridge even speeds up the migration, as travel by boat is far faster and easier than by foot across freezing mountain ranges.

We also know without a doubt that the Inuit and Aleut neighbors, the Athapascans, have had boats for a similarly long time and used them to travel. The Athapascans are a diverse group of peoples who made their homes in an incredibly wide range of environments. In the Subarctic, they are the Carrier and Kutchin tribes. Below the Subarctic region, but still in northern Canada, are the Dene people. From 1,000 to 2,000 years ago, according to archaeologists and anthropologists, many of the Athapascans migrated south and became today's Apaches and Navajos.

Dene, Apache, and Navajo elders from all three tribes tell a different story of the separation. By their traditional accounts, this migration happened much further back, some 12,000 years ago. The Dene, Navajo, and Apache oral traditions speak similarly about how the tribes separated. A giant was killed by the original tribe. When he fell, the people crossed onto the unknown new land across the back of this giant, which is the Thelon River in the Northwest Territories. What this story does metaphorically is describe the route taken by the tribe to the south.

The story of Athapascan migration does not end there. The Naishan Apache, also known as Kiowa Apache, split off from other Apache bands and lived on the southwest corner of the central plains, away from their desert cousins. The Hoopa also split off from other Athapascans and made their home in California. With such a history of incredible adaptability, there is no reason Athapasacan peoples could not have colonized most or all of North America. The Dene would have spread south and east perhaps all the way to the Atlantic Coast or as far south as the Great Lakes or even the Mississippi and Ohio valleys. The Hoopa would have occupied virtually all of the Pacific Coast, not just one part of California. The Naishan Apache would have spread to all of the Plains instead of just the region where the Plains area meets the southwest desert. Perhaps they would have gone farther east into the woodlands, meeting up with their Dene cousins.

As for the most famous Athapascans, the other Apaches and Navajos would have spread down into what is today northern and central Mexico. Conceivably there might have been Athapascan bands that split off and went even farther south, through the jungles into Central America and beyond, into the mountain ranges of South America. In South America they would have met, intermarried, and traded with, and perhaps fought with the Polynesians. On the east coast of Mexico and Central America, we would see the same pattern with Afro-Phoenicians, and farther north on the east coast of North America, the Euro-Phoenicians. With different technology and warfare traditions that fall somewhere between Europeans and Native Americans in the degree to which they practiced total warfare, Polynesian Americans and Phoenician Americans would have had more success against Europeans and less susceptibility to disease.

How would the Americas then look after 1492? It would still have been a region partly conquered and colonized by European invaders, but not nearly as completely. Some of the islands of the Caribbean would have become Spanish colonies, especially the smaller and more fertile ones best suited for sugar cane plantations. Parts of Central America, the east coast of Mexico, and the north coast of South America likewise would have fallen to the Spaniards. The Portuguese also would have gotten a foothold on the north coast of what is now Brazil, but they would have had a much harder time farther south where more Polynesians would have been located.

England and France were latecomers to the invasion of the Americas, and knowing that Spain and Portugal were having only limited success means they would have delayed sending their own armies and navies, but this did not happen in actual history. It is also quite possible that Europe could have been devastated by tropical diseases as deadly as the bubonic plague, spread from contact with the Afro-Phoenicians. This delay of several generations before the English and French arrived means the Natives of North America would have had more time to prepare and especially more time to recover from diseases spread by European fishermen and traders, or gradually would have gained immunity to these diseases. Likely, the English and French also would have faced wide-ranging alliances between Euro-Phoenicians, Afro-Phoenicians, and the Native allies of both. The Americas, from the fifteenth through the nineteenth centuries, would have resembled much more the pattern followed in invading Africa during the same time: coastal colonies but not conquests of entire continents.

How would this change the way Europeans think of nonwhites, not just Native Americans, but also blacks and Polynesians? As noted earlier, in real history, the conquest of the Americas and the wholesale slaughter of its people had to be justified, helping to create modern racism. If the conquest had been far more limited, then perhaps modern racism would never have been created or needed. Racism still might have been created by European philosophers, but this might have come centuries later or taken very different and more limited forms. At the very least, in our alternate history, racism is not as vicious or as widespread. Racism against Native Americans, Africans, and Polynesians might have taken on more of the qualities of the ideas called Orientalism, which Europeans were using to describe Asians and Arabs, seeing them as peoples who were exotic, hard to understand, but admirable and desirable too. Europeans would have seen Native Americans, Africans, and Polynesians as rivals in war and trade instead of subject peoples to be used or killed off without conscience.

How would any version of the United States be different without the Iroquois example to influence European philosophers and, indirectly, American government? Obviously any United States would be a smaller nation-state, not going inland very far from the Atlantic coast. Instead of copying the Six Nations model of federalism, would they instead have copied the Dene or Naishan Apache example? Athapascans tended to have decentralized bands for their political organization, which was why the Apaches proved so difficult to defeat. Would English colonists in North America have chosen a loose tribal organization in which leaders or chiefs were closer to counselors than to chief executives or legislators? Would the new Americans have practiced government by consensus instead of majority rule? Would we have a loosely affiliated "Bands of America" instead of a federalist United States of America? And how would the world be different without a powerful United States intervening in and often dominating other regions?

Would modern Europe and modern capitalism even have developed at all without the wealth of the Americas? As discussed earlier, after their first taste of success in conquering the Americas, Europeans increasingly saw themselves as the most advanced, most enlightened people in the world. Eventually, many of them believed in Social Darwinism and outright white supremacy. If the indigenous nations of

ANOTHER VIEW   The Afro-Phoenician Settlement of the Caribbean

The second most likely candidate for another diaspora to the Americas was the Afro-Phoenicians. Afro-Phoenicians, despite their name, were a mix of Middle Eastern peoples, North Africans, and sub-Saharan or people of black African heritage. In appearance, some probably resembled many of today's Arabs, while others looked like black people. Their culture was more Middle Eastern than African, with boats that resembled the galleys used by the Empire of Crete in its heyday. We know that the Phoenicians definitely traveled as far north as Iceland and as far south as around the "hump" of West Africa. The Phoenicians developed innovations like the keel and improved sails. Their ships were up to one hundred feet long, with a single purple sail used for signaling. Their sails were supplemented with oars and they could travel one hundred miles a day.

Some evidence suggests very strongly that the Afro-Phoenicians traveled to or even migrated to the Caribbean and perhaps the coast of Mexico and Central America. The most famous pieces of evidence are the enormous Olmec carved stone heads of warriors with very African features. There was also another branch of the Phoenicians that can be called Euro-Phoenicians. They intermingled with the local population in Britain and Ireland and quite possibly made their way to the east coast of North America. Historian Robert Hagen argues that the Euro-Phoenicians had a colony in what is today Virginia, and that Phoenician artifacts can be found in Pennsylvania.

Writings by ancient European scholars like Aristotle and Diodorus discuss the migration of Phoenicians to lands to the west beyond the Atlantic, driven there by warfare with the more aggressive Greeks. This migration began perhaps as early as the fourth century B.C.E. If the Afro-Phoenicians came to the Americas from the West African coast, the shortest and most likely route, in our scenario they settle into the Caribbean islands and perhaps the coasts of Mexico, Central America, or the north coast of South America. They trade, intermingle, and perhaps wage war with Athapascans already there. In the 2,000 years between their migration to the Americas and the Columbus invasion, the Afro-Phoenicians could have grown to number in the hundreds of thousands. Being from the Mediterranean and African tropical regions, they would have been exposed to and developed immunities to not just the same diseases as Europeans, but also to some illnesses that Europeans were more vulnerable to. The trade of African goods with Native Americans means the Afro-Phoenicians would have been continually exposed to the diseases back in Africa. Their immunities would have been developed when Europeans arrived.

Imagine the scene on an island in the Caribbean, 1492:

The captain led his men ashore. He planted the flag of Spain and proclaimed it crown lands in the name of Ferdinand and Isabella.

the Americas were rivals and not subjects, that sense of superiority would never have arisen. Economically, the flow of gold and silver, and later the flow of profits from sugar, cotton, and tobacco plantations, fueled the economic growth of Europe, providing a surplus to build what would become modern capitalism. If most of the gold and silver had stayed in the ground, Spain in particular would have become a far less powerful nation. Spain's ability to wage destructive wars against emerging Protestant nations in Europe also would have been lessened, meaning the Protestant Reformation would have been an easier, or at least less violent, experience.

What would have grown in Europe instead of capitalism and wars over religion? Would capitalism's two counterparts, fascism and communism, even have developed without having the system of capitalism

ANOTHER VIEW *The Afro-Phoenician Settlement of the Caribbean (Continued)*

Out of the woods came the islanders. To the captain's surprise, their skin looked like that of the Moors that Spain had been fighting for centuries, rather than like the people of India. But the islanders' dress was far different. Some of his men knew the Moors' language, but none of them could understand these people. If they were not the infidel, the captain reasoned, perhaps they could be won over to the one true Christian faith.

By nightfall, the islanders had the captain and his men on the run, hiding in their ships. By morning, the captain found his three small ships in running battles with the swift sailing ships of the islanders, ships that looked much like drawings of galleys from the days when Crete was a mighty empire. The captain retreated with his ships to a smaller island, restocking supplies before heading back to Spain. He vowed to return with a larger fleet for the riches he was sure were there and the converts he still hoped to win.

On the way home the captain was even more dismayed to see his men turning ill and dying from ailments they had never before encountered. With more time, men, ships, and at a great cost especially from new diseases, Captain Cristobal Colon and the conquistadores who followed were able to conquer some of the smaller islands. But the greater glory, power, and riches they sought mostly eluded them.

How would the Caribbean and the coasts of the two continents close to the islands then look after 1492? It would still have been a region partly conquered and colonized by European invaders, but not nearly as completely as it actually was. Some of the islands of the Caribbean would have become Spanish colonies, especially the smaller and more fertile ones best suited for sugar cane plantations. Parts of Central America, the east coast of Mexico, and the north coast of South America likewise would have fallen to the Spaniards. The Afro-Phoenicians, more than any other group, would have taken the brunt of the Spanish invasion. But because of both disease and Phoenician ships, that invasion would have been blunted if not entirely defeated in many places. It is entirely possible that Spaniards returning home would have brought new illnesses originally from Africa that would have reduced Europe's population as much as the bubonic plague had—by one-quarter to one-third. Such a catastrophe would have halted European invasion for two generations at least.

Farther north, after a prolonged delay of several generations, the English and French would still have invaded North America. But Europeans also would have faced alliances between Euro-Phoenicians, Afro-Phoenicians, and the Native allies of both. The Americas from the fifteenth through the nineteenth centuries would have resembled much more the pattern of Africa during the same time, with coastal colonies but not conquests of entire continents.

to defend or oppose? Europe might have remained more feudalistic, at least for a longer period of time. Or more likely, gold and silver would have flowed to Europe, but far less of it, and as part of trade and not as stolen wealth mined by Native slave labor. Apaches and Navajos in Mexico and Polynesians in South America would have traded gold and silver for technology, especially firearms, which they, in turn, would have used on both each other and on Europeans. In real history, English invaders traded firearms to Polynesian Maoris in New Zealand. Maori tribes fought each other, sometimes allying with the English against other tribes. Eventually the English succeeded in subjugating the Maori.

But this is not as bleak a picture as it might seem. The Maori today make up almost a fifth of New Zealand's population; in comparison,

Native people make up only 1 percent to 2 percent of the population in the United States. Maori leaders also are among the foremost indigenous rights activists in the world, and their influence has made New Zealand far more progressive than the United States in its treatment of indigenous rights and a host of other issues, and much more progressive than the countries of Latin America.

Even in the absolute worst-case scenario of using European weapons to divide and conquer, Athapascans and other groups could still have come out far better than Native Americans as a whole did in actual history. For example, the band government used by many Athapascans, such as the Apaches, would have made the conquest of these tribes extremely difficult or impossible. (Jack Page in his alternate history book *Apacheria* described how the Apaches could have stayed independent from outsiders.) Large parts of North and South America have no precious minerals to trade, so any intertribal wars were driven by the fur trade. In real history, the French fur trade brought in only a limited number of trappers and traders who intermarried into Native tribes far more than they tried to conquer them. Thus with more cohesive Native tribes and perhaps a lesser British presence, we are more likely talking about European spheres of influence on North America rather than total conquest.

Using the example of Africa once again, Africa was conquered and colonized by Europeans only in the nineteenth century, with some parts never conquered and virtually all the countries on that continent achieving independence within 150 years. This is what likely would have happened to all the peoples of the Americas if the Bering Strait land bridge had never opened. The world of the twenty-first century thus would have a number of heavily populated Athapascan, Afro-Phoenician, and Polynesian nation-states in the Americas regaining their independence in the mid- and late twentieth century. This alternate history also features a Europe with a far less racist and domineering past. A United Nations assembly in this scenario would have delegates for nations such as Apacheria and Dinetah (the Navajo nation) alongside the affiliated Bands of America. That is, assuming there would even be a need for a United Nations. With a later-developing capitalism and less need for either communism or fascism, both world wars probably never would have happened either.

Al Carroll

Discussion Questions

1. What methods do you think were used by people like the Polynesians and the Athapascan sailors to navigate out of sight of land in order to reach distant places like Hawaii, and the coasts of North and South America?

2. What reasons do you think explain why Africa was colonized by European peoples at first only on the coasts and never for more than 150 years, when North and South America were completely dominated by Europeans in the 500 years since contact by the Spanish explorers?

3. Why do you think Europeans adopted the idea that the peoples of North America were incapable of sailing or of developing advanced societies? What aspects of this myth of savagery made it easier for Europeans to conquer and colonize the Americas?

4. What methods do you think Europeans might have used to intentionally spread disease and to cause starvation among the peoples they encountered?

5. The European industrial revolution was funded and stimulated by trade from the New World. How would trade in goods like sugar and cotton help build up industries in Europe?

6. What sorts of constitutional arrangements could a modern nation have if it were organized in bands rather than in a federation of separate states? For example, if the United States were made up of 3,000 bands or local tribes rather than fifty large states, how would the national governmental legislature be structured?

Bibliography and Further Reading

Cowley, Robert, ed. *What If? 2: Eminent Historians Imagine What Might Have Been.* New York: G.P. Putnam's Sons, 2001.

Deloria, Vine, Jr. *Red Earth, White Lie.* Golden, CO: Fulcrum, 1997.

Diamond, Jared. *Guns, Germs, and Steel.* New York: W.W. Norton, 1997.

"Easter Island History: Thor Heyerdahl And The South America Connection." http://www.islandheritage.org/heyerdahl.html (accessed May 23, 2006).

Loewen, James. *Lies My Teacher Told Me.* New York: Touchstone, 1996.

"Our Languages: Dene—History and Background." http://www.sicc.sk.ca/heritage/sils/ourlanguages/dene/history (accessed May 10, 2006).

Page, Jack. *Apacheria.* New York: Del Rey, 1998.

Petit, Charles W. "Rediscovering America: The New World May Be 20,000 Years Older than Experts Thought." *U.S. News and World Report* (October 12, 1998).

Schmidt, Rob. "Stereotype of the Month." http://www.bluecorncomics.com (accessed May 23, 2006). Originally from "Tribe Challenges American Indian Origins." Paul Rincon. *BBC News Online Science Staff.* Also "Study: Native Americans Weren't the First." Jennifer Viegas. *Discovery Channel.* Discovery News.

Stannard, David. *American Holocaust.* New York: Oxford University Press, 1993.

Underhill, Ruth M. *The Navajos.* Norman, OK: University of Oklahoma Press, 1989.

"Wayfinders: A Pacific Odyssey." http://www.pbs.org/wayfinders/index.html (accessed May 23, 2006).

"Where the Buffalo Go: How Science Ignores the Living World." http://www.derrickjensen.org (accessed May 23, 2006).

TURNING POINT

The tribes of the Pacific Northwest yielded to white settlement in the 1850s. What if the Native Americans had not signed treaties that moved them from their territories?

INTRODUCTION

The Pacific Northwest is a large area that runs along the U.S. Pacific coast from Alaska to Oregon. The Native American tribes of the Pacific Northwest are as varied as the geography of the region. Although they are grouped together, each has distinctive characteristics, languages, and cultures. Archaeologists have dated the inhabitation of the area as far back as 10,000 years ago. The Pacific Northwest Native cultures were rich and elaborate.

In their early history, before written records, Native lore has recorded the stories of the creation of the land and the human people that came after the gods Raven, Coyote, and Crane. Raven embodied the characteristics of the spirit, humanity, the genius, the fool, and, of course, the bird. Coyote, the trickster, was responsible for giving to humans many of the resources they used, like salmon. Crane taught sharing. These are the basic tenets that the Native Americans traditionally lived by. The roles that these gods played in a family's history were reflected in the stories passed down from generation to generation.

Native Americans of the Pacific Northwest differed in many ways from the Plains tribes. The most obvious signs of these differences were the use of longhouses, cedar canoes, totem poles, and potlatches. Longhouses were the hubs of communal living for each village. Canoes were essential for daily life. Totem poles, although misnamed by European explorers, were the pictorial history of the family to whom they belonged. Totem poles were commissioned to record important events in a family's history. Potlatches, outlawed by the U.S. government in the 1860s, were important community celebrations.

Pacific Northwest Natives were considered rich by other tribes. They had bountiful food resources and abundant indigenous materials with which to craft items. Women spent time softening and saving cedar strips for use in weaving. They created mats, baskets, boxes, bedding, and even

An early twentieth century photo of Pacific Northwest Native Americans resting by a river. (National Archives)

clothing from cedar. The baskets and boxes were waterproof. The bedding and clothes were soft and supple. The skill of a woman's weaving was displayed on every item. They spent much time creating intricate patterns, and these patterns became part of a family's history.

Women spent most of their time gathering and preparing fruits, vegetables, and roots for winter meals. They dried most of their harvest. During the winter, they mixed dried items with oil they had distilled from fish to create nutritious meals. They also assisted men in fishing. Women and children split and dried the fish. They also harvested fish roe, or eggs, which they also dried.

Juan de Fuca, a Spanish sailor, is reported to have explored the Pacific Northwest in 1591. The Juan de Fuca Strait, which separates Vancouver Island, Canada, from Washington state, was named after de Fuca by Charles William Barkley in 1778. However, the exploration of the Pacific Ocean and Northwest coast was begun in earnest during the 1770s. From 1774 until the early 1800s the search for the famed Northwest Passage resulted in miles of coastline being claimed, mostly by England. European explorers such as Captain Juan Perez (1774), Captain James Cook (1778), and Captain George Vancouver (1792) added much to the knowledge and coffers of their countries.

Captain Juan Perez was under orders from the Spanish government to investigate Russian advances along the Pacific when he explored the Pacific coast from Monterey, now California, to the Queen Charlotte Islands, in British Columbia, Canada, in 1774. Although he sighted Vancouver Island and discovered Nootka Sound, which he called the harbor of San Lorenzo, he was prevented by heavy coastal fogs from landing. However, the Haida tribe took the opportunity to send a trading party in canoes out to his ship, the *Santiago*. They invited him to shore but he declined, worried that it might be an ambush. The Spaniards were impressed with the variety and quality of goods the Haida party had to offer for trade. It was noted in *Indians of the Pacific Northwest: A History*, by Robert H. Ruby and John A. Brown, that a blanket offered in trade for Esteban Jose Martinez's red hat "is most elegant for having been made by a people without culture."

Captain James Cook also encountered the Haida while searching for the Northwest Passage in 1778. With him on the voyage was a midshipman, George Vancouver. Captain Cook died in the Hawaiian Islands before being able to return to England. His four voyages circumnavigating the globe and exploring the Pacific greatly added to the knowledge and trading partnerships throughout the world.

George Vancouver, promoted to captain in Her Majesty's Navy, returned to the Pacific Northwest in 1792. His mission was twofold: He was to take over the English territory of Nootka Sound and to chart the Pacific coast. He was the first to gain entry to, and map, Puget Sound, naming it after his first officer, Peter Puget. It was American fur trader Robert Gray, however, who crossed the dangerous bar and explored the Columbia River in 1792, claiming the previously unknown area for the United States.

The Native Americans of the Pacific Northwest were skilled traders. They were eager to acquire European goods, which they often used as gifts during potlatch ceremonies to elevate their status. Although they traded furs, Pacific Northwest Natives were primarily fishing communities. The oceans were abundant with fish, shrimp, seals, and whales. The coastal peoples were not only skilled at harvesting nature's bounty, but they were also strong environmental managers. The First Salmon Ceremony is an example of this holistic approach to environmental conservation. Each spring, the first few salmon caught were ceremoniously prepared and served to the entire community. The remains of the fish were delivered back to the river to continue their spiritual journey.

The Lushootseed (from two words meaning "sea water" and "language"), who lived around the Puget Sound area, and other tribes initially welcomed European explorers and traders to their lands. Their generosity included advice and land. In return, the Europeans gave them trade goods and diseases from Europe. The diseases decimated much of the tribal population. Measles and smallpox wiped out up to 90 percent of the indigenous Pacific Northwest population. Moreover, the settlers were arriving by droves, displacing the remaining Native peoples. Life wasn't always peaceful between the two factions. Settlers were increasingly encroaching on Native lands. Native Americans often retaliated.

KEY CONCEPT Longhouses, Canoes, Totem Poles, and Potlatches

Longhouses were permanent structures unlike the teepees of the Plains Indians. They housed entire families, and in some cases, entire villages. These buildings varied in size, from 50 to 300 feet long, and were dug down into the ground; others were built at ground level. The idea of communal living was the same, regardless of the form the house took. The owner of the house was the oldest male of the family line. The basic layout of the longhouse allowed for a central fire and smoke hole in the middle of the house. The owner's space was at the rear of the longhouse. Here, also, were kept the treasures of the family.

Each family member had a space within the longhouse. Everyone had a personal space separated from the others by mats made from woven cedar strips and grasses. Mats were used for curtains and also for flooring and beds. Women spent much time gathering and preparing materials to create mats and other useful items from cedar. They had shelves and beds built into the walls. Elaborately woven baskets held many of the items they required for daily living.

Cedar canoes differed from birch bark and hide canoes. They were constructed from one tree. Some cedar canoes could transport more than 100 warriors. The red cedar trees, which were used to create the canoes, were felled with stone axes. They were hollowed out, and then shaped using water and hot stones. Cedar canoes were used for fishing, traveling, and hunting.

Totem poles were commissioned from master craftsmen for ceremonial occasions like births, deaths, and marriages. These poles could be displayed in front of the house, used as doorway posts, or placed as supports for the house. They were also used as coffin holders. Totem poles, translated as "man stands up straight" poles, were heraldic columns portraying the family history and its ties to the past. These poles chronicled the important roles and events that had occurred within the family. The Lushootseed and Makah tribes used posts, often carved or painted, within the longhouse rather than the totem poles of their northern neighbors. The

The "Sun and Raven Pole" of the Tlingit Indians restored by Native American workers at Saxman Indian Village, Tongass National Forest, Alaska. (U.S. Forest Service/National Archives)

The "Old Woman" pole, restored and erected at the Saxman Indian Village, Tongass National Forest, Alaska. (U.S. Forest Service/National Archives)

KEY CONCEPT *Longhouses, Canoes, Totem Poles, and Potlatches (Continued)*

Two Native Americans make their way down the Columbia River in Washington State, 1900. (Library of Congress)

banning of the potlatch effectively ended the creation of new totem poles.

A potlatch was an elaborate ceremony involving the giving away of goods. The potlatch served to strengthen community ties as well as to celebrate an important event. During this time, a totem pole was raised to commemorate the occasion. It was also customary to give each guest gifts according to his or her status or rank. Common gifts were pelts, blankets, weapons, and even slaves. The potlatch also reflected the host's wealth and prominence. Tribes that traditionally practice the potlatch include the Haidas, Kwakiutls, Makahs, Nootkas, Tlingits, and Tsimshians. It was this elaborate communal gift-giving that caused consternation among the missionaries and the government. The reason given for banning this practice was that it was considered opposite of the good Christian work ethic. The potlatch ceremony was banned in 1884. It was not officially reinstated by law until the 1934 Indian Reorganization Act. In Canada, the restriction was repealed in 1951. However, tribes often held informal, and illegal, potlatch ceremonies.

Tlingit Native woman in full potlatch dancing costume, 1906. (Library of Congress)

KEY CONCEPT   The Salmon Ceremony

Salmon were, and are, a very important part of the Pacific Northwest Native American culture. This is evidenced by the number of stories that relate how the salmon were given to the Native peoples. Many rituals focus on the salmon, an indication of how central to their lives the salmon was. The First Salmon Ceremony is one such ritual.

Each spring, two or three salmon, enough to feed the village, were caught in special nets. Extreme care was taken with these salmon. Once caught, they were swiftly killed with a quick severing of the backbone behind the head. They were prepared and served, overseen by the shaman or priest. Thanks were given for them and all the salmon to come. Each member of the village ate from the salmon, then the remains were returned to the river.

The early 1800s saw an influx of settlers. Puget Sound and the surrounding area in particular drew the attention of Americans looking to supply the growing country with lumber and foodstuffs. Christian missionaries also traveled into these lands. They came to convert and civilize. By the middle of the century, plans were in place to resettle the Native Americans to reservations.

Tlakluit Indian woman, sitting on the ground, placing salmon fillets on a wood plank, Washington State, 1910. (Edward S. Curtis/Library of Congress)

ANOTHER VIEW   Native Americans as Peacekeepers

In an alternate history, the Pacific Northwest Native Americans could have gone on to create their own militia that assisted in training other Native nations in their battles with white governments. They would have had the economic capability to outfit their own forces and provide instruction and intelligence operations to other tribes. They would have had the means to maintain diplomatic contact and covert surveillance with their neighboring tribes as well as the governments of Canada and the United States and other trading partners. They would have had to maintain a naval presence to patrol their fishing grounds and ensure that their rights were being upheld. Far from being a military force in the accepted sense, they would have been built as a frontline peacekeeping force.

TURNING POINT

During the winter and spring of 1854–1855, four treaties were signed in quick succession by Isaac I. Stevens, governor of the Washington Territory, with the Yakima, Wall Walla Cayuse, Lushootseed, Makah, Nez Perce, and the Coeur d'Alene indigenous peoples of the Washington and Oregon territories. These agreements were the Medicine Creek Treaty, December 26, 1854; the Point Elliot Treaty, January 22, 1855; the Nez Perce Treaty, June 18, 1855; and the Yakima Treaty, June 22, 1855. The lands that were ceded to the government were among the choicest lands available. They included Olympia, Tacoma, and Seattle (named after Chief Seattle, an important and powerful Lushootseed chief). He was one of the most feared and powerful Native leaders of the time.

Although each of the treaties varied slightly in content, the agreements' purposes were inherently the same. Stevens needed to have legal right to the property and lands in the possession of the various Native tribes in the Washington and Oregon territories. In exchange for ceding these lands over to the federal government, the tribes received allotted tracts of lands throughout the territories. However, the government held the right of easement for the use of public transportation through the lands and waterways within these reservations. It was also stipulated that whites were not to be allowed to reside on these reservations without permission from the tribes as well as the knowledge of the Indian agent. In total, the Native Americans ceded nearly seven million acres of land to the government during this time.

In addition, according to Elizabeth Von Aderkas in *American Indians of the Pacific Northwest*, Native Americans retained the right to take fish "from the usual and accustomed places" and to "erect temporary buildings for curing them, together with the privilege of hunting, gathering roots and berries, and pasturing their horses and cattle upon open and unclaimed lands." Additionally, provisions for specified plots of land were noted. In the case of the Yakima tribe, land was set aside for a township known as Wenatshapam Fishery, "not more than six miles square," according to Von Aderkas. In the treaty signed with the Nez Perce tribe, a tract of land was to be used by William Craig, a pioneer who had been living among the Nez Perce.

IN CONTEXT   Chief Seattle

Chief Seattle was a fierce warrior and skilled trader. He had actively sought out white traders to do business with. His presence and reputation were so powerful that he was sought out by the chief trader at Fort Nisqually, in 1833, to place his mark on a treaty foreswearing murder. So strong was his desire to create trade with Americans that he relocated to Olympia to further his contacts with white merchants.

The title of chief is not a hereditary one. Chiefs come forward, because of their skills, during the times that they are needed. In the case of Chief Seattle, he was a great orator and forward thinker during a time when the Lushootseed tribe needed guidance. Although Chief Seattle could see the benefits of trade and cooperation with the whites who were entering Washington territory, he did not realize the full impact of the treaties that were being presented.

Partly because of the differences in cultural outlook between themselves and the white settlers, the Native Americans considered themselves guardians of the land whereas whites viewed land as something to be possessed; the treaties were biased against the Native peoples. Chief Seattle saw the advantages that assimilation into white society could have for his tribe, but he failed to see the potential dangers of the treaties' clauses.

The Native Americans saw Seattle's efforts as duplicitous. They renounced his leadership. He maintained contact with all the tribes during the Indian Wars; however, he remained a firm ally of the Americans. By the time of his death, policies put into place by the American government had barred him from living in the settlement that bears his name.

The treaties provided for the creation of two schools on the reservations within one year of ratification. Also outlined were the provisions for the repair and maintenance of school buildings, as well as the equipping of each with books and furniture. Additionally, one of the schools was to be designated as an agricultural or industrial school. To this end, the government was to employ, for a period of twenty years, the teachers and the instructors for the schools. The instructors were to include farmers, gunsmiths, a tinner (or tinsmith), blacksmiths, carpenters, wagon and plough makers, and a superintendent of farming. Although the expertise of some of the employees varied within the wording of the treaties, the general composition of teacher abilities remained.

Also to be erected on each of the reservations, as stipulated in the treaties, was a general agency. This agency was to house the Indian agent and a doctor. The doctor was to be responsible for the administration of medicines and vaccines, and to advise in medical matters. The costs of the agency, as for the schools, were to be expensed to the government. The salaries of the Indian agent and the doctor were to be borne by the government for a period of twenty years.

Each of the treaties laid out the framework for compensation. In return for the land concessions, the government was to pay to the tribes varying amounts of monies in the forms of annuities paid out over a period of up to eighteen years, and at the discretion of the president of the United States. It was further stipulated that the cost and expense of provisioning, delivering goods and materials, as well as the repair and maintenance of the structures were not to be removed from the amount of the annual annuities paid to the Native Americans on the reservations. Finally, the cost of relocation, including various provisions to some tribes for clothing and household goods, was to be borne by the government. The method of payment was not monetary. Goods and services were given to the members of the tribes to the amount agreed upon within the treaty. It was further stipulated in the Point Elliot Treaty that annuities to the tribes could not be used to pay individual debt.

Furthermore, the treaties laid out the compensations to be given to each of the tribes and each of the chiefs, or headmen, as were due for duties that were to be carried out and performed. Inducements were built into the treaties that rewarded the tribes and individuals within the tribes who adopted a more civilized lifestyle. Reserved lands that were to be occupied by the resettled tribes would be fenced, cleared, and readied for cultivation at the cost of the federal government and the discretion of the president. For those individuals who would make a permanent homestead, fencing property, and raising livestock and crops, an additional allotment would be paid.

The government also identified obligations the tribes had toward the citizens of the United States. The Point Elliot Treaty, signed by the Salish, and each of the other treaties held that the Native tribes desired to exclude alcohol, "ardent spirits" from their reservations. This article in the treaties stipulated the intent to punish, through the withholding of annuities, any member of the reservation who brought in or consumed alcohol. Other articles stipulated that Native Americans were to remain friendly toward all citizens of the United States. They were to deliver, rather than conceal, any offenders who broke the laws. They were also to free any and all slaves. They were not to acquire or purchase other slaves in the future. The Salish tribes, centered around Puget Sound, had an additional stipulation: They agreed not to trade with the British post on Vancouver Island or other places outside U.S. jurisdiction without prior consent of the Indian agent.

Thus, the turning point in history for the Northwest Natives was the signing of these 1854–1855 treaties—agreements that further eroded the Native American culture and lifestyle and forced the assimilation of the Native Americans into reservations.

ACTUAL HISTORY

The Pacific Northwest Natives, their numbers already decimated by diseases brought from Europe by explorers, traders, and settlers, began their move to the reservations. The treaties were not approved of by the members of the tribes and this led to unrest and unease. The treaties were referred to as the "thief treaties" as they were often signed under threat of violence. Many people refused to move onto the meager reservations allotted to them. Others protested the amalgamation of tribes onto one reservation. Still other tribes, notably the Duwamish, were offended that they did not receive official recognition or a reservation during the treaty negotiations. Old Joseph, of the Nez Perce tribe, refused to sign a treaty. Other Nez Perce chiefs did sign. This led to the government's creation of "treaty'" and "non-treaty" Native Americans.

This unrest ultimately led to a series of wars known as the Indian wars. From 1855 to 1858, various tribes waged protests against the encroachment of the white settlers upon their traditional homelands. There were

IN CONTEXT Oregon

The claims of several nations to the Oregon region were crucial to the lives of the Native American populations of the Pacific Northwest. With the exploration of the Columbia River and the region by explorers from the United States and Britain, both nations laid claim to a vast area, bounded on the south by the present northern border of California at 42 degrees, and stretching north through the present states of Oregon, Washington, Idaho (and the most western parts of Montana and Wyoming), and including British Columbia. These lands were known as the Oregon Territory between 1818 and 1846. To the north of the Oregon Territory, Russia held Alaska, while to the south of the territory, Spain and then Mexico laid claim to land. Instead of settling the rival claims by England and America, the Anglo-American Convention of 1818 agreed to a short-term policy of joint occupation of the Oregon Territory. In 1837, the agreement was extended for another ten years.

During the 1830s and 1840s, however, the agreement began to break down, as white American settlers traveled overland and by sea routes to take up farming in some of the rich lands of the coastal and inland valleys of the Oregon Territory. Some Americans wanted the United States to lay claim to the whole territory all the way to the northern border with Russia, the line of 54 degrees, 40 minutes. The English, however, argued that their section should extend all the way south to the Columbia River, the present boundary between the states of Washington and Oregon. The English based their claims on the long history of exploration and trading by the Hudson Bay Company. With American settlers flooding into the region both north and

a number of murders and retaliations committed during this time. Kamiakin, a Yakima chief, led a series of attacks against government forces. Furthermore, miners, on their way to the Klondike gold rush, were crossing Native lands in increasing numbers. But it was the murder of Indian agent A. J. Bolon, considered an honest man, that is said to have officially started the wars in the Pacific Northwest. Kamiakin was blamed for the murder although he knew nothing of it until after it had happened.

Kamiakin, as well as other chiefs who had joined him in the uprising against white intrusion, met federal troops at the Topennish River on October 5, 1855. The battle raged for a month. During that time, the Native Americans lost 300 warriors, the soldiers lost 700 men. The Native Americans finally retreated to the Yakima Valley during the winter. However, they lost children and elders during the march.

In April 1856, government troops learned of Kamiakin's whereabouts near The Dalles. Five companies, assembled by Colonel Cornelius at Satus Creek, attacked. During the fighting, only one person from each side was killed. The troops regrouped at Five Mile Creek. Here, Yellow-Wash, a Klickitat tribe member, drove off most of the soldiers' horses. The Native Americans then advanced toward Colonel Wright's army from Fort Simcoe. The Battle of the Satus caused several chiefs to approach Colonel Wright seeking peace.

A bounty was offered for several Native chiefs during treaty negotiations in May 1856, including Kamiakin. The chiefs were insulted. The Native peoples began to fight among themselves; some wanted peace while others wanted to continue to fight. In September 1858, at the Battle of Four Lakes near Spokane, the Native Americans were defeated. Kamiakin eventually fled to Canada.

---

south of the Columbia in the 1840s, however, the English position weakened.

In 1844, Democratic candidate James K. Polk ran on an openly expansionist doctrine. Hoping to win northern support for a plan to admit Texas to the Union as a slave state, he held out for settling the Oregon question. Although most believed that Polk stood for claiming the whole Oregon Territory all the way to the 54–40 line, he quietly entered into discussions with the English to settle the issue by diplomatic negotiation. In June 1846, the issue was finally resolved, when Secretary of State James Buchanan (who later served as president) signed the Treaty of Washington. That treaty set the boundary at the 49th parallel, extending the existing line to the Strait of Juan de Fuca. There the agreed boundary took a southern dip, allowing the English to retain the whole of Vancouver Island, but guaran-

teeing to both nations freedom of navigation of the waters of the Strait of Juan de Fuca. Meanwhile, the United States had moved troops to the Rio Grande in the disputed lands between Texas and Mexico, and the war with Mexico had begun. Many Northerners felt that President Polk had betrayed northern interests by sacrificing to England the land above the 49th parallel that later became the Canadian province of British Columbia, while at the same time he actively supported the expansion of the southern slaveholding section with the war on Mexico.

Nevertheless, for the Native American population of the Pacific Northwest, it was clear that between the Canadian line of 49 degrees and the northern boundary of California, the flood of settlers from the United States would present a cultural onslaught over the following decades.

By the 1860s the economy of the Washington Territory was booming. Sawmills, to create the lumber needed for the shipbuilding and construction industries, were in full production. Prospectors flooded the territory like salmon swimming upstream. Settlers came to reap their own profits from growing or selling the goods needed by those on their way to the goldfields of the Klondike.

The Native Americans were the only ones who missed out on the boom. Pushed from their natural fertile land, and restricted from fishing and hunting, they became increasingly dependent on the government for their livelihoods. However, the government promises, made within the treaties, were slow to appear. Payment for horses and other goods, procured from the Native Americans during the Yakima Indian Wars and for the use of government troops, was slow or not forthcoming. The treaties took years to become ratified by the federal government. Payment was delayed even longer. Oftentimes, payment was forgotten. Treaties were being renegotiated although the original terms had not been met, or were being breached.

Furthermore, Native lands continued to be settled by whites. This was seen by the Native chiefs as an insult and as indication that the promises given in the treaties were worthless. In 1863, there was a renegotiation of some of the original treaties. Native Americans wanted additional compensation for the lands that were being used, in contravention of the treaty, for mining and agriculture. Old Joseph, of the Nez Perce, refused to sign as the new terms called for a reduction of the reservation to one-sixth of its original size. The Native Americans would receive no additional payments. Old Joseph resisted in part because the new treaty would remove the Wallowa Valley, a traditional homeland, from the

Nez Perce tribe. However, a Nez Perce named Hal-halt-los-sot, better known as Lawyer, signed the treaty. The U.S. government accepted his signature as the representative of the Nez Perce, although the people did not. According to *Indians of the Pacific Northwest: A History,* Old Joseph would not sign as "no man owned any part of the earth, and a man could not sell what he did not own." His son, Chief Joseph, heeded his father's words and vowed that he would never sell the land of his forefathers.

The signing of the treaty caused a rift in the federation of Nez Perce. Those, like Old Joseph and Chief Joseph, who did not sign were classified as "non-treaty." This created a separate group that was not entitled to any of the benefits laid out in the treaty. The "non-treaty" Native Americans went back to the traditional lands and tried to maintain their way of life. They were respectful of their Mother Earth. They did not want to raise animals and till the land. They considered the plowing of land sacrilegious. In 1873, Indian agents began to put pressure on the "non-treaty" Native Americans to move to the reservation. When they refused, threats of force were issued by General O. O. Howard. Chief Joseph, wanting to avoid war, asked for an extension of thirty days to gather his people and livestock.

During the time that the Native Americans were collecting their possessions, a group of young warriors killed four white men. The "non-treaty" Nez Perce were forced on a four-month, 1,300-mile trek in 1877. During that time, they were pursued and attacked by soldiers as they slept at Bitterroot Valley. Another battle was waged en route to Yellowstone country. By this time, Chief Joseph had led his people across four states. He finally agreed to lay down arms. His words, during his historic speech of September 1877 were, "I will fight no more forever," according to *Indians of the Pacific Northwest: A History.* In retaliation, Chief Joseph's people were sent to Bismarck, North Dakota; Fort Leavenworth; then Baxter Springs, Kansas, before being returned to northern Washington state to live on the Colville reservation.

The organization of government schools helped to further break down the traditional Native way of life. A stipulation in each of the treaties was to operate a school for all Native American children. In theory, this was to help them better acclimate to mainstream American society. In reality, some observers believe, it was to eradicate their traditional way of life. The schooling was to instill the white way of thinking into the Native children. Many of the schools were residential and the children were removed from their homes, placed with other children from other tribes, and forbidden to speak their own languages. Richard Henry Pratt, founder of Pennsylvania's Carlisle School, summed up the prevailing philosophy, "Kill the Indian and save the man," according to Edwin H. Chalcraft in *Assimilation's Agent: My Life as a Superintendent in the Indian Boarding School System.*

By the time the Washington territory was declared a state in 1889, it was well on the road to economic prosperity. Gold had been found in the Salmon River in Idaho, home of the Nez Perce, in 1877. Now the fortune seekers were on their way north. The Klondike and Alaska gold rushes solidified Washington territory's economic fortunes. The white settlers had begun logging in earnest in 1853, when the first steam-driven mill was built. The return of prospectors from the Klondike caused a building boom. They brought huge amounts of gold with them and were willing

KEY CONCEPT   Indian Schools

Indian schools were most often residential. The children were removed from their homes and sent to schools that were operated by private organizations like the Carlisle School, or religious groups. These schools were often used as a less-expensive option to operating federally funded schools.

Life for the students was often hard. It was physically demanding, as the students were required to provide all the labor that kept the school in operation. These tasks, or chores, were used under the guise of providing basic training in household or farming skills. The girls would learn to sew by mending uniforms, linens, and bedding. They learned culinary skills by working in the kitchens. Boys learned animal husbandry by caring for the stock, the chickens, cows, and pigs that provided the food that the girls prepared. They learned to farm and to repair tools and equipment. The focus on manual and domestic labor was indicative of the mainstream mind-set that Native Americans were incapable of learning complicated concepts and were best suited to menial jobs.

Their daily routines were governed by strict adherence to a system of bells or alarms. They woke up, ate, studied, played, and slept according to the bells. Any deviation from the routine was severely punished. Likewise, use of their own language was strictly forbidden and harshly punished. The severe discipline meted out to students who dared to run away was used to show the others the consequences of breaking the rules.

Many of the survivors of this system found that they no longer fit into either the Native or white system. They had lost the use of their language. Some never regained fluency in their mother tongue. They didn't fit into white society; their skills were not sufficient to propel them into mainstream jobs. They had lost the ability to communicate with their elders. This led to increased breakdown of families and an increase in substance abuse that still plagues Native Americans today.

to spend it lavishly. As the news spread of the Klondike strike, men and women traveled toward the north. The stream of prospectors bought goods in Seattle, often outfitting themselves before they boarded ships. A second boom followed when news of a new gold strike in Alaska filtered out. Gold prospectors also used overland routes, which had prompted the Native unrest earlier and continued to aggravate the tensions between the Native Americans and the whites.

The first cannery had been built at Mukilteo in 1877 and the processing of salmon became an economic mainstay. Salmon was shipped all over the world. Oysters from Puget Sound were harvested and shipped from the mid-1800s. The expansion of the transcontinental railways to Tacoma in 1883 allowed more transport of goods into the interior states as well as ports to the east.

In 1890, Washington state passed a law wherein private citizens could purchase tidewater land. The Bush Act, passed in the same year, stipulated that any person who purchased tideland and found it unfit for oyster cultivation could have the deed revoked. The first fish hatcheries were established in 1895. Fishing in the early 1900s was at its peak. Huge nets were used to haul thousands of fish daily from the rivers in Washington state. However, by the 1950s, Puget Sound was considered the sixth most polluted area in the United States. Native Americans had little profit from these ventures. They were marginalized and kept apart from not only mainstream society but also from their traditional way of life by the encroachment of civilization. Some Native Americans fared better than others. Those who found work in the logging, fishing, and milling industries did better economically than their counterparts who stayed on the reservations.

Washington's resource-based economy had a series of upturns. Related to technological developments like band saws, and clear-cutting for lumber, and refinement of growing and canning techniques for the fishing industry, Washington rode each wave. The world wars created demand for ships and lumber and increased the need for canned fish.

The Indian Reorganization Act of 1934 was designed to decrease government involvement in the regulation and the overseeing of Native American affairs. The act, which outlined the return of control over assets (notably lands), sought to reduce the depletion of reservation resources and to build a sound economic foundation, and was actively pursued until the outbreak of World War II.

However, the construction of dams along the Columbia River and its tributaries caused a massive decline in the salmon stocks. The first major dams, the Bonneville (1938) and Grand Coulee (1941), were hydro-electric projects. More than 400 dams harness the Columbia's massive 21-million-kilowatt–generating capacity. This has come at a huge price. Spawning salmon have to jump the dams to reach their traditional breeding sites. The attrition rate of these salmon has been as high as 35 percent per dam. Fish ladders have helped to a degree, but not enough to save the Snake River Sockeye and the Willamette Steelhead salmon from inclusion on the endangered species list.

The 1970s saw massive movements toward structured self-government. The American Indian Movement (AIM) created a twenty-point manifesto asking for the return and restoration of Native American and treaty rights. In support of the Native Americans, actor Marlon Brando refused in 1972 to accept his second Academy Award as Best Actor for his role in the *Godfather*. Instead, he sent a Native representative to the awards ceremony to deliver the speech he had written. In it, according to the American Indian Movement ("A Brief History of AIM" at http://www.aimovement.org), he said, "I think awards in this country at this time are inappropriate to be received or given until the condition of the American Indian is drastically altered. If we are not our brother's keeper, at least let us not be his executioner."

Many of the Native American tribes in the Pacific Northwest have reestablished councils and organizations by which they are reclaiming governance and control over their lands. They continue to fight for their lands and their rights.

ALTERNATE HISTORY

In the winter of 1854, the governor of the Washington Territory, Isaac I. Stevens, wanted to meet with the Native Americans to discuss the creation of treaties that would move them from their traditional lands and place them onto other lands, and away from the oncoming invasion of American settlers from the east. Had the Native Americans refused to sign and had they not fought among themselves, the territory would not have been settled by whites as quickly. Stevens had to try to take the land legally, even with the coercive threat of violence. The lands of the Pacific Northwest Natives would have ceased to be considered part of the Washington Territory. In essence, they would have become an independent, autonomous nation, the Pacific Northwest Federation.

Had the Native Americans had a stronger solidarity and cohesive leadership, they would have been able to stave off the advance of the settlers and prospectors. From the time of the arrival of the first explorers, the Native Americans had learned many things. They had watched while the sailors manned the rigging of the tall ships. They had seen that the block and tackles used by the crews had been able to lift easily the heavy sails that no one man could move alone.

They might have applied this technology to their own fishing methods. The Native Americans' huge traps and smoking and preserving methods could have become an important export. They could have continued to trade their surplus with all the ships from Europe as they wouldn't have signed away their rights to multinational trade, as outlined in the treaties prepared by the U.S. government. They would have been able to become an autonomous federation, complete with their own ambassadors and armed forces.

This economic boon would have resulted in an increase in population, as the tribes' standard of living would have improved. The Native peoples would have been able to repopulate their tribes, which had been decimated by earlier outbreaks of measles and smallpox. Having acquired an immunity and having a healthier lifestyle would have helped the Native Americans to recover from the diseases that had reduced their numbers so dramatically in the first part of the century.

The Northwest Native Americans would have been able to use the skills given to them by their spirit ancestors to further refine their salmon-fishing prowess. Their preservation methods for the fish as well as the roe, or caviar, would have been acceptable for the long journeys the ships would be making back to Europe. The watertight baskets, with their elaborate outer designs, could have become a much sought-after status symbol on the continent, as were the furs that were brought back with the traders.

The Native Americans were an observant and intelligent people. They would have heard of the big mill operations and could have allowed a trusted white man, like William Craig, to negotiate and set up a mill where they could mill their own logs for sale and export. Native Americans could have employed many of their own people both in the mill and the production of dogfish oil that was used as a lubricant for the mills.

They could have used the same block-and-tackle technology to ease the production of the fish oil from being heavily labor-intensive to a much more easily managed task. In the same vein, they could have used the logs to construct booms that, like cranes, could move large quantities of fish directly to a specially built longhouse, after they had been cleaned and gutted. There, the women and children could smoke large quantities of salmon.

As each of these smoker-longhouses could have been built and maintained next to the rivers where the salmon were traditionally caught, the disruption to the Native lifestyle would have been minimized. Traditional lifestyles and ceremonies could have continued as before. Without the ban on potlatches, the economy of the Pacific Northwest Native Americans would continue to flourish. In the alternate history, the Native Americans would have redistributed their wealth regularly and amassed slaves, not through war as often as through bargaining with other tribes who were still warring. This redistribution would have further strengthened Northwest tribes' position as leaders. The ties, forged through the regular potlatches, would have enabled them to maintain a united front against the persistent push of settlement into their lands. They would have been able to provide a united and lethal front from which to repel additional attacks from U.S. government troops. Like Chief Seattle, they would have watched the troops and would have followed the development of armaments. With the money they would have accumulated, they could have purchased the newest weapons and had them ready and at their disposal in case of future attacks from the army.

The coming of the railways could have been a potential problem for them, because with the railways came workers and those looking to settle into new lands. However, given their new economic strength, the Native Americans would have been able to negotiate beneficial settlements. Had they been able to negotiate with the railroads, they could have procured transportation agreements that would have given them favorable rates for the movement of their lumber, fish, and seafood products to the east.

They would have been able to hire and oversee the professionals they would have needed to help them develop the skills necessary to function within the white world. They would have been able to hire teachers, blacksmiths, mill hands, and interpreters to further the Native American goals.

The gold rushes of the late 1890s would have created a boon for the Native city of Seattle. The whites who had remained there would have pledged allegiance to the Salish tribe in return for their continued occupation of Native lands. The Native Americans would have become the purveyors of vegetables and meats for the prospectors and miners traveling to and from the goldfields.

The Native Americans could have used all the skills their spiritual ancestors had provided to them in an effort to manage their environment effectively. They would have seen that the removal of so many salmon was causing a hardship on the fish population. They could have created special holding ponds for the roe where they would have overseen the hatching and growth of the fry. They might have reduced the consumption of caviar that the European aristocracy had developed a taste for. This would have driven the price up and created additional demand for better conservation methods to ensure future supplies.

The Native Americans had learned that being generous toward others did not always apply in their dealings toward non-Native peoples.

They would have become even more skilled in business, commerce, and trade. The Pacific Northwest Native Americans would have been able to remain on their homelands and raise their children in the ways of their people. However, they would have also insisted that the children learn of the white world in order to preserve their own.

The environmental skills and continued control over their lands would have impacted the development of the Columbia River as a hydroelectric source. This, in turn, would have eliminated the destruction of millions of acres of habitat. The Native Americans would have needed this land. In the alternate history, their sound ecological practices and sharp business skills would have propelled them into an enviable position. They could have devised a system of green dams that would have used the power of the rivers to create the energy needed without the wholesale flooding caused by the super dam projects like the Bonneville and Grand Coulee dams. Other dam projects could have helped with irrigation and flood control. While they couldn't have controlled the development of other dam projects in Canada or in the areas outside their borders, they would have been in a very advantageous negotiating position to ensure that they would be adequately compensated for any environmental damages.

The Pacific Northwest Natives could have faced a population explosion as soon as the early 1900s. As they had basically become an advanced form of a hunter-and-gatherer society, their need for land was increasing as the tribes expanded, moving from place to place, while trying to minimize the impact they were having on their precious Mother Earth. Families would be creating ever-larger longhouses as their members lived longer and had more children. Natives of the Pacific Northwest had always lived in semi-autonomy. Each village operated basically independently of the others but had strong ties to other villages through intermarrying and potlatch ceremonies. With the longer life spans and increased health of their members, families would have realized that they were having a negative impact on their environment.

In the alternate history, the outbreaks of World Wars I and II would have put an increased strain on the environment as Native business-people struggled to maintain the balance between industry and ecology. As an independent federation, they would not have had to participate in the war. The Indian Militia would have been maintained as a security measure. They might have declared themselves a neutral nation, like Switzerland.

With their strong environmental practices, the Pacific Northwest Federation might have become a leader in positive environmental practices. This could have led to a tertiary industry as the area became an eco-tourist destination. Having been able to preserve traditional lifestyles, the Native Americans could have also become an object of anthropological study by researchers who wanted to view a parallel societal structure that had managed to survive the onslaught of Western civilization.

The population would have stabilized in the mid-1900s. The tribes would have managed their health and environment in an effort to

maximize benefits they and the environment would receive. With sufficient revenue from trade, they would have been able to have a strong
preventive health program. The standard of living would have been
very high in relation to tribes living in the United States. According to
their traditional tribal society, the programs would have been socialist
in nature. The health care would have been universal in keeping with
the philosophy of wealth distribution.

The Pacific Northwest Federation would never have had the
upheaval of being removed to a reservation and having their children
taken from them and forced to receive a mainstream education. The
tribes would not have suffered the family breakdowns, substance
abuse, and identity questions that Native Americans faced after they
moved off their lands and onto reservations.

The people of the Pacific Northwest could have become the poster
people for the correct way to live with the environment.

Deborah Clark

Discussion Questions

1. Following the American Civil War (1861–1865), the United States
   Army engaged in numerous wars against Native American peoples to
   suppress their independence and to acquire control of their lands.
   What factors had to be present in the alternate history case of the
   Pacific Northwest Federation that would lead to the survival of that
   state as an independent nation?

2. The United States acquired Alaska from Russia in 1867 for $7.2 million
   (including the cost of bribes to congressmen). If Congress had failed to
   approve the sale, and if Russia had retained Alaska and developed an
   interest in supporting or taking over the Pacific Northwest Federation,
   how would that have changed the history of western North America?

3. The British had originally claimed the Oregon Territory, including the
   lands now in the province of British Columbia and the U.S. states of
   Washington, Oregon, and Idaho. The extension of the U.S.-British
   boundary on the 49th parallel to the Pacific Ocean was established in
   the Oregon Treaty of 1846. If the alternate-scenario Pacific Northwest
   Federation had appealed to Britain to rescind that treaty and establish
   a protectorate over their independent state to prevent U.S. control,
   what would have been the consequences for British-American relations in the 1860s?

4. The Native American peoples of the Pacific Northwest used lumber
   in making canoes and for the construction of buildings before any
   established contact with Europeans. Other aspects of their advanced
   technical skills are mentioned in this chapter. How would such
   sophisticated material culture have helped them in resisting takeover
   of their lands by the United States?

5. One factor in weakening the resistance of the Native American population to European conquest was the introduction of diseases to which the Native Americans had little immunity or resistance. Why was there so little resistance to European diseases and how did this factor make a difference in the European conquest?

Bibliography and Further Reading

Aderkas, Elizabeth von. *American Indians of the Pacific Northwest.* Oxford: Osprey Publishing, 2005.

American Indian Movement. "A Brief History of AIM." http://www.aimovement.org (accessed April 26, 2006).

Boyd, Robert, ed. *Indians, Fire, and the Land in the Pacific Northwest.* Corvallis: Oregon State University Press, 1999.

Chalcraft, Edwin H. *Assimilation's Agent: My Life as a Superintendent in the Indian Boarding School System.* Lincoln, NE: University of Nebraska Press, 2004.

Chief Seattle Arts. "Chief Seattle." http://www.chiefseattle.com (accessed April 26, 2006).

Diomedi, Alexander. *Sketches of Indian Life in the Pacific Northwest.* Fairfield, WA: Ye Galleon Press, 1998.

Peabody Museum. "Potlatches." http://www.peabody.harvard.edu (accessed April 26, 2006).

Ruby, Robert H., and John A. Brown. *Guide to the Indian Tribes of the Pacific Northwest.* Norman, OK: University of Oklahoma Press, 2003.

Ruby, Robert H., and John A. Brown. *Indians of the Pacific Northwest: A History.* Norman, OK: University of Oklahoma Press, 1988.

University of Washington Library. "Alaskan Tlingit and Tsimshian," "Native Americans of the Pacific Northwest: An Introduction," "Salmon, the Lifegiving Gift," "The Lushootseed Peoples of Puget Sound Country," "Totem Poles: Heraldic Columns of the Northwest Coast," "The Makah Tribe: People of the Sea and the Forest," "The Nez Perce," "Washington State and Tribal Sovereignty." http://content.lib.washington.edu (accessed April 26, 2006).

Archaeological evidence suggests California Natives never developed Bronze Age technology. What if these peoples had created Bronze Age iron weapons and tools?

INTRODUCTION

If you ask them where they come from, they will tell you, "We have always been here." They will tell you that their traditions are as old as time itself, and that they sprang from the land itself. They are the First People, the Native Americans whose ancestors entered the Americas many thousands of years ago and settled and prospered. They will tell you how they became the 500 Nations of the North American continent and how their technology helped them to adapt in order to live in their homeland. And if you listen long enough, you can hear the story of their fall and how all that they once had was taken away from them.

There is a lot of debate about when humans first entered the American continent and how many times large groups of them crossed the Bering Strait area from Siberia into Alaska. Scholars agree that the best available evidence shows that North America was well colonized by the First People as early as 12,000 years ago. Currently there is a lot of debate in the archaeological community about how much earlier humans might have entered the North American continent. Recent archaeological findings in Chile, Alaska, Texas, and the Carolinas suggest that a large group of Amerind language speakers arrived in America about 20,000 years ago. However, University of South Carolina archaeologists announced in the fall of 2004 that material from the Topper archaeological site shows that humans had colonized the Americas as early as 50,000 years ago. Many archaeologists dispute this finding, but the new material adds weight to the evidence showing that the Clovis culture (10,000–9,000 B.C.E.) was not the first significant Paleoindian tradition in the Americas.

Along the western coastline of the United States are Paleoindian sites that are between 10,000 and 11,000 years old; most of these sites cluster in and around San Diego County in California. These sites show how people of that time were adapting to significant global climate changes. Their ancestors were born during the Pleistocene Ice Age, when the Laurentide Ice Sheet and other massive glaciers covered parts of North America as far

KEY CONCEPT Bronze

Bronze is the earliest known alloy, or blend of two metals. Developed in the Middle East about the year 3500 B.C.E., the alloy was made from blending copper and tin. Since the two ores are available in California, a bronze-age technological revolution in California before the arrival of the Spaniards and other Europeans was a real possibility. When copper and tin are blended in the right proportions, the resulting alloy is stronger than copper but still easily worked. Both tin and copper are soft metals, but the alloy of the two, because of way the crystalline shapes at the microscopic level blend, comes out harder than either.

Bronze was developed in the Eastern Hemisphere only after there was a metal industry using copper. Copper and gold were both worked in Mexico in the era before the arrival of the first Spaniards, so it is quite possible that copper working—and the accidental discovery that copper and tin, when blended, made a superior metal—could have occurred in the Western Hemisphere before the arrival of the first Europeans. Such a development would most likely have taken place where both copper ores and tin ores were found, such as California.

Bronze is harder than copper yet easier to cast, and more readily melted than iron. Furthermore, it is harder as a metal for making weapons, blades, and tools than pure iron. Also, bronze resists corrosion, turning slightly green with a coating that keeps out further oxidation, whereas iron can rust deeply. When iron was substituted for bronze around 1000 B.C.E. in the Eastern Hemisphere, iron became more

south as Idaho. Glaciers began to push through the land, shaping the landscape by grinding down mountains and carving through river valleys. As temperatures dropped to their coldest level during the Last Glacial Maximum, fresh water was bound up in glaciers and the ocean level gradually dropped.

Land along the continental shelves emerged from the oceans, making it possible for humans and animals to travel to previously isolated areas such as Ceylon, Ireland, the British Isles, Indonesia, and Australia. In the area between Alaska and Siberia, the continental bridge called Beringia emerged from the sea. As the glaciers slowly crept forward to shut off Siberia and lower Asia from North America, animals and humans trapped in this area of ice and snow retreated into the broad, dry grasslands and tundra of Beringia.

Although the glaciers never intruded fully onto this land bridge, the haven wasn't destined to last forever. As the Glacial Maximum passed and the climate warmed, the world began to thaw slowly. Across the globe, the vast continental ice shields began to melt and retreat, releasing their stores of fresh water into the oceans. Coastal ocean environments changed from salt water to brackish water and the sea level began to rise slowly, permanently flooding low-lying areas. Large hurricanes and typhoons became more common as the ocean itself began to warm. Across the world, warmth brought shifting weather patterns that created grasslands in areas that once were desert, created forests in areas that once were grasslands, and brought drought to the areas that would become the Sahara desert, the Gobi desert, and the great deserts of the southwest United States. Beringia began to disappear under the rising water levels.

With glaciers blocking the land to the west, humans and animals were forced out of the flooding Beringia tundra onto the North American coast. Alaska and Canada still lay buried under the Canadian Ice Shield, but in abundant and cheaper than tin. In the Eastern Hemisphere, one of the major areas for mining tin was in Cornwall, Britain, and the tin had to be carried great distances by ship and overland travel in order for metal workers to make bronze there. Although iron was cheaper, as a metal it had few real advantages over bronze for use in weapons, tools, and other fixtures, such as hinges, door-studding, or shields. Considering the hardness of bronze and its resistance to corrosion, it would have remained the dominant metal if it had not been so expensive because of shipping costs.

Because bronze was such a strong metal, compared to gold and copper, its use caused a technological revolution. Gold and copper had been used almost exclusively, both in the Eastern and Western Hemispheres, as decorative metals for jewelry, adornment, statuary, and in the Eastern Hemisphere, also as mediums of commercial exchange. But bronze, because of its superior qualities, led to wider use of metals in much more utilitarian functions, especially in weaponry. The people who possessed bronze and bronze weapons tended to win out in warfare over people using only flint, stone, or wooden weapons. Furthermore, the development of metal tools (such as hammers, chisels, adzes, hatchets, gouges, and drills) would soon lead to improved woodworking and construction. So a bronze revolution in California could have put that region far in advance of other areas of the Western Hemisphere, and in a position to resist and adapt to outside influences.

the region of present-day California, Nevada, and Arizona there existed the best of all environments—open woodlands and pastures with abundant water teeming with wildlife and coastlines and rivers full of fish. It is along these coastlines that we find some of the earliest traces of the people who came from Siberia via the Beringia land bridge.

These immigrants lived much as their Siberian ancestors did, in small groups made up of one or more families who slept in cave shelters or temporary open-air camps and followed migratory herds of large game animals. They constructed shelters from locally available materials such as bone, tanned hides, brushwood, reeds, and grasses. They wove plant fibers into baskets, sandals, mats, and fishing nets. They gathered seeds and ground them into flour with mortars and metates. They knew how to make beads, and they developed a variety of stone tools, from tiny microblades to the large, heavy Clovis spear point. They also brought with them their dogs, the first domesticated animals in the Americas.

They adapted to the new environment by changing their food gathering techniques. Fisheries were an important source of food along the coastline, and tribes such as the Chumash developed ways of catching different species of fish, including hook and line, seine, netting, and fish traps. Nuts, seeds, and berries were also an important part of the diet, and acorns became an important staple as methods were developed to extract the tannin and grind the nuts into nutritious flour.

TURNING POINT

The turning point for these Native Americans came around 5000 B.C.E.; the age of the birth of civilizations. Up until this point, Native peoples had been technologically equal with the rest of the world. As the world

KEY CONCEPT The Holocene Hypsithermal

The Holocene Hypsithermal occurred some 8,000 to 3,000 years ago and was a period of weather that was warmer and drier than the conditions immediately preceding it. It was responsible for changing weather patterns and contributing to ecological pressures that caused the shift of both humans and animals to different areas.

entered the Holocene Hypsithermal Climate Interval, temperatures across the globe began rising and a long period of global warming started. Extended dry seasons shrank lakes and marshes and decreased the water flow in creeks and rivers; some forests became replaced by grasslands and some grasslands became desert. Ocean levels rose and coastal fishing areas disappeared permanently.

As the number and variety of prey animals dwindled, a shift in hunting and gathering techniques occurred. In the Old World, these pressures crowded people into river valleys where permanent settlements were formed and the earliest civilizations emerged. In the New World, people responded to the climate pressure by moving and by changing hunting and food production methods.

Early North American hunter-gatherers focused on food that might take longer to acquire but was easy to process, such as meat from large animals. With prey becoming harder to find, the focus switched from easily processed foods to those that were more locally available but took some time to process. Acorns became an important part of the diet, and a number of techniques evolved to rinse the tannin from the acorn meat and to grind it into flour for baking.

At a time when the Old World was learning agriculture and animal domestication, life in the New World still remained based on a semi-nomadic lifestyle. Plant and animal resources were managed informally, and controlled burnings were used to create areas that were desirable for some types of plants. The new way of managing food resources was more efficient than the old lifestyle, and there was a corresponding population increase.

As groups grew larger, the problem of maintaining order and organizing everyday life became a more complex task. Subgroups—political, ceremonial, economic, social, and professional—began to form in these communities. There was no organization at a tribal level, rather, each village was headed by its own chief. Larger communities might have had several chiefs, each of whom was in charge of a particular area of village life such as fishing, boat making, or hunting. Gender was no barrier to power. Men or women could lead villages, and the villages themselves were autonomous entities in much the same way that the Greek city-states were. All adults shared in the decision-making process for the group.

Social organization was along patrilineal and patrilocal structures. Women married into families that lived in other villages whereas men retained membership with the tribe and family into which they were born. Lands and food sources were not owned, although in some areas, families controlled access to fishing rights. Resources were shared with other members of the village, and excess food as well as baskets and jewelry and other goods were exchanged along an extensive network of intertribal trade routes.

Part of the reason for their long and peaceful history was the abundance of natural resources in California. In some areas of the world, fierce competition for food and raw materials resulteds in sharply divided societies and the rise of a system of castes or classes, but the tribes of California remained as their ancestors did—autonomous bands with egalitarian principles. For thousands of years there were few permanent settlements, and most tribes followed a "seasonal round" where they moved to different locations according to what foods were in season.

Agriculture and horticulture were slow to arise in this setting. Basketry took precedence over pottery for most of the history of the California tribes, and some technologies such as metalworking never developed. By 1000 C.E., tribes such as the Luiseños had settled into permanent villages and were beginning to develop farming techniques. Hunting changed with the introduction and spread of the bow and arrow, which was far more accurate than the spear and atlatl. Concepts of ownership became stronger among groups throughout the state during this time period, with some tribes claiming certain land areas as their territory and denying access to other groups. Tribal societies became more structured and specialized as ceremonial, social, and political subgroups formed in the largest villages. Wealth and status became important divisions in society, particularly among the northernmost tribes of California, Oregon, and Washington.

This period of stability was interrupted by another long-term climate shift that caused social and economic changes throughout the Americas. A series of extended droughts began in North America around 1000 C.E. and lasted until shortly before the arrival of the Spanish Conquistadors. The Anasazi, Hohokam, and Mogollan cultures all abandoned their former lands as a partial consequence of the drying up of their local water resources. The drought was especially severe in the San Juan region of California from 1270 to 1300 C.E.

As resources were stretched to their limit, populations declined. Tribal conflict on the Great Plains and in the Southwest increased in response to limited access to good water sources. More time was spent on growing and finding food, and the quality of life decreased in villages and settlements in those areas hit hardest by the climate changes.

Although the Old World and the New World were on a relatively level footing in terms of society and technology in 8000 B.C.E., the combination of abundance and a semi-nomadic lifestyle caused a technological gap in the two populations. Late development of pottery and agricultural practices widened the division. Social disruptions caused by periods of drought after 1000 C.E. furthered the problem. By the time that the Old World discovered the New World at the beginning of the sixteenth century, the technology gap between the two hemispheres was vast.

ACTUAL HISTORY

Although the California Indians lived a largely peaceful existence in a land of plenty, Europe was a place of almost constant war. Dense populations, limited living space, and limited resources meant that there was a constant state of conflict in Europe, northern Africa, eastern Russia, and the Middle East. Oceans, mountain ranges, deserts, and steppes kept expansion and conflict limited to neighboring regions, but as kingdoms and empires acquired ocean-going ships capable of long sea trips, they began voyages of conquest to other areas of the world.

What they were looking for was gold. Gold could buy armies from other countries, and gold could buy the very latest weapons and teachers to show how to make those weapons and how to use them. European society was emerging from feudalism. It was possible for someone who had been born a peasant to buy his way into a different class. The conquest of Montezuma and the discovery of Aztec gold started a gold rush to America, bringing people who were eager to exploit the people and resources in the new land to raise their own social status.

Tantalizing rumors about seven "cities of gold" led to several Spanish expeditions into the interior of Central America and northward into the United States along both the Pacific coast and the Gulf of Mexico. They found no gold, but on the peninsula of Baja California they did find Stone Age tribes and good harbors that could shelter ships coming from the Philippines. The Spaniards quickly moved in and occupied the area and explored northward, finding only a few tribes and fishing grounds that were of no interest. The Natives of California were left in peace for another one hundred years.

By 1700, European interest in California renewed. Spain's grip on the New World had weakened. The defeat of the Spanish Armada at the end of the sixteenth century opened up the Americas for exploration and colonization by the Dutch, English, and French. In Mexico, the harsh practices of the Spanish colonial policy led to numerous revolts among the indigenous peoples that threatened the stability of the Rio Grande region. Spanish claims to the Pacific coastline were being challenged by the incursion of Russian fur traders south of Alaska and the presence of English traders in Hudson Bay.

Spanish Viceroy Jose de Galvaz proposed a plan to consolidate the Spanish power in the New World by establishing missions along the coastline from Baja California northward to Sonoma. A group of Franciscan friars together with soldiers made their way to the area of San Diego that is now called Mission Valley. While some of the soldiers continued north to Monterey, others stayed behind with the priests to protect them as they set up the first mission. The priests attempted to contact the local Native peoples, to persuade them to convert to Christianity and learn to become "civilized." The Native Americans were unimpressed

The friars tried offering gifts to convince the Native peoples to convert, but to no avail. Relationships grew increasingly tense, culminating with an attack on the mission in which a priest was killed and the church was burned to the ground. Retaliation by the Spanish troops was swift, and they kept up the pressure as supplies, colonists, livestock, and more

KEY CONCEPT   The Paleolithic Era

The Paleolithic Era, also called the "Stone Age," was the first clearly definable stage in the history of human technology. It begins with the first invention of the stone axe, about 2.5 million years ago by our ancestor, *homo habilis*. Stone tools and the Stone Age last until people settle into stable communities and develop agriculture and tools other than those they knap from flint and obsidian.

troops arrived at the mission. Within five years, the Native peoples were defeated by superior firepower. The survivors were forced to convert and join the mission system as novices. It was a scenario that was repeated countless times as the Spanish went on to establish a total of twenty-one missions in California.

With the colonists and soldiers, a new nightmare was introduced in the form of European diseases. Maladies such as smallpox, diphtheria, syphilis, pneumonia, and chickenpox periodically ravaged the tribes. Traditional healers and shamans could provide no protection from these illnesses, and frightened parents, desperate to save their children, would bring their families into the missions to seek aid. The priests would offer the best care that European medicine of that time could provide. Those who survived and their families were converted to Christianity and became religious novices, to serve Spain as feudal peasants in America.

The life of a religious novice was brutal. The friars had promised the Native peoples that they would be converted to a good religion, civilized, taught skills and a trade, taught how to farm, given livestock, and eventually given land—the land that their own tribe had owned—to farm. In practice, they were little more than slaves or indentured servants. Adults were segregated into single-sex buildings. Family groups were separated, and children were taken from their parents and sent to live in barracks. Women were often taken by the soldiers as concubines and those who resisted were raped.

Any sign of rebellion was immediately suppressed. Punishment was harsh, even for minor crimes, and brandings and executions were common. The mission Natives attempted to fight back in a series of revolts during the 1800s, but these were answered by ruthless acts of retribution from the soldiers

In 1821, Mexico achieved independence from Spain and California became a province of the Mexican Republic in 1823, bringing changes to the treatment of Native peoples. Under Spanish rule, land grants to individuals were few in number and the title to most land was in the hands of the crown. Under Mexican

An Athapascan Hupa female shaman from northwestern California, poses for a portrait wearing shell headbands, necklace, and holding two baskets. (Edward S. Curtis/Library of Congress)

IN CONTEXT The California Missions

Along the Camino Real (King's Highway) from San Diego to San Francisco and north to Sonoma in the last quarter of the eighteenth and first quarter of the nineteenth centuries, a chain of missions was founded a "stiff day's march" (thirty miles—the "march" was on horseback) apart from one another. These missions established Spain's claim to Alta (Upper) California. This claim was urgent in the late eighteenth century, for although Spain had claimed this territory since the early 1500s, it was barely explored, there were no Spanish colonies or settlers there, and the Russian fur traders were rapidly proceeding down the California coast in search of sea otter. By 1812, the Russians had established Fort Ross just eighty miles north of San Francisco Bay. Establishing missions seemed to be a quick way to colonize and hold the area for Spain. Eventually there were twenty-one missions in the chain along the Camino Real, which was similar to an earlier chain of fourteen missions set up along the Baja California coast by the Jesuit priest Father Kino.

Colonial settlement was developed under close cooperation between the military and the clergy. Sometimes, as in Mexico, the acquisition of territory was a military conquest, consolidated under the clergy and later given over to civil authority. In some areas, like California, the Indians were thought to be docile, so the clergy opened the frontier with only a military escort.

Alta California was far from bases of supply and civil authority. Also, no riches were thought to exist in California. No land routes other than Native trails existed in California, or places where food, water, and supplies could be obtained—at least, that was what the Spanish thought when they examined the problem with their own cultural bias.

Father Junipero Serra, a priest in the Franciscan order, is considered to be the "father of California." Serra was born on the island of Mallorca, Spain, in 1713. He joined the Franciscan order in 1730 and taught philosophy at the university on his home island. He decided to give up this career in 1749 in order to convert the Native peoples of North America to Christianity. He worked for nine years among the Pame tribe at a mission north of Mexico City and in 1768 was made president of the Baja California missions. Serra was a small man

(5 feet 2 inches) who walked thousands of miles during his lifetime. When in residence at the Carmel, California, mission, he lived in a small cell furnished only with a cot of boards, a single blanket, a table and chair, a chest, a candlestick, and a gourd. The Franciscans are an order with a vow of poverty, and Serra certainly lived up to this vow. Serra was an intense man who loved the natural beauties of the world, a sweet man who instilled devotion in his followers. But he could also be a fierce fighter if angered, and he had a dark side. He often dramatized his sermons by scourging himself with chains, pounding his chest with heavy stones, or searing his skin with tapers. For years he had an abscess on his leg caused by an insect bite for which he refused to seek treatment; thus, he walked with a limp. Father Serra's statue is one of two that represent California in the U.S. Capitol at Washington, D.C.

In June 1769, Father Serra arrived by mule in the vicinity of San Diego Bay. He had traveled overland from Mexico City. The missions in Baja California were taken away from the Jesuits by the Spanish and put in the hands of the Franciscans, and Serra was chosen to head them. But before he could get under way, orders arrived to missionize Alta California, beginning at the two most important mapped ports, San Diego and Monterey. The military/civil portion of the 1769 expedition was led by Don Gaspar de Portola. Two ships carried part of the force, while the others, including Serra, went overland. Scurvy took a terrible toll on the passengers, with at least one-quarter of the shipboard men dying of the disease. The survivors, after meeting at San Diego, set off for Monterey under Portola. On July 16, 1769, after Portola's departure, Father Serra raised a cross at the site of the first mission in Alta California in San Diego. Native Americans soon came into the camp out of curiosity. They began stealing items, then finally attacked the camp and were driven off. A stockade was built. Meanwhile, Portola made it to Monterey Bay but did not recognize it from the verbal descriptions left by earlier explorers. He led his men back, starving, to San Diego, and was ready to abandon the project altogether. However, Father Serra stubbornly insisted upon staying with his new mission, even if his military escort left him behind. A relief ship was weeks

IN CONTEXT   *The California Missions (Continued)*

late in coming, and Portola put pressure on Serra to leave. The ship finally arrived at the very last moment, loaded with food and supplies. Father Serra's mission project was saved. Serra took the new ship to Monterey, where on June 3, 1770, the second mission was dedicated. A presidio (military fort) was built at Monterey, but the mission was soon moved four miles south to Carmel. Father Serra was designated as Father-President of the Alta California missions, and Carmel became his headquarters until the end of his life.

The padres and their handful of military guards would be, by themselves, poor colonizers. They needed the help and support of colonists or converted Native peoples who could tend crops and manage livestock. While the padres were sincere and enthusiastic in their desire to preach the Gospel, the soldiers who accompanied them were recruited from the lowest ranks of Spanish society. They pursued the Native women, causing conflict with tribes. For this reason presidios and missions were soon established some distance from one another (five to six miles) within areas that had both. Army recruiters were also urged to seek married soldiers and to encourage them to bring their wives with them into the new country.

Because the military had had such a bad effect on the Native population, Serra went to Mexico City in 1772 to plead his case before the viceroy. The military commander in California refused to discipline his men for depredations against the Native peoples, insisted that he was in ultimate charge of the province, and even dared to open Serra's mail. As a result, the government gave Serra full control over the military in his district, and authorized more missions. This is one of the only instances in U.S. history when the ultimate authority in a territory or state was religious rather than military or civil. Once the way was cleared to found more missions for the chain in 1773, they were created as fast as supplies, soldiers, and missionaries arrived to support them. The government had specifically authorized the founding of a mission farther north, on the great bay named San Francisco. This was accomplished in 1776. After founding nine missions and walking thousands of miles from one to another, Father Serra died in 1784 at age seventy-one. He was succeeded by

Father Fermin Lasuen, a man every bit as capable as Serra, who added nine more missions to the chain. Lasuen died in 1803 at the age of sixty-seven. Both men are buried in the Carmel Mission.

There were an estimated 100,000 Native Americans in California. It is estimated that California was crowded with more Indians per square mile than any other portion of the pre-European United States. They were primarily hunters and gatherers, living in a bountiful land in which they did not need to raise crops or livestock to survive. Religious concepts were complex and subtle. Early mission records prove they were very healthy people, and at least three of their Native remedies have found their way into the modern pharmacopoeia. They lived in villages near streams, the ocean, or groves of live oaks. Their homes were conical in shape, with the Chumash building some that were sixty feet in diameter. They made baskets so tightly woven they would hold water. Their thirty-foot boats, made of planks for use on the ocean, have been judged to be the finest made by Native American tribes. It was difficult to make such contented people see the wisdom of conversion to Christianity and acceptance of a radically different lifestyle. Factions formed within tribes, which became part Christian and part non-Christian, and these were very destructive. One of the major problems in communicating with and teaching the Indians was language. Between Sonoma and San Diego alone there were groups who spoke six different languages, each with many different dialects.

A mission was only one of three agencies used by the Spanish to colonize territory. In California it was the most important, more so than pueblos (towns) or presidios (forts). In California, presidios were set up to protect the missions, not to colonize the province. Attempts were made to start pueblos, but the Spanish had an impossible task in convincing colonists to move to Alta California, so far away on the frontier. In 1777, fourteen families agreed to Spanish conditions and founded the first pueblo in Alta California at San Jose. In 1781, the second pueblo was founded by a motley group of forty-four people who were rounded up in Baja, made many promises, and marched northward to the future site of Los Angeles. The third pueblo was Branceforte, founded in 1791 with convicts and prostitutes evicted from Mexico. The pueblos did not do well (only three were founded in the eighteenth century), and the citizens who lived in them chafed under the restriction of not being allowed to own land. Land grants were issued to military men as rewards for service or to aristocrats, but even these were rarely given out. Technically, the land used by the citizens at pueblos was owned by the government. The padres consistently opposed land ownership, claiming that they needed the open ranges to support the huge herds of mission cattle. The government upheld the wishes of the padres.

Because there were no inducements to settle pueblos, and presidios were meant only to guard the missions, it was up to the missions to do the work of colonizing in Alta California. Most missions were founded near the coast so they could be supplied by sea. Others were created a short distance inland up the valleys; none penetrated too far inland. Compared to pueblos and presidios, a mission was inexpensive to launch—one or two padres, a handful of soldiers, and a load of supplies—and it later became a self-supporting entity. The primary purpose of a mission was to Christianize the Native peoples, but its other major purpose—perhaps the real, if unstated one—was to colonize and hold territory for Spain. Spain wanted to use converted Native peoples to hold its territory, changing these

Native peoples eventually into Spanish citizens. This method of colonization should be contrasted with that of the English, who were most often unwilling to let other cultural groups come to full citizenship in their colonies.

The padres originally wanted to teach the Native peoples in their own languages, but there was such a profusion of tongues that Spanish was used instead. In addition, the Native vocabularies contained few words for things that could not be seen, heard, touched, or tasted. The padres, of course, taught about the Christian religion. They were unsuccessful in teaching many Native peoples to read and write. The padres tried to teach administrative duties, and when this failed, decided to teach Native peoples a system of "trades." In California this included raising crops and caring for livestock. Because the missions had huge herds of beef cattle, the Native peoples were taught the trade that today we would call ranching. In effect, they became the first cowboys, called vaqueros. Other trades carried on in missions included tanning, blacksmithing, and winemaking. Women also learned to cook, sew, spin, and weave. In 1834, just before the missions were secularized, the Indians at the twenty-one California missions herded 396,000 cattle, 62,000 horses, and 321,000 hogs, sheep, and goats. They also harvested 123,000 bushels of grain. The padres came to teach the Indians religion, but the only way they could

rule, local governors were encouraged to give tribal lands in the form of grants to citizens who wanted to establish ranches for raising cattle, although the law of 1824 granted Native Americans the right to live in their own Native villages. In 1834, the secularization of the missions began. Under this process, the large religious centers became large landed estates that were put under the control of wealthy Mexicans and influential immigrants such as John Marsh and John Sutter. The ranch owners needed a readily available pool of labor to work their new estates and took advantage of a lack of unity among the local Native groups to coerce tribes into working for them. Some owners, such as Sutter, attempted to negotiate treaties with the Native peoples who were living on the land grant, offering goods in exchange for labor. Many simply raided the tribes, stealing women and children for slaves.

A series of plagues in the mid-1800s further reduced the California Native American population to just 150,000—half of what it had been only seventy years earlier. The Mexican government of California finally collapsed in 1847, and in February 1848, the Treaty of Guadalupe

IN CONTEXT *The California Missions (Continued)*

reach them was through teaching trades. The unworldly, spiritual padres ended up administering huge farms and ranches.

The padres attracted Native peoples to the missions with presents of glass beads, clothing, blankets, and food. They gained the trust of the Native peoples and eventually convinced some to move inside the mission complex. Once the Native Americans consented to join the mission, they could never again leave without permission. They were taught the Christian faith and expected to attend services several times each day. They were taught the rudiments of several trades, then assigned to perform the work for which they showed proficiency. Each Native American had to spend a specified number of hours each week making adobe bricks and roof tiles, building walls, working at a handicraft, or tilling the fields. To relieve monotony, the padres celebrated nearly every feast day on the liturgical calendar, many including processions, fiestas, games, and celebrations. The Native peoples were well fed, with three big meals each day, thus ending their hunter-gatherer lifestyle forever. In many of the missions, Native peoples were granted a two-week vacation every five weeks to go back to visit their villages. Not all Native peoples responded well to the mission lifestyle. Some rebelled, some ran away, some even set fire to the buildings and led revolts. Runaways

were hunted down and brought back for discipline, usually two days in the stocks. Native resistance was greatest in the areas north of San Francisco and along the Santa Barbara Channel.

At the close of the mission period, there were 31,000 Christianized Indians living in twenty-one missions under sixty padres and 300 soldiers. Historians have been divided into two camps over the mission system; some said it was bad, others that it was good. In defense of the mission system, it is said that the padres were devoted to the Native peoples they taught and were sincere in their desire to Christianize and "civilize" them. The missions offered a peaceful way to acquire and hold new territory, gradually making the Indians full citizens of the empire. Critics of the system call it a thinly disguised form of slavery, forcing a culture and religious beliefs on a people with no attempt to keep the traditional culture of the Native peoples. Once the missions were secularized, the Indians tried and failed to return to traditional ways of life. The introduction of Europeans brought diseases to the Indians that killed thousands. On balance, it can be said that the Spanish treated the Native peoples far better than their American successors in California, who killed Indians indiscriminately with guns and further diseases, then herded the remainder onto reservations in the most worthless portions of the state. (National Park Service)

Hidalgo ceded sovereignty of Mexican lands to the U.S. government. For the tribes of California, this change in government brought no improvement for the Native peoples.

On January 24, 1848, James Marshall discovered gold at the site of John Sutter's sawmill, and the great American Gold Rush began. It would usher in decades of unimaginable horrors to the tribes of the intercoastal mountain area. Within a year, 100,000 gold seekers from across the world descended on the area and a virtual reign of terror began against the tribes that lived in the areas of the Sierras where gold was plentiful. When the tribes fought back they were declared a nuisance.

Vigilante paramilitary troops such as the Eel River Minutemen formed—troops whose only purpose seems to have been to kill Native peoples and kidnap their children. Death squad militias and miners killed over 100,000 Native peoples during the first two years of the Gold Rush. By 1850, there were fewer than 70,000 Native peoples alive in the area.

The California government enacted a series of laws that took the right to vote away from the Native peoples and stripped them of other rights,

KEY CONCEPT   Epidemics

Epidemics have always been shapers of human destiny and human culture, occurring when new cases of any disease appear in a population at an unusually high rate over a short period of time. They enter a population from an outside source such as an animal or plant or new people from another region, and spread quickly within the nonresistant group. They seldom kill every member of the infected population, but mortality rates can be very high. Ebola has a mortality rate of 50 percent to 88 percent, and in the Middle Ages some areas had a mortality rate for the bubonic plague of 90 percent.

including the right to control where their own children lived and went to school. Other clauses allowed Native Americans who were accused of "loitering" to be sold to the highest bidder. The children of these vagrants could also be sold as indentured servants. Bands of kidnappers raided Native tribes, murdering the adults and stealing the children to sell to the slave markets. These harsh laws were repealed in 1866 when the state was forced to comply with the terms of the Thirteenth Amendment of the U.S. Constitution, which abolished slavery.

While the state of California was permitting these activities, the federal government sent commissioners to find a peaceful way to settle problems with the California Native peoples. By 1852, this group had negotiated 18 treaties with 139 entities that they classified as "tribes;" treaties that set aside nearly one-third of the land in California for Native use.

The California state government was outraged because the treaties gave large tracts of rich agricultural land and areas with commercial mining value to the Native peoples. They instructed the California senators to oppose ratification of the treaties and the Senate went into secret session to discuss them. During this session, ratification failed and the treaties were then placed in secret files where they would not be discovered for another fifty years. Congress did establish federal Native American reservations and tribes were moved onto these lands.

The reservations were placed in the hands of supervisors who used the lands to line their own pockets. Complaints and problems with the superintendents were numerous, and in 1870, the government turned control of the reservations over to the Quaker Church. While this ended the corruption complaints, the church was very intolerant of Native traditional beliefs and Native Americans found themselves once again the wards of a church (having previously suffered the same fate as part of the mission system under the Catholic Church).

Drought struck in the 1870s and the desperate tribes turned to their religion. A messianic cult movement began, called the Ghost Dance, based on the belief that the world was ending and the dead would return with the disappearance of the whites. Terrified whites quickly moved to suppress it and make it illegal. Social ills and starvation continued to take a heavy toll. But as their situation worsened, outrage began growing in the white community and a number of notable citizens, including Helen Hunt Jackson, became activists to force the government to redress some of the wrongs. The

KEY CONCEPT   Helen Hunt Jackson and *A Century of Dishonor*

Helen Hunt Jackson (1830–1885), writer and activist, was one of the early voices calling for the end of the U.S. government's abusive Indian policies. She turned toward activism after attending a lecture in which Chief Standing Bear described the brutal conditions by which the Ponca tribe was removed from its Nebraska reservation. Angry at what she heard, and further angered at the abuses her research uncovered, she wrote the classic *A Century of Dishonor*.

When the book was published, she sent a copy to every member of Congress. Although she never lived to see the kinds of reforms she dreamed of, her efforts constitute a landmark in Native American reform and helped bring about the beginning of public awareness for the problems of the displaced Native nations. Her very popular novel, *Ramona*, which was intended to further educate Americans about the Mission Indians, has become a cultural icon.

government idea of mending the problems was to set up the Indian boarding school system.

Some Native peoples gathered enough wealth and power to begin trying to deal with the American government in a different way. The Cuperno tribe began a lawsuit to prevent their eviction from their tribal lands at the Warner Ranch. Other Native peoples bought their land, though their hold on this property was shaky because they were not recognized as citizens of the United States. With the rediscovery in 1905 of the "lost" treaties, Native Americans and their supporters began a drive to have the terms of those treaties enforced and found that they were more successful battling in the courts than they had been battling with weapons. In 1928, Congress passed a Jurisdictional Act that allowed the Native peoples to sue the federal government and to be represented by the attorney general.

In 1924, the Native peoples were again granted citizenship. Many took the opportunity to send their children to local schools, and the era of the Indian Boarding School began to wane. In the late 1940s, Native Americans began to establish and take control of organizations designed to help their own people. During this time, three important Native groups arose: the Native American Church, the National Congress of American Indians, and the Federated Indians of California. They became some of the major social and political forces for the tribes as they moved forward to the twenty-first century.

The 1969 occupation of Alcatraz Island by a group called Indians of All Tribes was the beginning of a new era of Native American affairs. Young, educated, skeptical Native peoples began to take a very active interest in what had been done to their people, and they began lobbying

POMO INDIAN BASKET · CALIFORNIA

INDIAN COURT
FEDERAL BUILDING
GOLDEN GATE INTERNATIONAL EXPOSITION
SAN FRANCISCO 1939

Poster for the Indian Court exhibit at the Golden Gate International Exposition in San Francisco, showing a Pomo basket. (WPA/Library of Congress)

universities for Native American courses. Major universities began offering courses in Native American culture and history, and powwows and other Native American cultural events grew in popularity. Tribes banded together to reestablish traditional ceremonies, to encourage language retention, and to begin removing impediments to the exercise of traditional tribal religious practices.

At the beginning of the twenty-first century, the tribes are still struggling with issues that plague many other Native Americans—poverty, lack of access to resources, poor education, and fragmenting social structure. Many have taken their cause to the internet, using electronic communications to preserve and offer education about tribal heritages, languages, and economic opportunities as well as to coordinate social activities such as powwows.

ALTERNATE HISTORY

Why does one group of people develop iron weapons and tools while another one living in a similar area never goes beyond stone tools and baskets? There is no single good answer, but part of the answer lies in what kinds of technology they develop and whether they have a nomadic lifestyle or settle in one location. Both groups develop tools suitable for their lifestyles and their environments, but the materials available and the methods of processing raw materials are very different in the two groups. Over time, these differences can progress so that one group develops a significant lead over the other in weapons, tools, and agriculture.

The first Natives of California brought with them a variety of technological developments, including the atlatl, spear, fishing nets, boats, weaving looms, and baskets. If social and climate changes had prompted the Natives of California to settle permanently in one area, both pottery and agricultural practices could have emerged at a much earlier date and the Native peoples' fate would have been considerably different.

Learning to make pottery from clay confers a number of advantages on a group emerging from the Stone Age. In order to make good pottery, high temperature ovens need to be developed. Once a group has ovens of this kind, it's possible for them to extract iron from some hematite ores and to make bronze if tin is available. Mass production of ceramics and metal objects also becomes possible as these ovens become more sophisticated.

Pottery also represents a more insect-and-rodent-proof method of food storage. Better storage means that larger quantities of food can be kept against hard times, which leads to stable population levels during climatic stress and population increase during periods of normal local climate. As population centers get larger, societies change to become more complex structures. Idea exchange and experimentation take place at a more rapid pace in larger groups, and roles of individuals within that society become more diversified and specialized.

California would be uniquely suited to support an emerging Bronze Age civilization because it is a land of considerable commercial mineral wealth. In addition to pottery-quality clay deposits, copper and silver and gold are available throughout the state in "placer deposits"—pure

Baskets made by Mission Indians, photographed in 1924. (Edward S. Curtis/Library of Congress)

metals washed down from sources in the mountains. Other metal ores occur throughout the state in sufficient quantities to be mined, including a tin ore called cassiterite, as well as lead ores and zinc ores and several types of iron ores including hematite and magnetite.

A Bronze Age America would have had both advantages and disadvantages in dealing with the first Europeans to make contact with them. In addition to bronze vessels and weapons and objects of art and ritual, they would also have had items made from gold, which is found in numerous placer and surface deposits in the intermountain areas of Northern California. A European gold rush to California would have started in the early 1500s, shortly after Spanish and English ships returned to the Old World with reports of the wealth of the California tribes. But conquest would not have been possible if California had entered the Bronze Age. The bow was still the main weapon of warfare in Europe in the 1500s, and well-organized bands of Bronze Age hunters turned warriors could have easily blocked any attempts by the Spanish or English to establish a base on the coastline.

The only way that the Europeans could have gained access to gold would have been to barter things for it that the Native peoples found more valuable—horses, perhaps, and iron tools and guns. Here, the French had a distinct advantage. They were among the earliest Europeans to enter the North American continent, but they could not afford to send the same number of soldiers and colonists as England and Spain and the Netherlands. So the French approached the tribes in small groups, seeking to trade and to form alliances rather than seeking conquest. This was an effective method along the east coast and would have won them allies in California, particularly among the Chumash who had already established an extensive system of trade routes. It would have been a win-win scenario for both parties. The French could have negotiated for land and a harbor for their ships and gold in exchange for guns, cloth, steel tools, and horses. They could have added to their wealth further by taking these goods to tribes that lived along the edge of the Rocky Mountains and trading with them as well. A network of trades and alliances could have ensued and by 1700, on the west coast as well as on the east coast, a French-Native alliance would have been a power bloc that would not have been easy to conquer.

The rise of a Bronze Age civilization and earlier contact with the Europeans would also have given the tribes of California better resistance to diseases brought by the whites. As long as they had a nomadic or semi-nomadic hunter-gatherer lifestyle, they were particularly vulnerable to diseases from outside. Hunter-gatherers seldom came into contact with disease in any form. They lived in small, isolated groups and moved frequently. Disease problems caused by sewage and rotting food did not occur among nomadic people because when an area began to smell too bad, they simply moved away from that location. Transmissible diseases would make enough of the group ill so that they would stay in one location until the disease had run its course. They would not come into contact with other groups to spread the infection to other people, and thus would have had a very low resistance to diseases introduced from other parts of the world.

Living together in larger groups in Bronze Age villages and towns would have made the Native of California better able to resist European diseases. Smallpox, measles, tuberculosis, and the other killing diseases of Europe would have affected all the tribes, but the impact would have been far less powerful than it actually was. Diseases unique to the California area would have arisen in a Bronze Age population and while the adults would have been mostly immune to them, the Europeans would have found them debilitating and fatal. Such diseases could have wiped out enough soldiers to have reduced the number of forts that the Europeans place on the west coast.

Instead of being enslaved by the Spaniards early in the sixteenth century, the Natives of California would have been able to remain fairly autonomous. As tribes along the eastern coast did, they would eventually have learned a system of writing and would have begun to document their beliefs and history. If the history of the rest of the Americas had remained unchanged, the Natives of California would have had to deal with the indirect consequences of European conquests in North and South America. From bases in Mexico, the Spanish could have conquered Baja California, whose inhabitants had little contact with the rest of the world. But they could not have established by conquest a series of presidios or forts throughout California because they would have lacked both manpower and firepower to deal with the Native peoples and because their position as a global superpower would have been challenged by Portugal, Spain's former partner in South America.

Spain's political and military power would have been further tied up by growing problems with Mexico. Native revolts against the harsh colonial rule would have been fueled by rumors from the north that tribes had successfully managed to avoid being conquered by the Europeans, and small groups of refugees would have begun moving northward, seeking freedom. They would not have been welcomed into a California that was controlled by the existing tribes, but they would have been able to trade or raid to acquire guns for themselves. This would have enabled the remnants of the Aztecs and others from Central America to settle in armed camps and villages near the Rio Grande and raid the Spaniard estates of northern Mexico. By 1750, the Spanish forces would have been stretched too thin to maintain control, and Mexico could have gained its independence by 1775.

As France and Europe entered the Age of Enlightenment in the early 1700s, another export from the Natives of California would have made a significant contribution to society—their philosophy and way of life. By now they would have developed commercial fishing, trapping, and mining areas in California, but as people whose existence relied on their knowing the local environment well, they would have been more in tune to the damage being done by some processes. Because the land area was so large, they could have extracted the resources lightly, working one area for a while and then switching to another area to allow the first to recover. Their egalitarian political and social structure might have been taken as one of the models for the new French Republic that rose from the ashes of the French monarchy.

The new American colonies would not have been seen as a threat to the way of life of the Natives of California. The European powers would still have been struggling with dreams of empire, with the English trying to recover from the loss of their colonies in the New World. Spain and Portugal might have begun a more subtle move for power by bringing in friendly missionaries and focusing their attention on a few tribes such as the Yokuts, who might have felt slighted by the Chumash with their coastal harbors and trade networks. The Spanish and Portuguese would have found it easy to promote distrust and suspicion among the desert tribes and begin their own trade network that would run through Mexico, making friends with the descendants of the Aztecs, who had originally fled from them, and supplying the Yokuts and Southern Paiute with guns.

By 1800, pressure would have begun to mount on the California Native peoples as tribes from the eastern seaboard and the Midwest would have fled the encroaching Europeans. More treaties would have been made and signed and broken. European power in the New World would have crumbled as their former colonies revolted and gained their freedom. The Natives of California would have found themselves sharing a continent with new nations that wanted to lay claim to as much land as possible. Other Native American tribes that had not developed strong alliances would now be overrun by these new countries.

The United States would have been a particularly powerful opponent. The U.S. government was on a campaign of expansion and colonists were pushing west at an alarming rate. Texas and parts of New Mexico and Arizona became part of the new republic. Railroads were beginning to encroach onto the Great Plains in spite of the opposition of the tribes of that area, and open warfare began between the Native peoples and Americans. American newspapers printed sensationalized versions of every skirmish, and many lawmakers in Washington, D.C., urged Congress to declare war against the Natives of the Great Plains. These tribes, which had continued their nomadic lifestyle, were far more vulnerable to vigilantes and militias than the tribes west of the Rockies. The free-ranging Shoshones, Nez Perce, and Comanches, with their large herds of horses, were tempting targets for gangs that captured and sold horses to the U.S. Army.

The army also moved westward as settlers pushed onto the Great Plains, carried along by the railroads. This mode of transportation moved large armies hundreds of miles in a relatively efficient manner, and by the beginning of the American Civil War, the Great Plains were added to the territory of the United States. The remnants of the tribes that once lived there would flee westward, to avoid being put on reservations. This flood of immigrants, who spoke many different languages and had many different cultures, would cause social and economic problems for the Natives of the west coast. The Civil War interrupted the American plans for empire, but the 1867 purchase of Alaska by the United States made it clear that it was only a temporary pause. The technological advantage was still on the side of the Americans, with their environmentally destructive manufacturing methods and farming practices.

The presidency of Theodore Roosevelt would bring matters to a head. With the signing of the Panama Canal Treaty, the way would be freed to bring the U.S. Navy quickly to the west coast to threaten coastal towns with bombardment. The tribes might approach Congress and after a long series of negotiations, the lands west of the Rockies would become part of the United States. It would not be an easy transition. Many whites would still view Native peoples as inferior races, and a long series of legal battles would ensue before the issue of property and mineral rights was settled.

The Great Depression would bring a lot of balance back into the situation. Now it would be the Native peoples who would have productive farms and lands and the whites who would be destitute and eager for jobs. California would become a strong economic power as a provider of food and raw materials, and a careful plan of economic development would begin, guided by the tribes. Other minorities would find California a welcoming place, away from the burgeoning racial tensions of the southern United States. California would become more of a melting pot than the rest of the country.

And so the California Native Americans would arrive in the twenty-first century, with most of their customs and languages intact, with a larger and more robust population—thanks in part to the development of pottery that gave them the ability to move from the Stone Age to the Bronze Age in time to deal with the arrival of the Europeans.

Mel White

Discussion Questions

1. How did the attitudes of the founder of the Jesuit order, St. Ignatius Loyola, impact the Jesuit priests' approach to the Native peoples?

2. Many tribes today have started gambling casinos in an effort to bring money into reservations. Opponents to the casinos argue that they bring an undesirable class of people into the area and contribute to gambling addiction. If a tribe that lived in your area wanted to start a casino, how would you vote on the issue—and why?

3. How might history have changed if the treaties of 1851 had been discovered immediately after the Civil War?

4. A number of tribal languages are threatened with extinction. Do you think they should be documented and studied but treated as dead languages (as Latin is today) or do you think the tribes should attempt to revive them as living languages? Why?

5. How would the course of history have been changed if the Spanish had found gold when they first arrived on the Pacific Coast in the 1500s?

Bibliography and Further Reading

Arnold, Jeanne E. *The Origins of a Pacific Coast Chiefdom: The Chumash of the Channel Islands*. Salt Lake City, UT: University of Utah Press, 2001.

California Department of Parks and Recreation. "Five Views: An Ethnic History Site Survey for California." Office of Historic Preservation, December 1988. National Park Service, http://www.cr.nps.gov/history/online_books/5views/5views1.htm (accessed April 27, 2006).

California Historical Society. "California History Online." http://www.californiahistoricalsociety.org (accessed May 11, 2006).

Centers for Disease Control and Prevention. "Factors in the Emergence of Infectious Diseases." http://www.cdc.gov/ncidod/eid/vol1no1/morse.htm (accessed April 27, 2006).

Flannery, K. V. "The Origins of the Village Revisited: From Nuclear to Extended Households." *American Antiquity* 67, no. 3 (2002).

Four Directions Institute of Native American Studies. www.fourdir.org (accessed April 27, 2006).

Houghton Mifflin. "Encyclopedia of North American Indians: California Tribes." http://college.hmco.com/history/readerscomp/naind/html/na_005400_californiatr.htm (accessed September 1, 2005)

Jackson, Helen Hunt. *A Century of Dishonor: A Sketch of the United States Government's Dealings with Some of the Indian Tribes*. Norman, OK: University of Oklahoma Press, 1995.

Larson, Daniel, John Johnson, and C. Mihaelsen. "Missionization among the Coastal Chumash of Central California: A Study of Risk Minimization Strategies." *American Anthropologist* 96, no. 2 (1994).

Laverty, Philip. "The Ohlone/Costanoan-Esselen Nation of Monterey, California: Dispossession, Federal Neglect, and the Bitter Irony of the Federal Acknowledgment Process." *Wicazo Sa Review* (Fall 2003).

Lesser, Alexander. "Cultural Significance of the Ghost Dance." *American Anthropologist* (January 1933).

Sousa, Ashley Riley. "They Will Be Hunted Down like Wild Beasts and Destroyed! A Comparative Study of Genocide in California and Tasmania." *Journal of Genocide Research* 6, no. 2 (2004).

Spicer, E. H. *Perspectives in American Indian Culture Change.* Chicago: University of Chicago Press, 1961.

State of California Online. "California Geological Survey." http://www.consrv.ca.gov/cgs/geologic_resources/gold/ (accessed April 27, 2006).

Straus, L. G., B. V. Erikson, J. M. Erlandson, and D. R. Yesner, eds. *Humans at the End of the Ice Age: The Archaeology of the Pleistocene-Holocene Transition.* New York: Plenum, 1996.

Plains Native Americans relied on buffalo herds for survival. What if disease struck the herds, leading to migration of these tribes?

INTRODUCTION

One of the most widely recognized and compelling symbols of the American West is a Plains Native American—often imagined galloping across the Plains on horseback, pursuing a thundering buffalo herd, and singling out one of the shaggy beasts for the kill.

Like the Plains Native American, the buffalo, too, symbolizes the American West. In fact, both have come to represent not only the American West, but America itself. This is because the spreading of the United States across the continent, from sea to shining sea, is a defining component of American history, and both the Plains Natives and the buffalo are important characters in that story. For generations, Americans have mythologized the saga of American westward expansion—Lewis and Clark's expedition up the Missouri River; pioneer wagons rumbling along the Oregon Trail; Sitting Bull, Crazy Horse, and Custer's "Last Stand" at the Little Big Horn; and the slaughter and near extermination of the massive buffalo herds that once stretched as far as the eye could see.

This history, though familiar to many, provides an opportunity to contemplate an alternative outcome to America's conquest of the West.

The Great Plains of America is one of the world's largest grasslands and a distinctive part of the American West. Its boundaries encompass parts of thirteen states, from the southern tip of Texas all the way into Canada, and from approximately the 98th meridian in the east to the foot of the Rocky Mountains in the west. To an observer standing on the Plains, the land appears either flat or slightly undulating, like large, gentle waves of earth. However, the Great Plains has a steady eastward decline, from over 5,000 feet above sea level at the base of the Rocky Mountains to an elevation of about 2,000 feet at its eastern edge. Denver, about ten miles from the base of the Rockies, is on the western edge of the Plains. On the steps of the capitol building is a marker indicating its 5,280-foot elevation, allowing Denver to call itself, quite literally, "the mile-high city."

One of the defining characteristics of the Great Plains is its aridity. The eastern edge of the Plains, the 98th meridian, runs just west of Fort Worth, Texas, a city whose tag line is "where the West begins." To the west of this line, rainfall is remarkably scarce, usually less than twenty inches per year. Making life tougher, this scarce rainfall is unsettlingly undependable. The 98th meridian also divides the tall grass prairies from the short grass plains. To the east of this line, the higher rainfall allows for the growth of taller grasses; to the west of this line, the sparser rainfall is more suitable for the short grasses. Trees on the plains are sparse, usually confined to the banks of rivers that have eroded channels into the land as the rivers flow down from the Rockies toward the Mississippi River.

Great Plains weather is marked by extremes. The Plains can be blistering hot in the summer and bitterly cold in the winter, as polar air masses bring strong, piercing winds with blizzards whipping across the open land. This unforgiving environment has profoundly shaped, and usually limited, the lives of its inhabitants for thousands of years.

One might imagine that this inhospitable environment was, for the most part, uninhabited—at least until Native Americans acquired horses from Europeans. However, this view is incorrect. Native people had migrated onto the Plains at least by 12,000 B.C.E., during the last Ice Age—and new evidence suggests that people may have visited the Plains thousands of years earlier. The earliest known Plains-dwellers belonged to the "big game tradition," a mode of living in which small bands of people hunted large game animals, following the herds wherever they went. One of the animals they hunted was the *bison antiquus*, a much larger ancestor of the modern day bison, the *bison bison*, commonly called the American buffalo. Scholars speculate that these bands of hunters were probably

Buffalo dance of the Mandan tribe of the American plains. (Artwork by Karl Bodmer 1833–1834/National Archives)

related by blood, perhaps consisting of a man, his sons, his brothers, and their families. Family-based groups residing with a family's male line are called patrilocal groups. Because these groups survived by hunting, and the responsibility of hunting belonged to men, it made sense for the bands to be patrilocal. Hunters used spears with flaked stone points that were good for short-range jabbing. Early hunters also killed game by herding them into kill zones or off cliffs, where the animals would plunge to their deaths and be butchered by band members waiting below.

In the thirteenth century, a widespread drought hit the American West and caused the population of the Plains to decline. Those who remained on the Plains gravitated toward the rivers and settled along the river banks. There, they established villages and raised crops—supplementing their diets by hunting bison or other game animals. Around the edges of the Plains, nomadic groups pursued game on foot, seldom venturing too far onto the Plains.

In the middle of the sixteenth century, new visitors arrived on the Plains. The Spaniards, under the leadership of Francisco Vásquez de Coronado, explored the American Southwest. In 1540 Coronado marched north from Mexico, or New Spain as it was then called, searching for Cibola, the famed and mythical "seven cities of gold" believed to lie undiscovered somewhere in America. A Plains Native guide told Coronado that somewhere in present-day Kansas was a city rich with gold. Coronado eagerly marched his men across the southern plains, an enormous expanse of level land, arriving at their destination in 1541.

Arapaho camp with buffalo meat drying in the background, photographed near Fort Dodge, Kansas, in 1870. (William S. Soule/National Archives)

What awaited him was the village of Quivira, a riverine settlement belonging to the horticulturalist Wichita Indians. In the village was an assemblage of thatched hive-shaped huts, but Coronado and his men found no gold. Dejected and angered, they executed their informant and trudged back to New Spain.

Coronado is sometimes given credit for introducing horses to the Native people of the American West, after all, when the Spanish discovered the New World, there were no horses living anywhere in the Western Hemisphere. This Coronado scenario is probably incorrect, because there are no accounts of Native Americans owning horses until over a century later.

Instead, it seems that Native people acquired horses in the middle of the seventeenth century. Colonial Spaniards raised horses in their northernmost settlements, and sometimes Native American ranch hands would leave the Spanish settlements and return to their original communities, taking a few horses with them when they left. By this method, and by trading and raiding, Native Americans gathered horses and traded them to neighboring tribes. By the late 1600s, trappers, traders, and explorers of European descent noticed horses among the tribes of the Southern Plains, and by the middle of the 1700s, explorers noted horses among the village-dwelling Mandans of the upper Missouri. By the end of the eighteenth century, horses were common among tribes of the Plains, and when Lewis and Clark journeyed up the Missouri River in 1804, they did not consider the presence of horses to be unusual.

The spread of the horse to the Plains revolutionized Native American life. For centuries, the Native people who lived on the Plains had to reside

Blackfoot Indians on horseback, chasing buffalo near Three Buttes, Montana. (Artwork by John M. Stanley, 1853–1855/National Archives)

ANOTHER VIEW   George Catlin and Karl Bodmer

George Catlin and Karl Bodmer are two of the most famous artists of the American West. They each journeyed up the Missouri River during the early 1830s to document Plains Native American life. Both men were talented artists and produced dozens upon dozens of sketches and paintings of what they encountered. Catlin and Bodmer chose to visit the Plains because they believed that, unlike eastern Natives, the Plains tribes were still relatively untouched by American civilization. They each painted Great Plains landscapes; portraits of Native American men and women; illustrations of lodges, clothing, tools, and equipment; and scenes of religious ceremonies, hunting expeditions, and everyday life. Their artwork is colorful and compelling and has been widely reproduced in different media.

A tragedy that occurred shortly after Catlin and Bodmer visited the Plains has added to the value of their work. In 1837, a devastating smallpox epidemic struck the Mandan villages on the Upper Missouri. Catlin and Bodmer had stayed with the Mandans while visiting the region, and produced many paintings and textual descriptions of Mandan life. When the epidemic subsided, about 90 percent of the Mandans had died, and the remnant group, scarcely able to support itself merged with other tribes. Much of early nineteenth century Mandan history would have been lost if it had not been for the efforts of Catlin and Bodmer. Today, Native Americans look to these two men to learn more about their heritage.

Sioux Indians as portrayed in a painting by Karl Bodmer. (National Archives)

along the major rivers, where they farmed the fertile soil in the river bottoms, supplemented their diet with game animals, and had dependable access to water—a highly valued commodity on the Plains. They needed wood from trees for fuel and for building material, and trees grew in adequate supply along the rivers. Furthermore, because these rivers had eroded deep gullies in the soil, people could escape the bitter winds of winter by hunkering down in the dry river bottoms, where game animals also would congregate, offering a welcome opportunity for fresh meat. These Native Americans generally dwelled in villages, ranging in size from several dozen inhabitants to several hundred, and occasionally over a thousand. Members of a single tribal group occupied multiple separate villages distributed over a stretch of river. Women did much of the farming and managed the fields; consequently family groups were matrilocal, that is, they resided with a mother and her daughters. When a village's natural resources would dwindle, the village would relocate to a site with more abundant natural resources. Village life, while not without its dangers, was a relatively stable mode of existence. Because of this stability, village tribes developed social, political, and religious hierarchies, and these hierarchies provided cohesion to the villages, which in turn reinforced their stability.

When early explorers and traders visited these tribes in the eighteenth century, they found the villages to be centers of power and influence and ideal locations at which to conduct trade. The village way of life had initially developed without the horse; as the eighteenth century progressed, the village tribes, like the Mandans, Pawnees, and Arikaras, incorporated horses into their lives, but the tribes did not fundamentally alter their village way of life.

Other Native groups, though, were quick to adapt the horse. For the Sioux, Cheyennes, Comanches, Crows, Arapahos, and others, the horse radically changed their way of living. Prior to acquiring the horse, these groups lived on the margins of the Plains and were either *pushed* onto the Plains by stronger enemies—perhaps by a tribe that had acquired firearms from European traders—or *pulled* onto the Plains by the lure of easier living made possible by the acquisition of the horse.

Horses, unlike humans, are well adapted for life on the Plains. Horses eat grass, and there was an abundance of grass on the Plains. Even further west, in the drier, more elevated regions of the Plains, horses found much nourishment from the short grasses. In the colder months, these grasses dried into a nutritious hay-like form. On the grassy Great Plains, a horse could take its rider seemingly anywhere—horses proved extraordinarily liberating!

Mounted Native American hunters had greater range and speed than hunters on foot, allowing them to pursue and kill more game. Horses could carry more cargo than the traditional beast of burden, the dog. Horses could transport more hides to traders and allow their owners to acquire more personal possessions. The acquisition of European trade goods like metal pots, metal knives, cloth, guns, and beads made life easier and more comfortable for many Native Americans, and they eagerly participated in the fur trade.

Dependence on horses required their owners to accommodate their horses' need for fresh grass; tribes had to remain mobile, continuously

A Plains Native American village on the move across the Great Plains. (Artwork by Charles M. Russell, 1905/National Archives)

moving in search of fresh grass for their herds. In other words, by embracing the horse, the Native Americans had to become nomads. However, with millions of bison grazing on the Plains in the late eighteenth century, life as horse-mounted nomadic buffalo hunters was good. More and more Native Americans migrated onto the Plains to feast on abundant buffalo meat and participate in the booming hide trade.

 TURNING POINT

The late 1700s was a time of tremendous change on the Great Plains. Thousands upon thousands of Native Americans from many different tribes had wandered onto the Plains and become nomadic equestrian buffalo hunters. The populations of some of these groups burgeoned, as plentiful bison, growing horse herds, and expansive hunting ranges made for an easy living. Commercial routes to Spanish, British, and later American trading houses extended farther onto the Plains, and white traders ventured up rivers and onto the Plains in increasing numbers. The village dwellers, already living in established communities, at first prospered economically. Their villages were centers of trade, and their inhabitants found themselves in the enviable position of middlemen. They traded their crops and horses to the nomads in exchange for buffalo hides and horses, which in turn they exchanged with European traders for metal tools, weapons, decorative beads, and other items, which they in turn used either for themselves or for further trade with the nomads. Sometimes the nomads acquired European trade goods from traders on the Missouri and exchanged them with the village dwellers for a variety of items. In short, the villages became the hubs of trade on the Great Plains.

The village dwellers, and to a lesser extent the nomads, also suffered ill effects from their engagement in the European trade networks. As traders and trade goods pushed farther onto the Plains, Native Americans were increasingly exposed to Old World diseases, and they suffered greatly.

A thoughtful person might wonder how during any period of revolutionary change an alteration in one, or several, of the revolutionary forces might affect the outcome of the transformation. With any variation would revolutionary change have still occurred? If so, how might the outcome have been different? Old World diseases had a devastating impact on Native American communities; diseases not only reduced indigenous populations, but they also limited the ability of the Native Americans to respond effectively to the challenges posed by European contact. What if an Old World disease, perhaps from a European cow, horse, or pig at a Saint Louis trading post, mutated and spread to the bison herds? This disease might have been easily communicable and exceptionally harmful, thinning herds dramatically over the course of a decade. In such a scenario, the history of the Plains from that time to the present might well have played out very differently from the way it actually did.

ACTUAL HISTORY

No such massive epidemic destroyed the bison herds in either the late eighteenth century or any other time since. Instead, bison roamed the Plains in great abundance until the 1830s and 1840s, at which point their numbers began a steep decline and were quickly plummeting toward extinction by the 1870s. This near extinction hastened an end to the nomadic buffalo-hunting way of life that had so recently flourished on the Plains.

The interrelatedness of the buffalo and the Plains Native Americans has a long history. It dates back thousands of years to a time when the big game hunters preyed upon the massive *bison antiquus*. In the so-called proto-historic period, the period in which the only surviving written records are the scattered accounts of explorers, traders, and missionaries, European travelers expressed amazement at the size of the Plains buffalo herds. Coronado, on his trip to Quivira, was the first European to glimpse these massive herds. Later travelers did so, too, and by the early nineteenth century, the size of the Plains buffalo herds had become legendary. One traveler, crossing the southern Plains in the 1830s, reported seeing a bison herd that blanketed the country for three days. He calculated the herd must have spanned 1,350 square miles, an area larger than the state

A photograph taken in 1872 titled "Trail of the Hide Hunters" of buffalo lying dead in the snow. (National Archives)

of Rhode Island. American travelers in the early nineteenth century wrote fantastical accounts of the buffalo herds they saw. Although many of the accounts were likely exaggerated, their exaggeration attests to the awe and amazement that the travelers felt when viewing the herds—they had never seen anything like them before.

Current scholarly estimates place the total number of bison on the Great Plains around 1800 to be between 25 and 30 million. The number of bison, therefore, was more than three times greater than the number of people in today's New York City, and greater than the current population of Texas, America's second most populous state.

Plains Indians were especially resourceful in using buffalo carcasses to obtain not only food and hides, but other materials as well. The famous Sioux Chief Red Cloud remarked:

> His meat sustained life; it was cut in strips and dried, it was chopped up and packed in skins, its tallow and grease were preserved—all for winter use; its bones afforded material for implements and weapons; its skull was preserved as great medicine; its hide furnished blankets, garments, boats, ropes, and a warm and portable house [the tepee]; its hoofs produced glue, its sinews were used for bowstrings and a most excellent substitute for twine. (Dary, 1989)

KEY CONCEPT   Buffalo Hunters

"Let them kill, skin, and sell until the buffalo is exterminated, as it is the only way to bring lasting peace and allow civilization to advance."

—General Philip Sheridan in *The Destruction of the Bison: An Environmental History, 1750–1920* by Andrew C. Isenberg

Some 40 million buffalo or bison were estimated to have lived on the Great Plains. They roamed freely, Native Americans hunted them for food and other necessities, and a harmonious ebb and flow between man and beast prevailed. In the 1860s, after the Civil War, new army posts were established on the Plains. The army contracted with local men to supply buffalo meat to feed the troops. Railroad companies did the same to feed their construction crews, and soon the availability of work for the buffalo hunter increased in the West.

Also known as Buffalo Bill, William F. Cody, perhaps one of the most successful buffalo hunters, is said to have killed 4,128 buffalo in eighteen months working for the railroads. Some buffalo hunters killed more than that, perhaps an estimated 150 in a day. A great demand kept the hunters in business.

When the railroad tracks were laid, the "iron horse" and buffalo met. Delays occurred as buffalo herds took perhaps half a day to cross the tracks. The railroads saw a way to capitalize on this and solve a problem. They advertised hunting by rail, a sport for the "fun" of killing because the dead buffalo were simply left.

Buffalo chips (dried buffalo droppings) were another important resource. Quick burning and relatively odorless, they were used as fuel not only by Native Americans, but also by trappers, explorers, and American pioneers. Buffalo chips were especially valuable because wood for fires was not plentiful on the Plains.

Scholars like Elliot West point out that Native Americans used buffalo robes and hides as trade items to exchange for resources they themselves could not produce. For example, buffalo hides could be traded for agricultural produce, such as corn; lightweight and durable manufactures, such as cloth blankets and clothing; metal tools, like knives, needles, and cooking pots; and various niceties of life, like coffee, tobacco, alcohol, sugar, and decorative beads. The acquisition of these items through the hide trade made it easier for Plains-dwellers to adopt the nomadic, buffalo-hunting way of life, after all, the buffalo provided almost everything they needed, either directly or indirectly. In the nineteenth century, many tribes became dependent upon the buffalo for subsistence, survival, and prosperity. Ironically, nomadism and dependence on the buffalo, while at first overwhelmingly advantageous, ultimately proved disastrous to the Plains Native American buffalo hunters.

In the late eighteenth century, the balance of power on the Great Plains began to shift. The village dwellers began to diminish in power while the nomads began to gain it. One factor in this shift was illness; village tribes suffered from repeated epidemics of Old World diseases. These diseases, which included cholera, smallpox, and whooping cough, are called virgin soil epidemics because the stricken population bore no previous immunity to the disease. Consequently, virgin soil epidemics proved especially devastating, sometimes causing fatality rates higher than 50 percent. Disease often followed trade routes, being introduced by

In the east a demand for buffalo robes became an incentive to kill more of the animals. The skins were used as coats and lap robes in sleighs and carriages. Leavenworth, Kansas, became a trading center for the robes. Tanneries found a new use for buffalo hides as the drive belts for industrial machines, and the demand for them increased. Buffalo bones were ground into fertilizer and their tongues were served in fine restaurants. All this meant year-round work for former seasonal buffalo hunters who contracted with the army and the railroads.

The Native Americans were becoming increasingly angry and resentful of the demise of their food supply at the hands of the white man. This period was at the height of the Indian Wars. The demand for buffalo by hunters and the subsequent shrinking herds were factors that led Native Americans to the reservation system of living and altered their lifestyle and culture.

When the great era of the buffalo ended, there were an estimated 1,200 to 2,000 surviving buffalo left in the United States. Fortunately, early conservation efforts led to the establishment of Yellowstone National Park in 1872. This was the world's first national park and on it was preserved a small buffalo herd. Still, buffalo were being killed on federal land, so in 1894 the Lacey Act was signed into law, prohibiting the killing of any wildlife in federal preserves. The bison was saved from extinction. Today it is estimated that there are over 150,000 bison on public preserves and in private hands. Ironically, the buffalo's existence rests in the hands of the same group that tried to exterminate it: man. (National Park Service)

direct or indirect contact with Europeans. The village dwellers, whose villages were centers of trade, frequently fell victim to these epidemics. Because inhabitants lived in close proximity to one another, diseases spread quickly throughout a village. In contrast, the nomads, who followed buffalo herds and were usually far away from the villages, were more likely to avoid these epidemics.

To make matters worse for the village dwellers, they were increasingly subjected to extortion by the nomads, who were steadily growing in number and might. These nomads, particularly the Sioux, frequently chose to use force, or the threat of force, to obtain food, horses, and trade goods from the villagers. The nomadic ones occasionally faced food shortages and could avoid starvation by taking needed supplies from the village tribes. Mutually agreeable trade arrangements sometimes occurred only when the nomads did not have the force of arms necessary to steal.

Disease, extortion, and warfare extracted a high toll from the village dwellers. The Arikaras, it is estimated, dropped from a pre-epidemic population of 16,000 to fewer than 1,000 in the 1850s. Not only did populations plummet, but loss of life also weakened the social, political, and religious hierarchies that helped stabilize the villages. In the late eighteenth and early nineteenth century, the Mandans, Hidatsas, Pawnees, and Arikaras, all village dwellers, repeatedly consolidated their villages to compensate for population loss and defend themselves against the nomads. Eventually, for protection against these tribes, particularly the Sioux, the village dwellers allied themselves with the United States and placed themselves under the federal government's care. During the Plains Native American wars of the late nineteenth century, in which the U.S. military attempted to subjugate the nomads, the village tribes provided scouts and warriors to assist the Americans against their longtime enemies, especially the Sioux.

Meanwhile, as the village tribes were experiencing a collapse, the nomads were growing in number and expanding onto the Plains, taking

Sioux tepees photographed by the Signal Corps of the U.S. Army. (National Archives)

advantage of the massive buffalo herds and increasing trade opportunities. On horseback, the nomads, like the Sioux, Cheyennes, Crows, Arapahos, and other groups, ranged far and wide on the Plains, each tribe more or less patrolling its own hunting territory. They would spend the warm months of the year in small patrilocal bands tracking the buffalo herds, and in the winter they would camp in the sheltered river bottoms. During the summer, the Plains tribes often gathered in large groups to renew their shared identity and cultural bonds, usually performing the Sun Dance and other sacred rituals. Continued horse raiding by the men ensured an ample supply of horses for the band, and men rose in stature by distributing some of the horses they captured or buffalo they killed to the less fortunate band members. Nomadic tribes did not have a formal social, political, or religious hierarchy as the village tribes did; instead, the nomads tended to have a more individualistic, egalitarian, and fluid existence.

The nomads faced mounting pressures in the 1830s and 1840s as the buffalo herds began to diminish. Many history books blame the railroad construction crews, the American hide hunters, and the so-called sport hunters for nearly wiping out the herds between the late 1860s and the 1880s. These groups were undeniably major contributors to the bison's catastrophic decline, but before the 1860s, other factors were reducing the size of the herds.

First, the Native Americans themselves were thinning the herds. Horse-mounted hunters were so effective as bison-killing tools that they were killing buffalos more quickly than the animals could reproduce themselves. Hunters were motivated not only by the need to feed growing populations but also by their desire to obtain European and American trade goods from the hide trade.

KEY CONCEPT   Liebig's Law

In 1840, scientist Justus von Liebig published a book in Europe entitled *Organic Chemistry and Its Application to Agriculture and Physiology*. In this book, Liebig outlined what he called the "law of the minimum," which subsequently became known as "Liebig's Law." Liebig argued that no matter what abundances of resources existed in an organism's environment, the organism's survival, growth, and reproduction are instead determined by the *minimum* availability of necessary resources. In other words, if the summertime food supply on the Plains would support 100 million bison, but

the wintertime food supply would support only 25 million bison, the total herd size would not exceed 25 million, which is the lowest or minimum level of food available during a yearly cycle.

This law of minimums often applied to the Plains environment. Native Americans and overland emigrants often consumed or destroyed plant life along the rivers that was a minimum resource for the buffalo during the cold winter months. With the decreased availability of these plants, the buffalo population dropped steeply.

Second, the overland emigrants, traveling from the Missouri River across the Plains to Santa Fe, California, and Oregon, diminished the herds, too. It was not necessarily that the emigrants were killing too many buffalo for meat, but their wagon trains trampled the grasses, their livestock ate the grasses, and the emigrants themselves damaged the fragile river bottom ecosystems—not only allowing their animals to overgraze the grasses but also chopping down the scattered trees for fuel and for building materials. The steadily growing stream of overlanders became a flood after 1849 when gold was discovered at Sutter's Mill in California. This torrent of overlanders—tens of thousands of them—coincided with a dry period on the Plains. The rainfall on the Plains in 1825–1849 marked the wettest season on the Plains in centuries, but the ensuing dry years coincided with the deluge of overlanders in the 1850s. This coincidence of drought and wagon trains was unfortunate for the grasses, which in turn was unfortunate for the buffalo, which in turn was unfortunate for the Native Americans.

By the 1850s and 1860s, the nomadic tribes were feeling economically and geographically pinched. With the herds dwindling, the nomads had to range farther and wider to find buffalo, and tribes increasingly clashed with one another over hunting territory. The Civil War (1861–1865) temporarily slowed American westward expansion and tied up the U.S. military in the East. However, Americans would again rush onto the Plains after the war. In 1862 Congress passed the Homestead Act, making government land in the West inexpensively available to the general public, and after the Civil War, Northerners and Southerners, blacks and whites, and native-born and foreign-born emigrants surged westward again. Railroad companies, too, secured easy title to land on the Plains as they built their transcontinental rail lines across Native American hunting territory. And various gold and silver strikes across the West, in places like Denver and the Black Hills, brought ravenous prospectors into direct contact with the nomads.

The results were predictable. The Native American nomads resented these intrusions, and, feeling increasingly desperate because of the dwindling herds, they lashed out at each other and at the homesteaders, miners, railroad crews, and the U.S. military. Some indigenous groups, such as the Crows, ultimately allied themselves with the Americans against their more numerous enemies, the Sioux. Other groups, such as the Sioux and Cheyenne, frequently chose to protect their interests by force of arms.

To avoid conflict, government officials negotiated with tribal representatives, coaxing or forcing the Native people to accept fixed tracts of land that were geographically isolated from white American interests. Many Native Americans saw no alternative. They had become so heavily dependent on the buffalo that with the severely dwindling herds many were neither able to feed themselves nor obtain any commodity to trade for food. Native Americans accepted agreements in which they surrendered their independence in exchange for a small tract of land and the promise of government rations. In a particularly striking way, the buffalo herds had given the Native Americans independence and a new way of life, and the disappearance of those herds had destroyed that new lifestyle and left them largely dependent on the U.S. government.

Compliance with these treaty agreements was difficult. On the one hand, the federal government's authority on the Plains was limited, and the government was often unable to control the actions of its citizens. In some cases, the military tried to act as a referee, preventing American settlers and miners from intruding on Native American lands, but usually the military was unable to do so. On the other hand, the fluid, unstructured, individualistic nature of the nomadic tribes made it difficult for tribal leaders to coerce all the members of their society to abide by treaty provisions. For example, the Sioux under the leadership of Red Cloud and Spotted Tail agreed by the 1870s to live peacefully on government reservations; at the same time, other Sioux decided to follow Crazy Horse and Sitting Bull, refuse to negotiate with the government, and hold onto their nomadic horse-and-buffalo culture as long as they could.

This situation brought about the Battle of the Little Big Horn. Although many Sioux accepted the federal authority and confined themselves to government agencies, other Sioux, many of them young men and warriors, either refused to relocate to the government reservations or slipped on and off them when it suited them, hunting whatever buffalo remained on the northern Plains. In 1875, after the Black Hills gold rush had begun, the federal government issued an ultimatum to the free-roaming Sioux to report to the reservations or be considered "hostile." Many Sioux ignored the warning, and in the late spring of 1876 the U.S. army dispatched several columns of soldiers to arrest the free-roaming Indians. On June 25, a detachment of troops under George Armstrong Custer attacked a massive encampment of Sioux, Cheyenne, and Arapaho, who had gathered to perform their annual Sun Dance. Custer's men were woefully outnumbered, and were decimated by an Indian counterattack.

Americans were outraged at the magnitude of the Sioux victory and redoubled their efforts to subdue the Plains Natives militarily. The U.S. army and their Native American scouts relentlessly pursued the Sioux and their allies throughout the winter of 1876–1877, eventually forcing them to surrender. Ironically, Custer's "last stand" had proved a "last stand" for the Sioux as well. With the surrender of Crazy Horse in May 1877, the era of the free-roaming, horse-mounted, buffalo-hunting nomads had come to an end.

The close of the nineteenth century saw the Plains Native Americans confined to reservations—some in Oklahoma, others scattered about on the Great Plains, usually on land deemed economically undesirable by Americans. Today, this reservation system still remains. Some Native Americans have chosen to leave the reservation communities and try their fortunes in mainstream American society. Others continue to reside on the reservations. Because many Plains reservations are isolated and on land of marginal economic value, many who live there have social problems such as unemployment, substandard health care, low income levels, substance abuse, and a general lack of educational opportunities. Despite these setbacks, reservations provide their residents with segregated living space, a sense of cultural identity, and significant political autonomy.

ALTERNATE HISTORY

How might have Plains Native American history been different if the bison herds had been wiped out several decades earlier than they actually were? Hypothetically, the agent of decimation could have been disease—perhaps a disease common to horses, cattle, swine, or some other sort of Old World livestock. This disease might have mutated and made a trans-species jump to bison, and perhaps this mutation would have proved both exceptionally deadly and exceptionally contagious among bison.

St. Louis would have been an effective base for the transmission of this disease. The city was established as a trading post in the 1760s, and like New Orleans further down the river, it had residents and visitors of French, Spanish, British, Native American, and African descent. The city was strategically located, sitting near the confluence of the Mississippi, Ohio, and Missouri rivers. Many early traders who explored the Missouri operated out of St. Louis.

This disease, perhaps developing in the 1770s, would have decimated the herds. Buffalo are herd animals whose instinct is to congregate—for the most part, except for a few old bulls, buffalo are not solitary wanderers. Consequently, the disease could have spread rapidly through the herds, carrying away millions upon millions of animals over the course of a decade or so. By the 1780s, their number might have dwindled to a mere 1 to 3 million, the survivors existing in small, scattered, isolated herds that had to face the disease as it repeatedly cycled across the Plains.

If the bison herds had been thus affected, Indian history on the Great Plains might have been quite different. By the 1780s, when the imagined disease had dramatically thinned the herds, many Native people had already migrated onto the Plains and become nomads. The nomads' response to this ecological catastrophe would have been to leave the Plains. They were almost completely dependent on the bison herds, and the inhospitable Plains environment would have offered them no alternative resources for survival. In other words, on the Plains, a depopulation of the bison would have led to a depopulation of Native Americans.

The nomads would likely have left the Plains by several routes. Some might have retreated into the Rocky Mountains—this is from where the Comanches, the dominant nomadic group on the Southern Plains, originally came. Other groups, like the Sioux, Cheyenne, Arapaho, and Crow, might have retreated off the Plains and receded into the prairies and woodlands to the east where they had previously resided. Still others might have migrated to the more fertile, dry river bottoms where the village-dwellers lived.

The nomads who migrated to the river bottoms would have encountered the village tribes like the Mandans, Hidatsas, Arikaras, and Pawnees. These nomads might have chosen to cooperate and integrate with the village tribes, to coexist separately with them, or to destroy or subjugate them by force, to acquire their resources.

No matter what the means of interaction, the longer-term results would have been similar: Old World diseases would have decimated whatever Native people remained in the villages. Despite the diminished number of bison, traders and explorers would still have penetrated the region, bringing their destructive pathogens with them and making it possible for virgin soil epidemics to whipsaw back and forth across the area. These epidemics would have ensured that the human population of the river bottoms would remain low.

After the buffalo herds had all but disappeared from the Plains, the region would not have been an appealing ecosystem to most Native Americans, especially those who relied principally on hunting and gathering. Some tribes living on the margins of the Plains would have periodically forayed onto the grasslands to hunt deer, antelope, or small animals. However, the availability and quantity of game would not have been high enough or dependable enough to sustain many people, especially year-round, through the long, inhospitable winters.

The difficulties of year-round life on the Plains would not have been insurmountable. For a people to live on the herdless Plains, they would have to have been particularly resourceful. They would not only have to have been able to hunt and gather, but also to farm extensively. They would also have needed domesticated animals not only to be beasts of burden but also renewable sources of meat, leather, fur, milk, and other materials.

Cattle, for example, would have provided meat, leather, milk, and muscle power to pull a plow. Domesticated horses would have provided mobility and muscle power, which could have been channeled to domestic, military, or commercial ends. Sheep would have been a source of meat, leather, and wool. Goats would have given leather, meat, and milk. All of these animals grazed on grass, which was abundant on the Plains, and all could have been used as commodities for trade. Domesticated livestock was not only readily available but is also readily renewable. In a nutshell, domesticated livestock would have made human life on the Plains sustainable, more so than it had been for the village dwellers who had domesticated only dogs, and later, horses.

Who might these Native Americans be, and from where might they have migrated? They could have come from any number of Eastern tribes who had, through extended contact with Europeans and Americans, developed a tradition of formal agriculture and livestock husbandry, and a lesser dependence on hunting and gathering. A lengthy acquaintance with Europeans and Americans would also have given them a better understanding of white culture, politics, and trade practices.

The most striking example of such a group is the Cherokee Indians. The Cherokees were a numerous group of people living in the American Southeast. They are one of the "Five Civilized Tribes," called so by European Americans because these Native peoples had been remarkably successful in adopting many aspects of white American life. In the 1700s and early 1800s, the Cherokees had shifted away from hunting and more toward agriculture and animal husbandry. They raised corn, beans, squash, potatoes, watermelons, apples, peaches, and other crops such as tobacco and cotton. Some Cherokees even used African slaves to labor in their cotton fields. The Cherokees owned horses, cattle, sheep, and goats, and made butter and cheese from milk. They used metal hoes, plows, axes, and other tools. They built weaving looms to weave cotton fabric and established their own blacksmith shops. They made wooden boats, wagons, and carts for transportation. In the 1800s, they even developed their own written language and produced a Cherokee newspaper, and many Cherokees spoke English. The Cherokees lived in towns or villages, and intermarried, sometimes extensively, with whites. In fact, the most famous Cherokee chief of the nineteenth century was John Ross, who was seven-eighths white and only one-eighth Cherokee.

After the American Revolution, many Cherokees felt pressure from westward-moving American settlers. Over the years, this pressure increased, ultimately resulting in Andrew Jackson's forced removal of the Cherokees in the 1830s to Oklahoma—a diaspora the Cherokees called "The Trail of Tears." In the decades prior to their removal, many Cherokees had decided to move across the Mississippi voluntarily. Perhaps they believed that the pressures from American settlers in the east would only lead to trouble.

These Cherokee emigrants, and other Eastern tribes like them, might have found the nearly vacant but fertile river bottoms on the Great Plains a suitable alternative living environment. Perhaps by 1830, there would have been dozens of Native American villages, occupied by Cherokees or other Eastern groups, scattered along the banks of the Missouri River and other major Plains rivers like the Platte River in Nebraska, along which the Oregon Trail ran. Here, these "eastern" tribal villagers would achieve a modest prosperity, raising a variety of crops, grazing their livestock on the grassy Plains, and supplementing their diet by hunting deer, antelope, and the occasional buffalo that wandered into their territory.

These villages would prove safer than those of the "western" village-dwellers because they would not have to face the predatory actions of the nomads—the lack of bison on the Plains would have removed the nomads from the Plains environment. Furthermore, these Eastern groups had been exposed to Old World diseases for generations

"Burning the Range" by Frederick Remington.
(National Archives)

and had intermarried with Europeans, thus inheriting some of their genetic immunities. Consequently, these Native Americans might have had a greater immunity, if only slightly so, to these diseases than did the nomads or the western village-dwellers.

By the time the emigrant wagon trains rumbled across the Plains in the 1840s and 1850s, the Cherokees and the Eastern village-dwellers would have been firmly established along the river banks. No strangers to Americans and Europeans, these Native Americans would have known what emigrants needed, how to communicate with them, and how to negotiate with them. The Native Americans would have traded horses, cattle, and other livestock to the emigrants, along with farm produce and other trade goods in exchange for manufactured items that were difficult for the Native people themselves to produce. Most emigrants would have been seeking the greener lands of Oregon and California, or the gold and silver mines in the mountains, and would not have tried to wrest the Native Americans' land from them by force. Instead, the emigrants would have been grateful to receive assistance from the Cherokees and eastern village-dwellers, and goodwill and friendship would have characterized the relations of the two groups on the Great Plains.

Occasionally, a few emigrants might have decided to abandon their transcontinental trek and reside in the tribal villages, at least for a little while. Furthermore, small bands of other eastern tribes, pushed westward by the pressures of American expansion, would also have drifted into these riverine villages. Too small in number to impose their will upon the villagers, these refugee Native people would have quietly settled into the village community. Handfuls of emigrants, scattered refugee bands, and an assortment of frontier traders and drifters would have been absorbed into these steadily growing villages, and the ethnic divisions in each village would have become blurred. In time, villages would be known less by their tribal affiliation than by their geographic location. For example, "Red Deer's Village" might become known as "Near-the-Bridge Village" or "Bridgeport."

Because of the tradition of goodwill and friendship on the part of the village Natives, Congress, in passing the Homestead Act, would have recognized existing land claims in and around Native American villages, or at least granted first refusal rights to people already settled there. In this manner, there would have been nothing similar to the Plains Indian Wars that actually characterized the 1860s and 1870s. And there would have been no establishment of isolated Native American reservations on economically marginal land with the familiar array of social challenges that accompany them. Instead, Cherokees and other tribes would have continued to intermarry, ethnic divisions would have continued to blur, and these riverine Plains villages would have become large towns and small cities. Longtime residents would have enjoyed a certain insider status that would have given them slight leverage in social, political, and economic matters. However, these small Plains cities would have had to face the same challenges that faced all twentieth-century Plains communities. The hard reality of life on the Plains and shortage of opportunities caused many Plains citizens to leave their farms, towns, and small cities and head for larger urban centers like Denver, Lincoln, Omaha, Topeka, and Oklahoma City. Some communities collapsed, and others held on, but the success or failure of these communities would probably have been determined by factors other than their eastern Native American heritage.

Francis Flavin

Discussion Questions

1. What factors in the Great Plains environment shaped the development of human societies there?

2. Given the history of relations between village people and nomads in the Great Plains, what factors would have worked in favor of collaboration and cooperation if the food source of the nomads had suddenly vanished? What factors would have worked against such collaboration?

3. If the bison and the nomadic peoples of the Great Plains had already vanished before the great migration to California and Oregon by European Americans in the 1850s, how would that migration have been different?

4. In the alternate history presented in this chapter, a form of cultural and ethnic integration is suggested as a possible outcome of the collapse of the nomadic way of life on the Great Plains. What are the positive and negative results for the culture and well-being of the populations that would have arisen from such a process?

5. The Liebig law of the minimum applies to many situations that involve the impact of human practices on the natural environment. In what other contexts, either in the contemporary world or in history, have human activities threatened or affected the environmental balance?

Bibliography and Further Reading

Brown, Dee. *Bury My Heart at Wounded Knee: An Indian History of the American West*. New York: Holt, Rinehart and Winston, 1970.

Calloway, Collin G. *One Vast Winter Count: The Native American West before Lewis and Clark*. Lincoln, NE: University of Nebraska Press, 2003.

Dary, David A. *The Buffalo Book: The Full Saga of the American Animal*. Athens, OH: Ohio University Press, 1989.

DeMallie, Raymond J. *Handbook of North American Indians*, vol. 13, *Plains*. Washington, DC: Smithsonian Institution, 2001.

Holder, Preston. *The Hoe and the Horse on the Plains: A Study of Cultural Development among North American Indians*. Lincoln, NE: University of Nebraska Press, 1970.

Isenberg, Andrew C. *The Destruction of the Bison: An Environmental History, 1750–1920*. New York: Cambridge University Press, 2000.

Lamar, Howard R. *The New Encyclopedia of the American West*. New Haven, CT: Yale University Press, 1998.

McLoughlin, William G. *Cherokee Renascence in the New Republic*. Princeton, NJ: Princeton University Press, 1986.

Neihardt, John G., *Black Elk Speaks: Being the Life Story of a Holy Man of the Oglala Sioux*. New York: William Morrow, 1932.

Sandoz, Mari. *Cheyenne Autumn*. New York: McGraw-Hill, 1953.

Sandoz, Mari. *Crazy Horse: Strange Man of the Oglalas*. New York: Alfred A. Knopf, 1942.

Sandoz, Mari. *These Were the Sioux*. Fern Park, FL: Hastings House, 1961.

Utley, Robert M. *The Indian Frontier, 1846–1890*. Albuquerque, NM: University of New Mexico Press, 2003.

West, Elliot. *The Contested Plains: Indians, Goldseekers, and the Rush to Colorado*. Lawrence, KS: University Press of Kansas, 1998.

West, Elliot. *The Way West: Essays on the Central Plains*. Albuquerque, NM: University of New Mexico Press, 1995.

The Anasazi were peoples who lived in the American Southwest. What if these Native Americans had developed better farming techniques, such as irrigation, and dominated the area?

INTRODUCTION

The Anasazi are thought to be ancestors of today's modern Pueblo Native Americans. They lived in the Colorado Plateau country of southern Utah, southwestern Colorado, northwestern New Mexico, and northern Arizona sometime after 1 C.E. to about 1300. "Anasazi" is a Navajo word that has come to mean "ancient ones" or "ancient people," but the word itself is sometimes translated more literally as "enemy ancestors." Recent research traces the Anasazi to groups of early archaic peoples who practiced a wandering, hunting, and food-gathering lifestyle from around 6000 B.C.E. until the last millennium B.C.E. With the introduction of maize into the food supply sometime during this last millennium, the early southwest cultures began to rely increasingly on agricultural practices. It is during this transition period from the last centuries B.C.E. to the first few centuries C.E. that the southwest people began to develop into the distinctive Anasazi culture that we know today.

Archaeologists have defined several prehistoric cultures in the American Southwest. In the Four Corners area of Utah, Colorado, New Mexico, and Arizona are groups known today as the Anasazi (prehistoric Pueblo) who began constructing permanent hamlets and villages within the Colorado Plateau's canyon and mesa country. Mogollon peoples lived along the rim of the Colorado Plateau and in the mountains of eastern Arizona and western New Mexico. The Patayan occupied the area along the Colorado River in western Arizona. Finally, there are the Hohokam, (pronounced ho-ho-KHAM), who settled in the central and southern parts of Arizona.

Although these early Anasazi (known as archaic people) continued to move around in pursuit of seasonally available foods, an increasing amount of effort was being placed on the growing of crops and the storage of surpluses. Over time, these changes in daily focus led to a cultural change that reflected more the needs of a permanent rather than a mobile or wandering existence, and signs of a settled environment begin to appear. This new village/farming lifestyle encouraged individuals to rely

IN CONTEXT   Who Were the Anasazi?

The Anasazi were the ancestors of modern Pueblo Native Americans now living in New Mexico and Arizona. There never was an "Anasazi" tribe, nor did any group of people call themselves by that name. *Anasazi* is only a descriptive term of Navajo origin. Archaeologists applied the term to villagers who lived and farmed in the Four Corners between the years 1 and 1300 C.E. Most of them were probably ancestors of today's Pueblo people. After 1300, the heartland of this culture shifted southward but the culture never disappeared. The modern Pueblos are about twenty independent tribes living in New Mexico and Arizona. There is extensive literature available about the culture of modern and historic Pueblo people.

When the Anasazi or Pueblo culture began is a matter of definition, because there is no single event or trait that defines it. Archaeologists identify cultures by shared traditions in architecture, crafts, and other characteristics. At present they see the earliest traces of this culture dating back to at least 1 C.E., or as early as 1500 B.C.E., through characteristic kinds of basketry, sandals, art, tools, architecture, settlement pattern, and incipient agriculture. According to Pueblo oral traditions, different groups came from different directions and points of origin before joining together to form the clans and communities of today.

The ancestral Puebloan homeland was centered in the Four Corners region of northwest New

more and more on domesticated crops such as corn, beans, and squash, and also spurred the creation of new ideas and technology. A more stable lifestyle causes people to redefine how they view time and place. It seems that as individuals become more settled, there is a co-evolution in the use of decoration and art along with new ideas about the need for storage and housing. For the early Anasazi people, the developments were expressed in the construction of exquisite baskets and sandals, crafts for which we have come to refer to them as the Basketmakers.

Most cultural developments reflect the needs of people as they seek to adapt to their environments. And by the first century C.E., clearly recognizable regional variants or subcultures had begun to emerge within the southwest landscape. The eastern branches of the Anasazi culture came to include the Mesa Verde Anasazi of southeastern Utah and southwestern Colorado, and the Chaco Anasazi of northwestern New Mexico. The western Anasazi included the Kayenta Anasazi of northeastern Arizona and the Virgin Anasazi of southwestern Utah and northwestern Arizona. To the north of these Anasazi groups (north of the Colorado and Escalante rivers in Utah), there was a heterogeneous group of small-village dwellers known collectively as the Fremont people. With the exception of the Fremont, these early groups stored their goods in a variety of pits and circular cists that were often lined with upright stone slabs and roofed over with a platform of poles, twigs, grass, slabs of rocks, and even mud. Their houses were also sturdier than those of their archaic ancestors, although they had not yet used stone nor had they finished their designs with stucco.

By 500 C.E., the early Anasazi peoples had settled into a well-developed farming-village cultural society. Although they probably still practiced some seasonal traveling and continued to make use of wild resources, they were increasingly becoming farmers living in small villages. Their houses were well-constructed pit structures, consisting of a hogan-like superstructure

IN CONTEXT *Who Were the Anasazi? (Continued)*

Mexico and northeast Arizona, and in adjacent areas of Colorado and Utah, where their occupation lasted until 1280 or so. By 1300, the population centers had shifted south, to the Rio Grande Valley in north-central New Mexico and the Mogollon Rim in central Arizona, where related people had already been living for a long while.

Modern Pueblo people dislike the term *Anasazi*. The word offends many who consider it an ethnic slur. This Navajo word means "ancient enemy" (or ancient stranger, alien, foreigner, or outsider). Modern Pueblos speak several different languages, and do not share a common term for

their ancestors. The Hopi word is *Hisatsinom*, but other groups do not use it. "Ancient ones" and "ancestors" are adequate but rough translations for such terms.

The term *Anasazi* came into wide use about seventy years ago.

Today, however, no doubt remains that these prehistoric people were ancestral to modern Pueblos, who insist that their ancestors did not permanently "abandon" their former territories. Modern Pueblo people still make pilgrimages to ancestral village sites, have oral histories about them, and maintain shrines in the Four Corners region.

built over a knee- or waist-deep pit, often with a small second room, or antechamber, on the south or southeast side. Their settlements, which have been found scattered widely over the canyons and mesas of the southern Colorado Plateau, were generally small and consisted of one to three houses and up to a dozen or more structures.

Between 600 and 900 C.E., a number of developments took place in the Anasazi way of life. These village dwellers began producing more varied types of pottery with distinct differences in usage. There were also new large, communal pit structures that may have served a religious or political purpose. The bean was added to corn and squash as a major supplement to the diet, and the old *atlatl* (spear thrower) was replaced by the bow and arrow. We also find their housing being constructed above the ground during this period, with increased use of the pole-and-adobe building style. We are not sure why, but there were also major shifts in settlement patterns, as populations began to concentrate in some locations while completely abandoning others. Archaeologists refer to this gradual evolution toward a more stable farming/village lifestyle as the Puebloan period in Anasazi culture.

Anasazi civilization is divided into periods, with the Pueblo I and II periods representing approximately 700 to 1050 C.E. The tendency toward aggregation evidenced in Pueblo I sites reversed itself in the 250-year period between 900 and 1150, a time when certain areas in the Anasazi domain experienced tremendous population growth. Climate evidence based on pollen samples and tree rings indicates that the period was relatively warm. If so, the carrying capacity of the land may have increased significantly, and with the increase in food and nutrition, population numbers multiplied rapidly. Pueblo II people dispersed themselves widely over the land in thousands of small stone houses that replaced the pole-and-adobe architecture so prevalent during the Pueblo I period. The surface rooms now became year-round habitations, and the pithouses (now completely subterranean) probably assumed the largely ceremonial role we associate with the pueblo "kiva" (a large underground room).

Pottery in the interior of an Acoma dwelling, photographed in 1900. (Henry Peabody/National Archives)

It was also during this period that small cliff granaries make their appearance as secure storage facilities.

The house style known as the unit pueblo, which had its beginning during the previous period, became the universal settlement form during this period. In the unit pueblo, the main house was a block of rectangular living and storage rooms located on the surface immediately north or northwest of an underground kiva. The redware pottery industry continued to flourish, and pottery seems to have been traded throughout much of the Colorado Plateau region. Interestingly, the redware tradition ended in the country north of the San Juan River by late in the Pueblo II period, yet it blossomed in the area south of the river around Navajo Mountain in the Kayenta Anasazi country. The reasons for this shift are unknown, and the problem is a fascinating one. Production and refinement of the black-on-white and the gray (now decorated by indented corrugation) wares continued uninterrupted in both areas, but the redware tradition migrated across what appears to have been an ethnic boundary.

An Acoma pueblo and its reflection in a pool of water, photographed by Ansel Adams, 1941–1942. (National Archives)

TURNING POINT

By 1150, Anasazi populations may have reached their peak. The preceding 250 years had been relatively warm, and as the landscape adjusted to new weather patterns, the population seems to have adjusted to new carrying capacity levels. The actual conditions behind this population explosion are not fully known. It is likely that natural population growth was only part of the cause, and that immigration from outlying areas may have been equally important in accounting for the sometimes tenfold increases in people. There is evidence of road-building among some Anasazi groups, although the purpose and extent of the roads is not fully known. In other situations, the Anasazi also experimented with simple water diversion schemes, the forerunner of irrigation techniques found in hydraulic civilizations in other parts of the world. These elements along with others suggest that greater integration among distant Anasazi groups was being thought of, but there doesn't seem to be any evidence that it succeeded in becoming operational.

There is some possibility that politico-religious-ceremonial differences may have become significant between the various Anasazi groups, intensifying the idea of territory within each of the drainage areas the groups occupied. Of course, as territory becomes important so does territoriality

---

IN CONTEXT   Anasazi Timeline

Pre-Anasazi Period

Archaic 6500 to 1200 B.C.E.: The pre-Anasazi culture that moved into the Southwest after the big game hunters departed are called archaic. The people subsisted on wild foods and hunters used stone-tipped spears and knives, *atlatl*, and dart or spear to hunt deer, bighorn sheep, and antelope. They moved regularly and gathered wild plants in season.

Anasazi Period

Basketmaker I: There is no Basketmaker I group yet. Archaeologists have reserved the space just in case more evidence surfaces indicating there was another group between late Archaic and Basketmaker II, or they decide to refine the Basketmaker II classification.

Basketmaker II (early) 1200 B.C.E. to 50 C.E.: These early Anasazi camped in the open or lived in caves on a

seasonal basis. During this period they increasingly relied on cultivated gardens of corn and squash, but did not yet have beans. They made baskets, which is the origin of the label for this period, but they had no pottery.

Basketmaker II (late) 50 to 500: We find construction during this period using shallow pithouses, storage bins or cists. Corn and squash are present, but not beans. They continued to refine their baskets, but did not experiment with pottery.

Basketmaker III 500 to 750: Deep pithouses are being developed, along with some above-ground rooms. There is some use of surface storage pits and cists. The bow and arrow has replaced the *atlatl*, the traditional thrown spear. There is experimentation with pottery, mostly plain gray and

---

as a behavior, resulting in more closed societies and a failure to share ideas. Although the Anasazi show signs of significant cultural development, they remained an environmentally bound society. They were reactive participants in their world, adjusting to the conditions nature placed before them, with elements of settlement competing with elements of mobility cross-competing as weather and climate dictated.

Increasingly, concentrated environmentally defined populations struggle greatly with climate change, particularly when that change is for the worse. The Anasazi's western neighbors, the Hohokam, were experimenting with irrigation in south central Arizona at the same time as the groups living in the San Juan River region of northwestern New Mexico. If indeed the various tribes failed to integrate and share ideas, then new ideas and techniques (especially the development of irrigation) remained local, creating sharper divisions in the overall southwest cultural fabric in a region where water was the driving limit of existence. This could be why we find evidence of several distinct territorial groups within the southwest region, rather than evidence of an integrated southwest culture.

Interestingly, the Maya, who as contemporaries of both groups exhibited advanced developments in science, mathematics, astronomy, and construction, remained just beyond the reach of the Anasazi world. The spread of maize in the last millennium B.C.E. suggests there was some north-south interaction among the various Native groups of America and Mesoamerica, but we don't see much in the way of other scientific developments being transferred or emulated.

What we do see, however, is that following the collapse of both the Mayan and Southwest cultures, a new high culture (the Aztec) begins to develop in a high plateau valley in central Mexico. There is little evidence to suggest that the Aztecs were a combination of the Mayan and Anasazi

---

some black-on-white designs. The cultivation of beans begins.

Pueblo I 750 to 900: Large villages and great *kivas* (large underground ceremonial rooms) appear. Deep pithouses are still in use, and there is some above-ground construction using jacal or crude masonry. There is a variety of pottery forms; the plain and gray style with neckbands is the most common. There is also some black-on-white and decorated redware.

Pueblo II 900 to 1150 Chaco flowers: This is a high period with great population growth. There are very large Great Houses and kivas as well as constructed roads in some areas. We find begin to find evidence of small groups of above-ground masonry rooms and a kiva makeup that is typical of the Pueblo style. Pottery consists of corrugated gray and decorated black-on-white forms in addition to some decorated red and orange designs.

Pueblo III 1150 to 1350: The period of dispersement. There are now very large pueblos, cliff dwellings, and towers. Pottery includes corrugated gray, elaborate black-on-white, red, and orange. The climate is cooling and most of the traditional Anasazi villages in the Four Corners area are abandoned by 1300.

Pueblo IV 1350 to 1600: Large pueblos are now oriented around a central plaza. Plain pottery begins to replace the corrugated style, and there is increasing use of red, orange, and yellow as the black-on-white form declines.

Pueblo V 1600 to present: During the first part of this era the Spanish military, church, and civil domination and rule of the pueblos drives the Pueblo religion underground. The number of Pueblos shrinks from more than one hundred observed in 1539 to possibly twenty.

---

cultures. But what if, in 1050 or so, the Anasazi had done more than create minor stream diversions using small dams? What if they had learned from the Hohokam and instead constructed canals and developed the true art of irrigation sufficiently to become a hydraulic civilization, "an empire of the north." The result might have changed the course of history.

ACTUAL HISTORY

By the beginning of the twelfth century, most of the world was thrust once again into a general climate cooling (the Little Ice Age) with increased rainfall and much cooler summers throughout the world's grassland regions. We know that by 1150, Anasazi settlements on lands north of the San Juan River, such as Mesa Verde in southwestern Colorado, were being abandoned. The Anasazi were by this time a settled farming people and very dependent on harvests of corn, beans, and squash for their existence.

It is uncertain how much they may have relied on domesticated stock, but the change in weather favored grassland production over that of crops that need time to dry in order to reach full productivity. The Colorado Plateau landscape at this time was probably very close to what we see today in the area: a dry, rocky land with scrubby trees and bushes where there was seasonal water. The canyons remained as fairly efficient shelters from the cooler conditions (up to 7 degrees colder on average on the Colorado Plateau), but increased water flows made the Anasazi farming techniques more and more problematic as time passed. Following the period of population explosion just prior to this time, local populations were hard-pressed to maintain social structure and existence in the case of crop failures.

KEY CONCEPT   Colorado Plateau

The Colorado Plateau is a physiographic "province," a region distinct from other parts of the West. Originally named the Colorado Plateau by explorer John Wesley Powell, the plateau is in fact a huge basin ringed by highlands and filled with plateaus and mesas. Sprawling across southeastern Utah, northern Arizona, northwestern New Mexico, and western Colorado, the Colorado Plateau province covers a land area of 130,000 square miles. Of America's fifty states, only Alaska, Texas, California, and Montana are larger. The high, semi-arid region is actually a gigantic basin studded with a variety of landforms, ranging from 5,000 to 11,000 feet in elevation. There are rugged plateaus, slot canyons, mountains, river gorges with whitewater rapids, the Grand Canyon, and nearly every conceivable type of desert landscape.

Geologically, the Colorado Plateau is perhaps best defined by what did not happen to it in the geologic history of the American landmass. While the Rocky Mountains to the east and the basin and range country to the west were being thrust, stretched, and fractured into existence, the Colorado Plateau remained structurally intact. But a basin it

clearly is, and from nearly any vantage point the land drops away only to rise again far in the distance.

The Plateau is also the world's foremost museum of earth history. Each layer of rock represents an earlier epoch on the calendar of geological time. Scattered through these layers you can find fossil life forms that span the history of evolution from single-celled life to that of the dinosaur. At a single quarry in Dinosaur National Monument, for instance, scientists have uncovered the bones of three hundred dinosaurs representing ten different species. But animal life is not the only living presence. Here too lie the remains of 12,000 years of human occupation, spanning the entire temporal range of human prehistoric development from the Paleoindian culture to the modern Pueblo peoples.

Perpetually carved by erosion, the canyon lands of the Colorado Plateau form one of the most intricate landscapes on earth. It is a land of outstanding natural beauty and ecological diversity. The Colorado Plateau is also a wilderness. It is a remnant of the American frontier, a place where even contemporary human history hangs suspended in time.

We must remember that Anasazi agriculture in the east needed both rains and dry conditions to assure the best harvests. With rainfall increasing in both amount and intensity, harvests could have been reduced significantly. As a result, dwellers in certain locations probably experienced increased conditions of malnutrition and even starvation. We also know from Anasazi trash piles (called middens) that there were significant numbers of rodents around the granaries. Recent experience in the Four Corners region has shown that some of the rodents in the desert Southwest carry a deadly virus. With rodents having large supplies of grain to feed on, diseases that they carried could have easily wiped out entire villages in a very short time, had it been present. As people began to flee from the death and sickness, they would have carried the virus with them and only the most insulated canyon strongholds would have remained untouched. We would also see increased rejection of outsiders, as word of the sickness spread and small communities became increasingly aware of the danger outsiders might present. With people on the move, hunting activity would once again increase and many of the hunting grounds would have become over-hunted. It is possible that with the increasing cold, Native groups living further north on the Colorado Plateau might have moved south as the hunting grounds shifted with the climate.

With the exception of the Hohokam, these conditions ultimately led to the abandonment of many of the main Anasazi sites by the end of the

IN CONTEXT   The Anasazi Dinner Table

Although the Anasazi were farmers of corn, beans, and squash, they also hunted and gathered wild plants for food. Studies indicate that sometimes people depended more on wild foods than on farmed crops. Corn was dried and stored on the cob. Strips of dried squash hung in the storage rooms. Wild plant foods were also stored and prepared for cooking. Piñon nuts and sunflower and other seeds had to be winnowed and hulled before they could be cooked and eaten. Corn kernels were parched in jars that lay on their sides near the fire.

Women spent hours each day grinding corn into flour with *manos* and *metates*. Beans were soaked then cooked in large jars. Vessels full of stew or mush may have been placed directly over fires, or hot rocks were dropped into the contents. The women probably made paper-thin *piki* (a Hopi word) by spreading corn meal batter on a hot greased rock.

Mice and rabbits were probably more important sources of meat than larger game such as deer or bighorn sheep. Among the larger game animals, wild sheep apparently were more abundant than deer. Large animals were butchered at the kill site. Back at home the meat was roasted, stewed, or dried for jerky. Long bones were cracked to extract marrow, and hides were cured for other uses.

Turkeys were domesticated mainly for their feathers or as pets. They also were good for keeping bugs out of gardens. There is little evidence that turkeys or turkey eggs or dogs were eaten.

twelfth century and what seems to be a complete abandonment of sites by the start of the fourteenth century. In their place, other Native groups moved into the region. We find the Zuni and Navajo moving into the southern part of the Four Corners region, the Ute and Paiute to the west and north of the Four Corners, the Hopi in northeastern Arizona, and various bands of what today are Apache and Comanche in the south and west.

The first Europeans to see any part of the Southwest were probably Alvar Núñez Cabeza de Vaca and his three companions, perhaps reaching the Colorado Plateau in 1536. They were also the first to tell the fantastic stories of unbelievably rich cities such as the legend of the fabulous Seven Cities of Cíbola (the name given to a Zuni city Hawikuh).

The promise of silver and gold undoubtedly triggered the invasion of the Spanish Conquistador Francisco Vásquez de Coronado in 1540. As Coronado and his small army moved north, they too eventually reached Hawikuh, took it by force, and made it the center of their operations. But there wasn't any gold or silver there. Fearing they were being tricked, Coronado sent Captain Pedro de Tovar and a small force west in search of hidden treasure. But instead of treasure, they found extremely hostile local Native peoples and repeatedly fought battles with groups such as the Hopi. By the time the group had gone as far as the Grand Canyon, there seemed to be no change in the landscape and no easy way of crossing the great tear in the earth created by the Colorado River, and the group returned to Hawikuh. Coronado's failure to find great cities of gold and silver put an end to Spanish designs on the region, a condition that would last for the next forty years. By 1583 the rumors of gold seem once again to have surfaced in the Aztec capital, and the Spanish sent another expeditionary force north into Arizona in search of gold and silver. Although they did not find the wealth they hoped for, a group lead by Antonio de Espejo claimed the territory of the Hopis for King Philip II of Spain.

IN CONTEXT   Anasazi Pottery

Pottery and agriculture usually appear in ancient cultures at about the same time. Pottery is more practical for settled people who do not move frequently. Nomads commonly use baskets for storage and transport, but pottery better protects stored food from insects and rodents.

Much of the earliest Puebloan pottery is not decorated, but simple decorations (lines, dots, zigzags) appear at almost the same time as the undecorated pieces, around 575 C.E. in the Four Corners. In general, designs become denser and more precise over time up until about 1250 to 1300 C.E., which is the end of the Anasazi (or Pueblo) period in Colorado. Pottery designs from Colorado usually are bold geometric patterns in black-on-white, although sometimes they include obvious representations of birds or lizards, or humans. These geometric motifs seem to have originated from basketry decorations, in which straight and right-angle lines and stepped patterns were easier to create than curving forms.

We do not know what the geometric designs mean. According to the Pueblos, some of them signify clan affiliation. They may also represent family or village affiliation, or simply the potter's imagination. Many have been identified by Hopis and other Pueblo groups as symbolic of clouds, birds, bear claws, spider webs, water, friendship, migration, or other concepts.

Other kinds pf pottery included plain-surfaced and textured or corrugated cooking vessels. Black-on-red pottery from northern Arizona was traded throughout the Four Corners, as were red-on-buff styles from Utah. Shapes included jars, bowls, pitchers, ladles, canteens, figurines, and a variety of miniatures.

Firing was done with wood fuel at relatively low temperatures and apparently took place in earth trenches. To achieve a black-and-white result, the firing environment must be oxygen-deprived (reduction atmosphere) but without excess carbon, which would produce an all-black surface.

Southwest Native American ruins at Montezuma Castle National Monument, Arizona. (Edgar L. Perry/ National Archives)

The Spanish established a small outpost, wanting to make sure of their claim for the land, and once again they began to search for precious metals. During these expeditions, Spanish soldiers ventured as far to the east as central Kansas and portions of Oklahoma before returning to Santa Fe. Although they did not find cities of gold, they did find a grassland landscape rich in game.

Spanish colonists first settled in northern New Mexico in 1598. Don Juan de Oñate became the first governor and captain-general of New Mexico and established his capital in 1598 at San Juan Pueblo, twenty-five miles north of Santa Fe. One year later, he moved the capital to present-day Santa Fe. New Mexico was part of the empire of New Spain, and Santa Fe was the commercial hub. During the next seventy years, Spanish soldiers and officials, as well as Franciscan missionaries, sought to subjugate and convert the Pueblo Native Americans of the region. The indigenous population at the time was close to 100,000 people, who spoke nine languages and lived in an estimated seventy pueblos, many of which exist today.

Cliff dwellings in Pueblo Canyon, Sierra Ancha, Tonto National Forest, Arizona. (National Archives)

Ruins of cliff dwellings near Coon Creek, Sierra Ancha, Tonto National Forest, Arizona. (National Archives)

IN CONTEXT   The Social Structures of the Anasazi

Modern Pueblo groups that are believed to be descendants of the Anasazi share certain social patterns. Traditionally they are all matrilineal, meaning that clan affiliation is reckoned through the female line, and children "belong" to the mother's clan. They are matrilocal, meaning that husbands traditionally move into the bride's family household. Their society is matriarchal, meaning that homes and farmland are owned by and inherited from the mother, and a wife has the right to divorce and evict her husband. However, some kinds of civil and religious authority are usually reserved for men. Among the Hopi, for instance, the village chief or *kikmongwi* sometimes has been a woman, but usually the *kikmongwi* is a man.

Archaeological evidence is indirect, and does not usually reveal much about a people's beliefs, religion, political system, or social customs. Sometimes the geographic patterning of settlements in the landscape—or the placement of buildings within a village—are indicators of social relationships. Otherwise, we can only assume that many cultural patterns are the same now as they were one thousand years ago, and the Pueblos tell us they were. For example, in recent times, men were the weavers, and they socialized in the kivas. In archaeological sites, we often find evidence of weaving in kivas. But our understanding of Anasazi rules of property and authority are still too vague for us to be certain about matriarchy. At least there

is nothing that would indicate that roles have been reversed.

Many modern Pueblo people believe their thirteenth-century ancestors were organized into clans and were governed by clan elders. Some archaeologists doubt that the clan system existed at that time because they see little evidence for it. They theorize that clans were a response to social and geographical dislocations about 1300 to 1400, and to the need for a new way to define relationships between new neighbors. In this view, clans represent people who previously migrated as a group and then settled with other groups to form a larger community.

It is very common to find popular references to the Anasazi civilization or Anasazi cities. According to the narrowest definition, a civilization is a society that includes cities. A city is a large settlement of people who are not primarily farmers, but who make a living through trade and/or the manufacture of specialized products. The cluster of large settlements within Chaco Canyon, New Mexico, during the period 1000 to 1100 might have approached the definition of a true city. But the Anasazi culture region was much wider than Chaco's sphere of influence. The vast majority of Anasazi settlements were clusters of farmers.

Recent research indicates that as the landscape grew more crowded over time, dispersed settlements aggregated into larger communities with settlements surrounding central core villages. There

---

For the next one hundred years, the only Spanish who bothered to venture west onto the Plateau were Franciscan missionaries eager to save souls. Their progress was slow, dangerous, and, as far as the Hopis were concerned, largely futile. What the Hopi did accept from the priests were Old World plants like wheat and peach trees and animals such as dogs, goats, and sheep.

The Spaniards were further discouraged by the raiding of the Apaches and Navajos, who at once saw the advantages of having horses and stole them whenever possible. In 1680, Pueblo Natives revolted against some 2,500 Spanish colonists, killing 400 of them and driving the rest back into Mexico. The conquering Pueblos sacked Santa Fe and burned most of the buildings. The Spanish were able to reconquer the Pueblo peoples of the southwest twelve years after the Pueblo Revolt of 1680, but they never did gain control of the Navajos or Apaches. The fluid ways of the Apache and Comanche confounded the hierarchical and bureaucratic ways of the

IN CONTEXT *The Social Structures of the Anasazi (Continued)*

is also increasing evidence of status differences among the Ancestral Puebloans, as seen by differences in architecture and burial possessions. But compared to many ancient societies, Ancestral Puebloan society appears to have been relatively egalitarian without well-defined class distinctions.

In a photograph taken from a church top in 1904, the Acoma pueblo is set before the vast New Mexico horizon. (Edward S. Curtis/Library of Congress)

Spanish, and the continued raiding of the Native peoples discouraged any significant white settlement on the Colorado Plateau for another 150 years.

Arguably, the greatest impact on human land use by the Spanish was the drastic reduction they caused in Native American populations by the introduction of European diseases. At the time of Spanish incursions in the 1500s, about 100,000 Native Americans lived in about 100 communities in northern Arizona and central New Mexico. Following the devastating 1780 smallpox epidemic, which seemed to have had little effect on the Navajo, Native American populations on the Colorado Plateau had become a small fraction of that number.

When Mexico gained its independence from Spain in 1821, the door opened to contact with the United States. Santa Fe became the capital of the province of New Mexico, and trade was no longer restricted as it had been under Spanish rule. Trading expeditions began reaching Santa Fe along what would later be known as the Santa Fe Trail in the early 1800s. As the flow of

KEY CONCEPT   The Spread of Maize

Maize or corn is a gigantic domesticated grass of tropical Mexican origin. The plant is used to produce grain and fodder that are the basis of a number of food, feed, pharmaceutical, and industrial manufactures. Cultivation of maize and the elaboration of its food products are inextricably bound with the rise of pre-Columbian Mesoamerican civilizations. Due to its adaptability and productivity, maize spread rapidly around the globe after Spaniards and other Europeans exported the plant from the Americas in the fifteenth and sixteenth centuries. Maize is currently produced in most countries of the world and is the third most planted field crop (after wheat and rice). The bulk of maize production occurs in the United States, People's Republic of China, and Brazil, which together account for 73 percent of the annual global production of 456.2 million tons.

Maize is the domesticated form of a strain of teosinte, a wild grass occurring naturally in isolated patches usually restricted to elevations between 400 to 1700 meters in the Mexican western Sierra Madre (Michoacan and Jalisco). The prairies, open woodlands, and roadsides of Mesoamerica also are the only Native habitat of several closely related wild Zea species that are called teosintes, a common name derived from the Aztec language of Guatemala.

In the late 1950s, about 1,300 Indians lived in the Taos pueblo, in practically the same buildings and under the same conditions as in the sixteenth century under Spanish rule. The mound at the left is an oven. (National Archives)

Maize appears to have been first introduced in the Old World in Spain. In 1498, Columbus wrote that maize was being grown in Castile. In the early sixteenth century, maize spread from Spain throughout the countries of Southern Europe, Northern Africa, and the Middle East that border the Mediterranean Sea, and to northern Europe. In 1753, when Linnaeus named maize according to his new binomial system, he combined the Greek word *Zea*, meaning grain, with the adopted Arawak word for the species name, *mays*.

Nineteenth-century botanists also proposed the great antiquity of maize cultivation in the Americas. During his five-year voyage around the world on HMS Beagle, Charles Darwin found ancient heads of maize on the coast of Peru. Recent archaeobiological studies of maize cobs and pollen, and of maize phytoliths (microscopic structures of silica) in food residues in potsherds and on ancient human teeth, indicate that Native Americans domesticated maize in Mexico more than 6,200 years ago.

Most social and plant scientists regard maize agriculture as a prime example of the co-evolution of a plant and its domesticators: as the plant and human society evolved, they each exerted strong influence on one another. Likewise, the domestication and improvement of maize is strongly related to the development of cultural complexity and rise of advanced civilizations in prehispanic Mesoamerica.

goods continued along the Santa Fe Trail, so did exploration of neighboring lands. It wasn't long before expeditions such as those of Zebulon Pike, James Fremont, and Jedediah Smith were sent into the Rocky Mountain region in search of wealth as well as a possible land route to California.

When Americans elected James Polk as their eleventh president in 1844, they ushered in an era of expansionism and war that would soon reshape the American Southwest. The new administration sailed along on a slogan of "Manifest Destiny," a phrase coined by an energetic newspaper editor in the summer of 1845. Before Polk's term of office ended, U.S. territory encompassed the former Republic of Texas, and the Oregon territory, including present-day Oregon, Washington, Idaho, and parts of Wyoming and Montana, had been taken from the British.

A number of prominent Americans opposed Polk's hawkish expansionism: Henry Clay, former president Martin Van Buren, Daniel Webster, and John C. Calhoun. But for Polk, the prize to be obtained, especially from a confrontation with Mexico, was simply too tempting to ignore. He wanted California at all costs; and, of course, it would not do to have a foreign country in possession of the land between the far west and the rest of the United States, so Mexico would have to give it all up.

In 1845, Polk sent Zachary Taylor (known as Old Rough and Ready, a veteran of the War of 1812) with an army to the Rio Grande. Taylor's troops were soon attacked by Mexicans, giving Polk the excuse he needed to ask for and receive a declaration of war against Mexico on May 13, 1846. At the Battle of Buena Vista in 1847, Taylor's troops, outnumbered 4 to 1, defeated Santa Ana, making Taylor a national hero and a strong choice for the U.S. presidency in 1848. By September 14, 1847, Mexico City had fallen to the Americans. Peace negotiations between the two countries finally culminated with the Treaty of Guadalupe Hidalgo on February 2, 1848. The treaty established the boundary between the two republics, which begins at the mouth of the Rio Grande in the Gulf of Mexico westward, with several jogs, to the Pacific Ocean; a huge tract of

KEY CONCEPT   Little Ice Age

Only 150 years ago, most of the world came to the end of a 500-year cold snap so severe that thousands of people starved. The Little Ice Age, lasting from about 1350 to about 1850, was characterized by advances of mountain glaciers in most parts of the world and occasional spells of unusually cold winters in North America, Europe, and Asia. It also changed the course of history. Dutch canals froze over for months, ships could not leave port, and glaciers in the Swiss Alps overwhelmed mountain villages.

Five hundred years of much colder weather changed agriculture, helped tip the balance of political power from the Mediterranean states to the north, and contributed to the social unrest that culminated in the French Revolution. The poor suffered most. They were least able to adjust to changing circumstances and most susceptible to disease and increased mortality. These five centuries of periodic economic and social crisis in a much less densely populated Europe are a haunting reminder of the drastic consequences of even a modest cooling of global temperatures.

former Mexican lands that included present-day California, Nevada, Utah, Arizona, New Mexico, and parts of Colorado and Wyoming.

In early 1906, the people of New Mexico and Arizona voted on an issue of joint statehood, but only the New Mexico voters approved the measure. By 1910, the citizens of the New Mexico Territory were able to draft a new constitution in preparation for statehood, with Congress voting to admit them to the Union as the forty-seventh state in 1912. The configuration of the country we know today as the United States was set.

ALTERNATE HISTORY

As the summer of 1150 progressed, it would have become clear that the crops in the San Juan River valley were not going to ripen as expected. The summer's heavy rains and strong storms would have damaged most of the corn crop, and the consistent flooding of the valley floor would have threatened the beans and squash crops as well. This would have been the third year in a row that the rains and cool temperatures of summer would have limited the harvest and most of the granaries would have been dangerously low. The year before, a group of hunters would have gone as far as the Black Mesa region to investigate stories they had heard of a group of people living far to the southwest in a desert, who had the power to send water where they wanted it and who harvested strange and delicious crops. They were called the Hohokam, but their existence was only a rumor, and the village elders might have forbidden contact, saying it was not right for humans to manage nature and such people must be possessed by spirits.

The rains would also have brought more rats, and there would seem to be nothing that could stop them from getting into the granaries and spoiling what were very precious supplies. Reports would be arriving of a terrible sickness that was sweeping north of the river, wiping out whole villages in a matter of days. In early August, the elders would have decided to explore three areas in case they might have to move the village, while one group would begin moving all the grain in the granaries from baskets to pots in an attempt to save it from the rats. Two groups would have been sent to the north along the courses of the two main rivers that flowed south into the San Juan from the north. Another group would have gone directly south from the Chaco Canyon compound, while a final group would have gone west to see if the story of the mystery tribe was true.

By early September, the southern scouting party would have sent a runner back to report that the main group had entered a desert and would proceed south for two moons before returning. A week later, most of the western group would return with baskets filled with corn, beans, and many new plants that could be used as a base for the next year's crops. They would have reported that these westerners were indeed a great people who moved the waters about the ground to grow crops in variety and abundance in a way they had never seen. More important, they would have agreed to teach their Anasazi brothers how to manage the waters themselves in exchange for a large supply of pots for storing harvests. The northern group would not have returned until early November. They would have sent several runners back, but none ever arrived in the village. They would not have found rich valleys where the village might be moved, but they would have found great herds of deer and would have spent the past months hunting and drying the meat in order to bring it back to the compound. They would also have found a strange rock that was golden like the sun and became soft to the touch after being in the fire pit for several hours.

By 1250, the Chaco Canyon Anasazi would have used the new irrigation techniques to expand their agricultural output more than threefold. The increase in production would also have brought about an increase in population, resulting in a gradual agricultural sprawl. There would have been increasing disagreements over water and who could use it, forcing the council of elders to create official water-use policies. To meet the housing needs, local builders would have begun experimenting more with stone construction and larger, multistoried, multifamily dwellings. Similar events would also have been under way at other Anasazi sites such as Canyon de Chelly and Black Mesa in addition to new enclaves developing to the east on the edge of the great prairies.

Workers would have found that the strange rock that was the color of the sun could be easily worked by hitting it with stones once it was soft. Although the gold would not have been valued as money or a form of riches, there would have been a strong ceremonial and decorative demand for it, particularly among tribes far distant from the few mountain sources where the Chaco Anasazi had found it. As demand grew, the supply of nuggets would have quickly diminished. Fortunately, in hunting for nuggets, many of the workers would have noticed thousands of tiny specks glittering in the sands along stream banks. The gold dust would have proved to be easier to work than the nuggets. When heat is added to them, the small flakes quickly become malleable and are easily worked into many desired shapes. Workers would have found the golden rock even along some cliff walls higher in the mountains, but they would not have been able to determine how to get it out of the hard rock.

By the start of the fourteenth century, the Anasazi domain would have spread throughout the entire southwestern region, extending from what is today Texas in the east to southern California in the west. Although there would have been a rather large separate group living in the Copper Canyon region of northern Mexico, the results of the few encounters that would have taken place would have left the American Anasazi more fearful of further exchange than hopeful. There would have been also several very aggressive groups of Apache and Navajo living in the great desert lands of northern Mexico, and despite the Anasazi's best efforts, these people would have refused to listen to talk of planting crops, preferring instead to herd small flocks of goats and sheep they had captured.

In 1536, Alvar Núñez Cabeza de Vaca and three companions would have wandered into the Anasazi world. Had the men's fortunes been better and they had not arrived half starved with their clothes in rags, they would have been taken for gods. But their skins would have been dark from exposure to the sun, and only their beards and several strange hard objects would give cause for wonder. The men would have been completely delirious when found, and would have spoke some strange language that every now and then had words the scout group might have recognized. Rather than wait, the party would have determined to bring them back to the Chaco Canyon compound and let the elders determine what to do.

When de Vaca would have awoken, the first thing he would have noticed was a gold cup placed beside his bed. He would not be sure where he was, but his mind would have raced with thoughts of having found the fabled Seven Cities of Cíbola and how rich he would become. The Anasazi would have been gracious hosts and as the men slowly regained their strength they also would have come to understand enough of the language to begin to talk more openly with their hosts. The Anasazi would have been interested in learning about the hard metal substance that formed the spear the men carried and were told there were many other wonders of hard metal that the foreigners used to help with work. The group soon would have told their hosts they needed to return to the south and find their companions, but that they would return and bring many items for trade.

Four years later the mighty Spanish entrada (expeditionary invasion) of Francisco Vásquez de Coronado would have arrived and the Anasazi world would be changed forever. Scouts would have returned with reports of the large group moving north, so the sight of the horses and glistening hats would not take them completely by surprise. When the leader would have greeted them in their own language they would have been even more at ease. The elders would have been told that the group had come to establish a trade center and that their visitors would be happy to trade any item for the yellow rock. Not placing any special value on the yellow rock, the Anasazi would have quickly agreed to terms. As time passed, Coronado would have realized that the extent of the riches of these people was equal to or greater than that of the Aztecs whom they had already conquered. More important, they had learned lessons in dealing with the Aztecs and those could be used here to exploit the mining operations. Despite the urge to get rich quick, Coronado would not have wanted to make a move until he had learned where the mines were located. Once that was accomplished and the region would have been fully mapped, the Anasazi would have been no longer important except as slaves and converts for the priests.

In actual history, by the start of the seventeenth century, the Spanish dream of having a great trading empire with gold and silver shipments flowing to the Spanish crown seemed to be taking form. Although the Anasazis' understanding of plants as medicine would have at first lessened the impact of the European diseases brought by the foreign invaders, the result in the end would have been the same devastation experienced by other Native Americans after such exposure, and by 1600 less than 10 percent of the original people would have been left.

Naturally, in both actual and our alternate histories, the other European nations responded to the stories of gold and wealth flowing out of the new world. The Spanish, of course, had tried to keep their find a secret, but the English, Dutch, and French were quick to respond as a series of colonies sprang up along the Atlantic coast of the new world. But colonization and exploitation of new land is a slow process, and for the next two hundred years population growth was anything but explosive.

By the time the thirteen colonies took that brave step in April 1775 of breaking from England and forming a new nation, the political geography of North America had several clear divisions. Generally, lands east of the Mississippi were associated with the new American states and several identified territories as one moved north toward the Great Lakes. The French were laying claim to a vast stretch of land west of the Mississippi and north of the Arkansas River and as far west as the eastern parts of Washington and Oregon. Coastal Washington and Oregon were still in dispute, as both English and Russian ships had visited the region. The rest of the land was considered either too wild to be controlled or clearly under Spanish domination. Spanish-controlled lands included Texas, Colorado, New Mexico, Arizona, Utah, Nevada, and California as well as the stronghold of Mexico itself.

At the start of the nineteenth century, increasing financial pressure from the Napoleonic Wars found France in financial trouble, and in order to raise cash, the French decided to sell some of their lands in America to pay off debts. American President Thomas Jefferson, hoping to finalize a sale before the Spanish could make an offer, was quick to respond and agreed to purchase France's claims. The French, however, were not eager to give up all of their lands, agreeing to sell those lands west of the Mississippi, north of the Arkansas River, then along a mix of boundaries to Oregon country. At the same time, the French Revolution and Napoleonic Wars had diverted Spain's attention from its colonies, leaving a vacuum in the coordination and control of New Spain and an increasing local desire for self-government.

When Ferdinand VII was forcefully removed from the Spanish throne, he was replaced by Joseph Bonaparte, Napoleon's brother. Local discontent in New Spain at this time was already seriously fragmenting governance there and unless quick action was taken, control might be lost forever. A Spanish priest, Father Miguel Hidalgo y Costilla, had already begun a small revolt against Spanish tyranny and cruelty using mostly local people (Creoles) as resistors. Realizing the unique opportunity before him, Bonaparte might have quickly mobilized his forces and sent his army to Mexico to gain control. At the same time, he could have made an appeal to the Pope in Rome to sanction his actions and help free the innocents from tyranny. By the time Bonaparte and his forces arrived in Mexico City, the Pope could have granted permission to Bonaparte to do whatever was necessary to restore decency and control of the church. In a meeting with Father Hidalgo, Bonaparte could have convinced the priest to help him unite all the Native peoples against Spanish control and take the land for France. Bonaparte then might have sent General Santa Ana north to secure the northern border and make sure Texas and the goldfields in the west were safe.

Less than three months from its inception, the mission to establish complete control could have been accomplished. In a bold move, Bonaparte would have severed ties with Spain and established a new government. France, England, and the United States would quickly have recognized the new government and sent envoys to Mexico City to establish formal relations. Mexico's northern states would now have included Texas, New Mexico, Colorado, Utah, and California with capitals established to organize colonization and development. Bonaparte would have realized the northern territories were not secure. They were, after all, more than one thousand miles from Mexico City. Not trusting the United States and other European nations to recognize Mexico's control of these northern lands, Bonaparte would have granted the Pope lands in the heart of Mexico City and in California that could be used as a seat for a western Vatican City. In addition, he would have agreed to allow the Mexican army to be used for the protection of church outposts.

In the outcome of this alternate history scenario, today Mexico would be the fourth-largest country in the world and the largest world economy.

Richard W. Dawson

Discussion Questions

1. Why did the Anasazi not develop irrigation on their own?
2. What other factors might have limited the growth of the Anasazi population?
3. How would the discovery of gold affect the Anasazi culture when the European explorers arrived?
4. In actual history, how did the United States acquire most of the lands of California, Arizona, and New Mexico?
5. How was daily life different during the Little Ice Age?

Bibliography and Further Reading

Ambler, J. Richard. *Anasazi: Prehistoric Peoples of the Four Corners Region.* Flagstaff, AZ: Museum of Northern Arizona, 1989.

Cordell, Linda S. *Ancient Pueblo Peoples.* Washington, D.C.: Smithsonian Books, 1994.

Cordell, Linda. *Archaeology of the Southwest.* Burlington, MA: Academic Press, 1997.

Ferguson, William M. *Anasazi of Mesa Verde and the Four Corners.* Boulder, CO: University of Colorado Press, 1996.

Ferguson, William M., and Arthur H. Rohn. *Anasazi Ruins of the Southwest in Color.* Albuquerque, NM: University of New Mexico Press, 1987.

Frazier, Kendrick. *People of Chaco: A Canyon and Its Culture.* New York: W. W. Norton, 1986.

Gumerman, George J. *The Anasazi in a Changing Environment.* New York: Cambridge University Press, 1988.

Gumerman, George J., and J. S. Dean. "Prehistoric Cooperation and Competition in the Western Anasazi Area." In Linda S. Cordell and George J. Gumerman, eds., *Dynamics of Southwest Prehistory.* Washington, D.C.: Smithsonian, 1989.

Matlock, Gary. *Enemy Ancestors: The Anasazi World with a Guide to Sites.* Flagstaff, AZ: Northland Publishing, 1988.

McNitt, Frank. *Anasazi.* Albuquerque, NM: University of New Mexico Press, 1957.

Morrow, Baker H., and V. B. Price, eds. *Anasazi Architecture and American Design.* Albuquerque, NM: University of New Mexico Press, 1997.

Parker, Kay. *The Only True People: A History of the Native Americans of the Colorado Plateau.* Denver, CO: Thunder Mesa Publishing, 1991.

Plog, Stephen. *Ancient Peoples of the American Southwest.* London: Thames and Hudson, 1997.

Stuart, David E. *Anasazi America: Seventeen Centuries on the Road from Center Place.* Albuquerque, NM: University of New Mexico Press, 2000.

Wills, Wirt H. *Early Prehistoric Agriculture in the American Southwest.* Santa Fe, NM: School of American Research Press, 1988.

The League of the Five Nations was a remarkable peace agreement among Native American Iroquois tribes. What if the League had expanded to include non-Iroquois tribes?

INTRODUCTION

As the first Europeans sailed west to explore and colonize the New World, something remarkable happened in the forests of North America. In what is now upstate New York, five Native American groups—the Mohawks, Senecas, Onondagas, Oneidas, and Cayugas—set aside their differences and formed a league of friendship and peace. Oral histories relate that sometime between the fourteenth and sixteenth centuries, two notable leaders named Deganawida and Ayonhwatha (Hiawatha) traveled from village to village to persuade other Iroquois to end their wars against one another. The two leaders used a bundle of arrows to symbolically represent their plan of union. A single arrow could easily be broken, they explained, but when many arrows were tied together, they were indestructible. The Five Nations, as they would often be called, agreed to unite for common defense and formed the League of the Hodenosaunee, or People of the Long House. The Iroquois would thereafter play a decisive role in the history and development of early America.

What is remarkable about the Iroquois confederacy is that such a league could be formed by diverse Native Americans who were in a state of near-constant warfare. The conflicts partly derived from the value that indigenous peoples placed on war as a means for men to distinguish themselves in battle. Gaining status as a warrior was a benchmark episode in a young male's development as he sought a marriage partner and a leadership role within the community. Perhaps more important to recurring hostilities were the cultural obligations that came with clan membership. When someone within the clan was killed, it was the duty of the male members of that clan to avenge the loss. These revenge killings led to an endless cycle of murder that kept differing tribal groups at odds. Thus, when the Five Nations constructed a long-standing peace and league of union, their achievement represented a watershed in the history of colonial North America.

The Five Nations were partly able to accomplish this feat because of the cultural commonality they shared. Mohawks, Senecas, Onondagas,

KEY CONCEPT   The Longhouse and Iroquois Village

An Iroquois village was made up of one or more longhouses, which were usually that: long houses. They ranged in length from about 60 feet to well over 220 feet, and were generally about 20 feet wide and 20 feet high. The framework of a longhouse resembled a large rigid basket made of wooden posts set into the ground, with other poles and saplings lashed to these to form the exterior walls and create the arched roof. A variety of trees were used to construct the framework: decay-resistant woods selected for the posts and poles set into the ground; strong, and sometimes flexible woods chosen for the remainder of the framework. The bark was probably peeled from these posts, poles, and saplings so they would be less likely to harbor insect pests. Bark from various kinds of trees was used to cover the framework, for interior partitions, and for covering the benches and shelves of the living space. Among the New York Iroquois, elm bark was preferred. Large sheets of bark were lashed to the exterior walls and roof of the longhouse. The Iroquois smoothed the rough outer bark surfaces so that water would run off them more easily.

A longhouse was home to an extended family where the elder women and men were the keepers of the community's traditions and histories. As "storytellers" they entertained members of their extended families while teaching them through the spoken word about their traditions, histories, and values.

The length of a longhouse was determined by the size of the extended family for which it would serve as a home. The interior of the longhouse was divided into a series of compartments or apartments about twenty feet long. Each compartment housed two families who shared a fire for heating, cooking, and light. The two family living spaces

"The Town of Pomeioc" North Carolina by John White. (National Archives)

KEY CONCEPT   *The Longhouse and Iroquois Village (Continued)*

were separated by a central aisle or corridor. This aisle ran the length of the longhouse from end to end, door to door. A longhouse, 220 feet long, could be the home of eighteen families, or about ninety people; a longhouse of sixty feet might serve as the home of four families or twenty people. The longest longhouse known from archaeological excavations was four hundred feet long and was probably the home of about thirty-six families, or 180 people.

Everyone living within a longhouse, except the husbands, was related through the mothers' side of the family and belonged to the same clan. After marriage, husbands moved from their mothers' longhouses into those of their wives. The eldest women in the longhouse were in charge of it.

The longhouse was a comfortable place to live, as long as you did not mind lots of family as neighbors. Each family's home was on a fur- and mat-covered platform, or bench, about five to six feet wide and about fifteen feet long, which extended along the exterior wall of the longhouse. The bench was built a foot or so above the ground and served as the family's living space: their bedroom, dining room, recreation room, and workroom. Large mats or skins could be hung in front of it for privacy, or for warmth during the cold of winter. Firewood was often stored under the bench, and one can only imagine how much firewood would be necessary for heating, cooking, and lighting in each longhouse.

About five feet above the bench was a shelf that served for storage and made a ceiling over the bench. The space between them was closed off at the ends by partitions, which made a cozy cubicle of the living space. This arrangement formed a storage "closet" between one end of the cubicle and the end of the compartment.

Most of the information describing the inside of a longhouse comes from Iroquois oral traditions and from descriptions written by European visitors to longhouses during the 1600s and 1700s. These sources tell us that the longhouse was packed not only with people but also with the things that they made and used. Extra animal skin robes and blankets, reed mats, wood splint baskets, and clay pots used for storage or cooking were most often kept on the shelf that served as the "roof" to the living compartment. This shelf was also used for additional seating during family meetings or during

storytelling on winter evenings. Depending upon how cold or hot and smoky the longhouse was, the shelf might also be used for sleeping.

Little has survived of these longhouses. Archaeologists find only indirect evidence of them in the form of dark circular stains in the ground, which they call postmolds. These mark the places were the wooden posts of a longhouse framework were once set; the posts have since rotted away leaving an organic stain in the soil. Areas of fire-reddened earth, some associated with fire-cracked stones, mark the locations of fireplaces. These are commonly found along the center aisle. Other archaeological features, such as filled-in storage or garbage pits, provide additional information about longhouse life.

The Iroquois were farmers. Corn, beans, and squash were their main crops. In the Iroquois village of four hundred years ago there was a strict division

"The Town of Secoton" by John White. (National Archives)

KEY CONCEPT *The Longhouse and Iroquois Village (Continued)*

of work by gender. Although men created the fields in the forest by cutting down trees and burning the unwanted wood and brush, farming was women's work. Women planted, cultivated, and harvested the crops, assisted by their children whom they brought to the fields with them. Elderly men also might assist them in the harvest.

Corn, beans, and squash are known today by the Iroquois as Our Life Supporters, or as the Three Sisters. Like sisters who worked together in the fields and who shared the same longhouse living space, corn, beans, and squash were often planted together in the same spot. Here they grew together and provided strength and nourishment to one another. Cornstalks provided a place for the vines of beans to climb; beans replaced some of the nitrogen in the soil, which the corn depleted; and the large, broad leaves of the squash and pumpkin plants shaded the ground, holding moisture in and discouraging weeds from growing.

Although the main harvest took place in the fall, another important event in the farming cycle was Green Corn time, usually sometime in August, when the corn was green or not fully ripened. Similar in consistency to our sweet corn, the green corn was harvested for immediate consumption. This occasion was one of the Iroquois' important seasonal ceremonies of thanksgiving.

Much of the interior of the longhouse was taken up with food storage, especially corn, beans, and squash, which were harvested in the fall. Dried ears of corn, their husks folded back and braided into long ropes, hung from the longhouse rafters. Shelled corn and beans were stored in large bark barrels placed in the storage rooms at either end, near the entrances to the longhouse. Slices of dried squash and pumpkin hung from sticks also suspended above, where the heat would dry them and smoke would help to preserve them. (George R. Hamell and William Rogers, courtesy New York State Museum)

Oneidas, and Cayugas all spoke the Iroquoian language, and this was a key mark of distinction from their Algonquian-, Siouan-, or Muscogean-speaking neighbors. Though the Iroquoian tongue was spoken by other indigenous peoples in the northeast, such as the Hurons, Petuns, Wenros, and Susquehannock, their exclusion from the league to some extent stemmed from sociopolitical differences between them and the Five Nations Iroquois. The Five Nations were most distinguishable by the longhouses in which they lived. These dwellings varied in size, with some as large as two hundred feet long and twenty feet wide. The longhouse was more than just a living space, however; it also served as the major form of organization of Iroquois villages and brought families and clans into larger alliances. These local identities and associations formed the core of the League of the Hodenosaunee and decisively shaped relationships within the confederacy as well as with nonmembers.

The Five Nations used their strength in numbers to extend their power and influence throughout the region. When Europeans first arrived on the continent, the Iroquois and their neighbors had already been embroiled in a series of "mourning wars"; the purpose of these wars was either to replace lost relatives or to mollify their spirits by killing or adopting other Natives into the avengers' clans and communities. The Iroquois were very successful in these wars, so much so that Algonquians in the northeast called them Hilokoa, which meant "the killer people." Indigenous warfare dramatically increased with the onset of European colonization in the seventeenth century. These wars intensified partly because of the diseases that explorers and traders carried with them into

Native American country. The indigenous people were unable to with-stand the debilitating effects of smallpox, measles, and other Old World disorders that swept through their villages with unrestrained force. The Five Nations in particular experienced significant population loss. The resulting demographic imbalance led to mourning wars on an unprece-dented scale, as Iroquois attacked nearby tribes and incorporated many captives into their clans.

Trade also intensified conflicts between Native American groups. Europeans brought highly desirable items to trade for beaver pelts and deerskins, items such as iron tools and weapons, glass beads, copper ket-tles, and wool blankets. The Five Nations recognized the power of this trade and struggled to assert themselves as middlemen between the new-comers and non-League Native peoples. The Iroquois, in an attempt to eliminate competition in trade with the Europeans, attacked Hurons, Neutrals, Petuns, and others with deadly success. Entire villages were destroyed as refugees fled west toward the Great Lakes, and those taken captive were incorporated into Iroquois communities. Eyewitnesses were astonished at the presence of so many non-Iroquois within the Five Nations villages. By 1668, two-thirds of the Oneida villages consisted of Algonquians and Hurons.

The League of the Hodenosaunee was therefore a means through which the Five Nations Iroquois could effectively incorporate other Native peoples into their clans and confederacy. This inclusion of diverse Native Americans, however, was no trifling affair; it involved complex rituals—sometimes including torture—wherein rival Natives were cleansed of their old identities in order to become Iroquois. As the colonial period

"Iroquois Fort Captured June 19, 1610" from *Brule's Discoveries and Explorations* by Consul Willshire Butterfield, 1898. (National Archives)

KEY CONCEPT   Smallpox

The European conquest of the Americas moved rapidly, partly because Europeans had superior weapons, used horses, and saw immense opportunities for riches in the land and mineral resources of the new territories. However, a factor that made the conquest much easier for Europeans was the spread of fatal diseases among the Native American populations, diseases to which the Europeans had some degree of immunity. Diseases spread so rapidly into the interior of the continent from the first contacts with Europeans that when European conquistadors and settlers arrived, they often found empty villages and even cities, already wiped out by the advancing plagues. The most catastrophic of the newly introduced diseases was smallpox, although other killer diseases included measles, influenza, bubonic plague, and yellow fever. Even mumps and whooping cough, regarded as childhood diseases in Europe, killed adult Native Americans who had never been exposed to them. Smallpox is highly contagious, spreads rapidly, and leaves a few survivors terribly scarred and sometimes blinded.

These epidemics had different effects in different parts of the New World. Among the first affected were the populations of the small islands in the Caribbean, where in some cases, every Native American was killed by the plagues. In the heavily populated regions of Mexico, Central America, and northern South America, the diseases also spread rapidly. It is estimated that in some of these areas, over 90 percent of the original population died, mostly from disease, in the first decade of European contact.

However, in North America, where the original population was more scattered, with only minor agriculture, few large settlements, and scattered villages, all of the diseases spread more gradually. Even so, people often fled in panic from communities that suffered outbreaks of smallpox or other diseases, leading to the spread of the infection. As refugees, they would carry the disease to new areas, and while moving overland, they could not care for those already weakened. Another factor that accounted for the presence of diseases among Europeans that were unknown in the Americas was that Europeans, Asians, and Africans had a long

progressed and imperial rivalries between Europeans intensified, the Iroquois confederacy would be challenged as never before. The fate of the League would largely be determined by how the Five Nations related to their Native American neighbors.

TURNING POINT

Disease, trade, and warfare were all parts of larger processes in the Atlantic World in which Europeans attempted to exert control over the territories and peoples they encountered. Native Americans were often caught in the middle of these imperialist designs, which intensified competition and conflict between indigenous peoples. The Dutch were the first Europeans to establish trading posts and settlements along the Hudson River, penetrating far into the interior of New York and in proximity to the Five Nations' sphere of influence. The Iroquois entered into alliances with the commercially minded Dutch because trade with them gave the Iroquois significant advantages over their poorly supplied neighbors. In what has often been called the Beaver Wars, because of the great

KEY CONCEPT   *Smallpox (Continued)*

history of domesticating animals, while in North America, the only domestic animal was the dog. Many pathogens had been transmitted from close living with animals, mutating into human diseases in the Eastern Hemisphere. Smallpox, however, is a strictly human disease, not carried by animals. As such, it spread most virulently in high concentrations of humans, accounting for its devastating effect in island populations and in the more densely populated regions of Mexico and Central America.

There is some evidence that smallpox was introduced into the Caribbean when African slaves were brought to the islands in the first years of Spanish exploration. By 1495, the majority of the indigenous population of Santo Domingo had died, and by 1515, over two-thirds of the Native American population of Puerto Rico had died, mostly from smallpox. Although many of the original residents in Mexico died through direct slaughter in warfare with Europeans as well as from other diseases, smallpox is estimated to have killed about 65 percent of the population of that region within the first decade after the arrival of Hernan Cortez.

Smallpox came to the lands that later became the United States, either from the West Indies or from Canada. Although no one is sure what disease swept through the northeastern Atlantic coast region from 1616 to 1619, many analysts believe that it was smallpox that reduced the population of Massachusetts and other Algonquin tribes there by over 90 percent.

Controversy surrounds the issue of whether smallpox was intentionally introduced on several occasions in order to assist in the conquest. There is evidence that the practice was suggested and implemented by the distribution of smallpox-infected blankets among Native Americans in the Ohio area by English troops under the command of General Jeffrey Amherst in 1763. Unsubstantiated and more disputed is the assertion that the U.S. Army deliberately exposed Mandans to smallpox in 1837, resulting in some 125,000 deaths. Others argue that, quite to the contrary, by the 1830s, the U.S. government was vigorously pursuing a policy of vaccination of Native Americans to prevent the spread of the disease.

---

wealth beaver pelts created, the Iroquois extended their control over rival Natives by attacking both Iroquoian- and Algonquian-speaking groups in the 1640s and 1650s.

The burgeoning influence of the Five Nations continued past mid-century, even after the English ousted the Dutch from New York in the 1660s. Indeed, the English recognized the power the Iroquois held not only by their strength in numbers but also by their strategic geographic positioning. Historian T. H. Breen, writing in *America Past and Present*, later echoed the meaning of these words when he rightly asserted that the Five Nations were "a formidable power in the Northeast, one that no colonial power could overcome without incurring unacceptable costs." The English, whose trading capabilities far surpassed those of the French in Canada and even of their Dutch predecessors, accordingly sought to cement alliances with the Iroquois and other Native Americans in the northeast.

In the 1670s, therefore, the Covenant Chain was established in an effort to solidify Anglo-Native alliances. The Covenant Chain was a series of economic and military partnerships created among the English colonists and certain Native American groups in the northeast. Interestingly, the alliance arose out of the ashes of the worst Indian war in New England's history. In the mid-1670s, Metacomet (King Philip) of the Wampanoags led a multi-ethnic Native revolt against the English set-

KEY CONCEPT   Tribe, Nation, and Confederacy

Choosing a precise terminology to describe Native American groups is sometimes difficult. The term "tribe," for instance, typically refers to societies largely organized on the basis of kinship, in which members espouse commitment to a common ancestry and culture. But the expression was rarely used before the nineteenth century, and scholars who study indigenous peoples in earlier periods have found this concept inadequate. Europeans during the colonial era, on the other hand, often employed "nation" to denote an autonomous Native American people and their territory. Nation, however, can imply many things to many people, especially in the twenty-first century, when "nation" and "state" are practically synonymous. Indigenous communities were far from being organized political states in the modern sense, so caution must also be exercised when relying on eighteenth-century definitions. Another term used to describe some Native American groups, particularly the Five Nations Iroquois, is "confederacy." In its simplest form, confederacy means an alliance of people for some common purpose. Members' actions and attitudes should therefore be representative of those who "have one body, one head and one heart." But rhetoric often did not meet reality, since the Iroquois confederacy included diverse members with sometimes dissimilar interests. The goal of the league was to reach agreement in decision making. If agreement could not be attained, members were free to act independently as long as their actions did not threaten the league as a whole. This strength of the confederacy created room for maneuver for individuals and subgroups, but it also created factions that ultimately led to the league's undoing as imperial competition and intertribal rivalries splintered the confederacy in the aftermath of the American Revolution.

Chief Red Cloud (Cayuga Nation) poses for a portrait in 1901, possibly at the Pan-American Exposition in Buffalo, New York. (C.C. Arnold/Library of Congress)

tlers. While successful at first, the uprising quickly ran out of steam when the Five Nations Mohawks refused to support the rebellion and instead assisted the English in order to assert even more supremacy over the fur trade. In response to this bloody war, English officials attempted to foster more congenial relations with New England's Native American population, and thus the Covenant Chain was born. The Iroquois used their elevated position in this partnership to extend their control over more Native peoples, especially the Susquehannock, Delaware, and French-allied Algonquian tribes toward the Great Lakes. The height of Iroquois power, however, was nearing its end toward the end of the seventeenth century.

Waging continuous wars against their indigenous rivals, the Five Nations made many enemies and overextended the reach of their domain. The French in North America were especially apprehensive about Iroquois expansion. Quite often, the Iroquois had proven themselves enemies of the French by repeatedly attacking France's Native American allies in the Great Lakes region. Unable initially to resist Iroquois advances, the French and their Native American supporters eventually responded by bringing war to the Five Nations' homeland. Ottawas, Ojibwas, Hurons, and others attacked the Iroquois and burned their villages. By the end of the century, warfare was not as beneficial as it had once been for the Five Nations. Many members of the league accordingly sought peace with the French, even if it meant changing the structure of the Covenant Chain with the English.

The immediate result of these imperial struggles and intertribal warfare was the Grand Settlement of 1701, in which the Iroquois announced a policy of neutrality toward both the French and English. Though the Five Nations thereafter turned their attention south to make war on Creeks and Catawbas, the

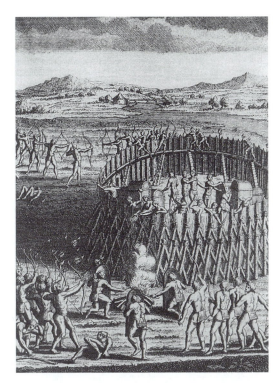

"An Attack on an Iroquois Fort" from *The Wilderness Trail* by Charles A. Hanna, 1911. (National Archives)

Grand Settlement somewhat stabilized their relations with Native groups in the northeast. The new peace allowed the Iroquois to increase their trade with former enemies, and these expanding commercial networks helped to improve relations with Ottawas, Wyandots, Miamis, and other Algonquians. The policy of incorporating other Native Americans into the confederacy continued, and this bolstered the weakened Iroquois League.

While the Five Nations Iroquois adopted individuals, families, and even whole villages into their league, they had never fully incorporated an entire tribe. All this changed in the wake of the Grand Settlement. Far to the south, in the Carolinas, an Iroquoian-speaking people known as the Tuscaroras were engaged in a vicious border war with English settlers and their Indian allies. By 1713, the Tuscaroras had been overwhelmed, and many of the survivors looked to the Iroquois confederacy for protection. With their military defeat, approximately 1,500 Tuscaroras made the long trek north and were soon after adopted into the Iroquois confederacy. Unlike earlier adoptions, however, the Tuscaroras did not become refugees scattered throughout the Five Nations; rather, they were incorporated as full-fledged members of the League of the Hodenosaunee in 1722, which was thereafter called the Six Nations. This unusual occurrence leads to an interesting question: What if such mergers had not ended there? How would history have been different if the Iroquois confederacy had spread to include other Native American nations, even non-Iroquoian tribes?

Group portrait of St. Regis Mohawk men and women in Native costume outside a log building, some on horseback. (W. S. Tanner/Library of Congress)

ACTUAL HISTORY

As it turned out, the Iroquois did not adopt entire tribes into the League. The addition of the Tuscaroras proved to be an anomaly, as the Iroquois continued their policy of incorporating small remnant groups while keeping larger tribes out of the confederacy. The Six Nations additionally persisted in treating their Native American allies as subordinates. Such subsidiary groups were known as "props of the Longhouse," for Iroquoian oral laws stated that Native peoples outside the Six Nations were described as supports of the longhouse. As the language implies, the Iroquois hoped to use such "props" to further their own interests. Historian Jane Merritt, writing in *At the Crossroads: Indians and Empires on a Mid-Atlantic Frontier, 1700–1763*, argued that the Iroquois were "colonizers" in much the same way the Europeans were, since they attempted to subjugate and exploit those who were not members of the league. In western Pennsylvania, for instance, the Delaware and Susquehannock became props of the longhouse, and the Iroquois accordingly used any means necessary to ensure supremacy over their Native American allies, even by selling their allies' lands to English colonists without their consent!

The results of such policies meant that allies of the Six Nations, such as the Delaware and Susquehannock, moved farther west toward the Ohio Country rather than merge into the league and thereby strengthen the confederacy. This failure to incorporate nonmembers as full political partners might seem surprising at first, since indigenous peoples in the northeast were part of the Eastern Woodlands Culture. Although they spoke a variety of languages, most northeastern Native Americans lived in permanent or semi-permanent dwellings, and clan membership formed the basis of social organization. These clans were matrilineal, which meant that a young male would be raised in his mother's household by his uncle rather than his biological father. Daily life revolved around a combination of hunting, fishing, farming, and gathering. Native Americans relied heavily on the "three sisters" for their sustenance—maize, beans, and squash. In these cultures women worked the fields as well as tended to a host of other duties. Iroquois women, in particular, also held positions of power, in that they could elect and remove clan chiefs as well as decide the fate of captives.

These cultural traits, especially those relating to gender roles, proved troublesome for Europeans, who thought Native peoples lived an idle, roving life and one where women, as one eyewitness scornfully noted, "wear the breeches." Thus, though Native Americans and Europeans were sometimes able to create a "middle ground" of mutual understanding and accord, as historian Richard White argued in *The Middle Ground: Indians, Empires, and Republics in the Great Lakes Region, 1650–1815*, their relationships were most often marred by distrust and discord. Cross-cultural conflict between Native peoples and newcomers increased as the eighteenth century progressed, especially as Europe's imperial wars reached the shores of America. Intense rivalries between the English, French, Dutch, and Spanish often threw the frontier into a chaotic maelstrom of violence and suspicion. The presence of Europeans and their colonists accordingly divided, rather than united, diverse Native peoples who sought to safeguard their own interests and their own individual communities. The Six Nations were no different. As they faced rapid decline through wars, disease, and Christian converts among their own people, the Iroquois responded by attempting to exert greater control over their Native neighbors in order to have more bargaining power with Europeans.

The most destructive and consequential colonial war on American soil revealed both the legacy of Iroquois domination and the fading power of the confederacy. The French and Indian War (1754–1763), also known as the

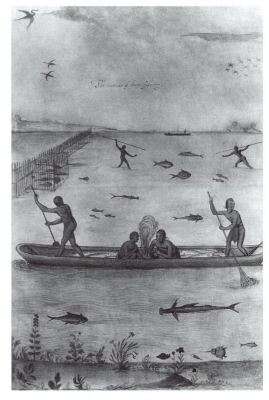

"Their Manner of Fishynge in Virginia." Watercolor by John White (a member of Sir Walter Raleigh's second expedition in 1585) of the Natives of what is now the northeastern coast of North Carolina. (National Archives)

Seven Years' War, witnessed English colonists recognizing the continued strength of the Iroquois League. At a congress in Albany, New York, Benjamin Franklin and other delegates lavished the Iroquois with presents and kind words in order to secure their favor. At the same time, however, the props of the Longhouse increasingly dismissed the authority of the Six Nations. The Delaware and Susquehannock, in particular, refused to acknowledge their subordinate status within the League. They instead joined other Native Americans in the Ohio Country to form a multi-ethnic confederacy, further revealing that the balance of power had shifted away from the Six Nations by mid-century. The French and Indian War also dismantled the Grand Settlement of 1701, in which the Iroquois had resolved to maintain a policy of neutrality toward the English and French. Throughout the course of the war, the Six Nations split into pro-French, pro-English, and neutral factions. This created divided loyalties within the league that further weakened Iroquois power.

While imperial rivalries between England and France greatly impacted the Iroquois and their indigenous neighbors, it was the American Revolution that proved to be the final death knell for the League of the Hodenosaunee. With France ousted from North America in the wake of the French and Indian War, the Iroquois and other Native peoples had to deal directly with the British Empire. Thousands of France's former allies revolted under the leadership of Pontiac, an Ottawa chief who resented British trade abuses and high-handed policies toward Native peoples. The revolt was eventually put down, but the British learned a valuable lesson from Pontiac's uprising; they needed to better organize their Empire in order to minimize such discontent on the frontier. This reorganization of their imperial system, however, ignited a firestorm among American colonists who protested higher taxes and their lack of autonomy. These protests culminated in a Declaration of Independence for the thirteen colonies and a nasty war with the mother country that lasted eight long years. As in previous wars, the Iroquois were not immune to the fighting—the American Revolution divided the Iroquois as never before.

At first, many in the Six Nations attempted to remain neutral. Both the Americans and the British, however, attempted to sway the Six Nations through diplomacy and gift-giving. The result was a marked split in the confederacy. Many Oneidas and Tuscaroras sided with the colonists, while the Mohawk, Cayugas, Onondagas, and Senecas generally favored the British. The Mohawk leader Joseph Brant was especially influential among all Iroquois as he persuaded many to attack American settlements on the frontier. When the British invasion of New York failed with General John Burgoyne's surrender in 1777 at Saratoga, the divided Iroquois were left exposed to American armies. Two years later, General George Washington ordered an invasion of the Six Nations' homeland that successfully destroyed scores of Iroquois villages and cornfields. American armies even burned the central longhouse at Onondaga that had contained the ceremonial council fire for the league for countless generations. Thereafter, the Iroquois called Washington the "Town Destroyer," for, as one Seneca headman related, "When that name is heard, our women look behind them and turn pale, and our children cling close to the necks of their mothers." By the end of the war, only two Iroquois villages remained untouched by the fighting.

The Revolution not only witnessed Iroquois fighting Iroquois but it also saw a considerable reduction in the population and territory of the Six Nations. Indeed, even before the war commenced, the Iroquois numbered only 7,000 compared to 22,000 in 1630. Population estimates for the Mohawk are even more dramatic. The Mohawk counted nearly 8,000 villagers in the early seventeenth century but only 640 were left by 1770. Without strength in numbers, as in former times, the Six Nations could not stem the tide of American expansion westward. Their situation worsened when the British ceded all claims to land east of the Mississippi River (excluding Canada) in the Treaty of Paris in 1783. To the Americans, this meant that Native Americans had no rights to the land, since most had joined the losing side. Many Iroquois, including Joseph Brant, left for Canada where the British had set up a limited amount of territory for Six Nations refugees. Others decided to stay in New York and tenuously held on to what little land had been left to them.

Skandogh, an old Oneida chief. Wood engraving by Whitney, Rochester, New York. Originally published in 1856. (Library of Congress)

These lands would further diminish in the aftermath of the Revolution. The Treaty of Fort Stanwix in 1784 was imposed upon the Iroquois by the United States in order for the young country to acquire more territory in Pennsylvania and western New York. The Iroquois were thereafter confined to small reservations scattered throughout the northeast and Canada. Alongside this decline in population and landholdings was a cultural disorientation that forever changed the nature of Iroquois life. With their hunting territory all but gone, the Iroquois were forced to rely on farming more than ever before. Since Iroquois men could no longer hunt and make war, many did not know how to cope with the changing circumstances. Into this depressed situation stepped Handsome Lake, an Iroquois prophet who led a nativistic movement that called for a rejection of alcohol and moral depravity. Handsome Lake also encouraged his fellow villagers to oppose land sales to whites, take up family-centered farming, and renew their commitment to traditional Iroquois ceremonies.

Handsome Lake's message reinvigorated the Iroquois by providing new ways to cope with the troubled times in which they lived. But in the aftermath of the Revolution, the Six Nations remained scattered, disunited, and unable to detach themselves from larger forces at work. During the 1830s, which is sometimes referred to as the Era of Removal, the United States followed a policy that sought to remove all eastern Native Americans to lands west of the Mississippi River. Even more Iroquois abandoned their reservations in New York, as many found no alternative but to leave the vicinity of whites. Those who remained in the

IN CONTEXT Nativistic Movements

The revival among the Iroquois inspired by Handsome Lake was not a unique phenomenon. By definition, a nativistic movement is an attempt to revive certain aspects of indigenous culture and accordingly slow down the pace of cultural change being imposed on them by an outside force. Such cultural resurgence can be found in many areas of North America during different periods of history. Preceding Handsome Lake, for example, was the Delaware Prophet Neolin, who led a spiritually charged awakening among Native Americans in the Ohio Country and Great Lakes in the early 1760s.

Neolin called upon his fellow Native Americans to shun much of white culture, warning them that a refusal to do so would mean death. Neolin is most well known for influencing the Ottawa leader, Pontiac, who forcefully resisted British rule following the French and Indian War. In much the same way did the Prophet Tenskatawa influence the great Shawnee leader Tecumseh nearly fifty years later.

As with other movements before, the new nativistic movement among the Ohio Natives was religiously motivated. Following his conversations with the Great Spirit, Tenskatawa told his people to

east encountered land speculators, invasive settlers, and government officials who did little to stop the further erosion of Iroquois lands that continued throughout the nineteenth century.

The Iroquois in the twentieth century likewise found it difficult to distance themselves from the trends that also impacted American society in general. The Great Depression brought even more economic hard times to the Iroquois. President Franklin Roosevelt's New Deal tried to counter this worldwide depression, but it was the onset of World War II that sparked the beginning of economic recovery in the United States. Numerous Iroquois found employment in the war industries, and countless others joined the armed forces to serve overseas, with many leaving the reservation for the first time because of these new opportunities. The postwar era witnessed the continued outmigration of many Iroquois, as they congregated in urban centers where the possibilities for employment were much greater than on the reservation.

In more recent times, there has been a surge in ethnic renewal for Native Americans across the country. During the Civil Rights era, many indigenous peoples were greatly affected by the protests that black Americans successfully used to gain equal rights. "Black power" for African Americans quickly translated into "red power" for Native Americans, who employed similar tactics to call attention to their plight. Many began to use the legal system effectively to eradicate discriminatory laws and gain victories in the economic realm. In the 1980s, for instance, federal legislation opened the way for new economic ventures on Native American reservations, including the right to operate gambling casinos. This has been a heated topic of debate among the Iroquois, as some see the advantages this influx of money brings into their communities, while others lament the cultural assault that naturally follows in the wake of such enterprises.

Nevertheless, the Iroquois have survived with their culture and identity largely intact, albeit greatly changed from the days when the Five Nations first formed their League of the Hodenosaunee.

IN CONTEXT *Nativistic Movements (Continued)*

reject those aspects of white culture, particularly alcohol, that were destroying Native American communities. More significantly, he and Tecumseh advocated intertribal unity, which resulted in a brief but unsuccessful challenge to the expansion of the United States during the War of 1812. Nor were such movements limited solely to Eastern Woodlands People. Perhaps the most famous nativistic movement occurred among the Plains Natives near the end of the nineteenth century. A Paiute named Wovoka spread his message throughout the American West at a time when most Native Americans had been forcibly subjugated and placed onto reservations by the U.S. military. Wovoka claimed that all white people would be taken away as buffaloes and that the indigenous people's ancestors would return to claim the land and live in peace. Wovoka's message spread quickly across the Plains, as many Native Americans participated in Ghost Dance rituals in order to hasten the arrival of the new age. White settlers on the frontier became alarmed at these Ghost Dance gatherings and called on the U.S. military to put down the resurgence movement. This led to one of the great tragedies in American history, the massacre at Wounded Knee, in which the 7th Cavalry brutally killed hundreds of Lakota Sioux.

ALTERNATE HISTORY

The year 1722 would have been a benchmark for the Iroquois confederacy in alternate history. Weakened by years of disease and warfare, the Five Nations would have had to find ways to stop their rapid decline. Adopting individuals and small remnant groups had worked well in the past, but such limited acts of inclusion would not have been enough to protect them from encroaching European settlers and hostile Native neighbors. When the Tuscaroras sought shelter within the league, the Iroquois recognized they had to expand their confederacy in order to maintain a prominent position in the northeast. The Five Nations thus became the Six Nations, as the Tuscaroras were formally adopted into the league as "younger brothers." Almost immediately following this event, however, something even more remarkable might have happened, something more powerful than the initial formation of the confederacy some two hundred years before. Iroquois leaders could have begun a policy of incorporating other tribes into the confederacy, not just as "props of the longhouse," but as full-fledged members. This strategy could even have called for the inclusion of non-Iroquoian tribes.

Iroquois leaders particularly would have had their eye on populous indigenous groups in the Ohio Country and the Great Lakes region. These included among others the Delaware, Susquehannock, Shawnee, and the many Algonquians who were closely tied to the French in Canada. Winning these Native peoples over, however, would have been no easy task. There was a long history of hostile relations between the Iroquois and their Algonquian neighbors, most recently dating back to the mourning wars and beaver wars of the seventeenth century. Leaders from the Six Nations would have had to find some common ground to erase the hard feelings between them. They could have done so in three ways. The first would have been to allow any tribe to join as full members, much as the Tuscaroras had done in 1722. This would have lessened feelings of inferiority and jealousy that would naturally result from being "props of the Longhouse" instead of equal members. The second approach the Iroquois could have used to win over former enemies might have focused on something that all Native Americans had in common: land. Land was important because it provided the inhabitants with food, clothing, and shelter. Perhaps equally as important, it gave Native Americans some degree of autonomy and a sense of identity.

The Iroquois might have thus stipulated that all members of the league, whether newcomers or the original Five Nations, could not sell any lands of member nations. If any tried to do so, those leaders and their immediate clan relations would suffer death.

The final method of luring western tribes into the League might also have proved to be the most consequential for the future of North America. Most Native Americans in the Ohio Country and Great Lakes were allied to the French. This presented major problems for the Six Nations who had long been tied to the English through the Covenant Chain. Though the Grand Settlement of 1701 had altered this relationship, by announcing a policy of neutrality, the Iroquois nevertheless remained closely tied to the British and their valuable trade. As the Six Nations sent diplomatic "feelers" to French-allied Natives, they would have found that those interested in joining the league would not abandon their French "fathers." Thus, if the Six Nations were to expand their confederacy and regain their strength in numbers as in former days, they would have to forsake the English and commit themselves fully to the French. After heated debate that could have dragged on for months, the Iroquois eventually might have reached a momentous decision: the Six Nations would renounce their policy of neutrality and become loyal allies of the French.

The British would have been both outraged and terrified. As news arrived almost daily that the Shawnee, Susquehannock, Delaware, Miami, Ottawa, Huron, Potowatomi, Chippewa, and others had joined the Iroquois confederacy, the British would have recognized their position in North America as becoming seriously undermined. Their frontier settlements from New England to Carolina would surely have felt the force of this new Native confederacy if it were provoked. Unfortunately for the English, these fears would have been realized most notably during the French and Indian War. As the English and French battled for control of the continent, the enlarged Six Nations might have changed their name to the Northern Indian Confederacy (NIC) and thrown their full support behind the French. As during the actual war, many French-allied Natives attacked English settlers on the frontier. Those who were not killed fled their homes by the thousands. In alternate history, however, this refugee crisis would have occurred on a massive scale. Most settlers would have sought refuge in the coastal settlements, while some might actually have returned to Europe! The frontier thereafter would have remained a vaguely defined and hostile borderland that separated the Native Americans and English settlers.

The significance of the French-allied Northern Indian Confederacy would not have ended with keeping British expansion in check. More important, the NIC would have protected the French in Canada from hostile incursions by British and American armies. Unlike actual history in which the French were defeated at Quebec, giving up Canada and withdrawing from North America completely, no such event would have occurred in alternate history. The French and their Native American allies would have fought the English to a draw and ended the war with the English firmly entrenched along the coast, while the French remained masters of Canada and the Mississippi River, including Louisiana and the port of New Orleans. The importance of this alternate event cannot be overstated. With the French and the NIC representing a formidable force in the interior, English colonists in America would have needed protection from the mother country. Though many would have resented the new taxes Britain imposed on the colonies to help pay for the immensely expensive war effort, few would have challenged the right of Britain to do so. With settlers more worried about France and the NIC than they were about independence, the American Revolution would not have occurred, and the British Empire would have remained intact.

The British colonies would have united in the wake of the French and Indian War. The war would have shown just how disunited the colonies were and the disadvantages this presented for their defense. Benjamin Franklin and others would have tried to encourage the formation of a United Colonies at Albany in 1754 but ultimately would have failed because neither the individual colonies nor Britain would have desired to sacrifice their sovereignty. The war, however, would have revealed that common defense was absolutely necessary if the colonies were to remain safe from French and NIC incursions. Thus, the United Colonies of Britain would have been formed in the wake of the French and Indian War.

The colonies would have joined together not to fight the British, as happened during the American Revolution, but to help their British brethren in the upcoming wars that once again plagued Europe and America.

As with Britain, which would have spent nearly four million pounds to fight the Seven Years' War, the French likewise would have incurred a hefty debt, which would have been partly due to their expenditures to the NIC. Thus, the French would have been similarly plagued by economic difficulties, ones that could not prevent the momentous French Revolution from occurring. With the rise of Napoleon in the aftermath of the revolution, the situation in North America would have been very different in alternate history. Instead of selling the Louisiana Territory to an expanding United States in 1803, Napoleon would have looked to maintain France's empire in America. This would have provided a very unique opportunity for the Iroquois and the NIC. As English settlers would have had no claims to lands beyond the Appalachian Mountains and would have been too weak to take it by force, the United Colonies of Britain would have remained relegated to the east coast. The NIC, with aid from the powerful French military, would thus have been able to check American expansion. In the actual Napoleonic Wars, which lasted until 1815, the French fought the British in Europe and America. Rather than face each other as bitter foes, which occurred in actual history, the British and Americans would have fought side by side against a common enemy. The English and their colonists might have attempted to drive the French out of Canada and split asunder the NIC but to no avail. The war would have ended with a peace that officially recognized the boundaries of the NIC and temporarily guaranteed their future security.

Wars for empire would not have ended there. Western Europe modernized and industrialized in the nineteenth century, and a new round of imperialism ensued in which France, England, and Germany in particular looked to exploit lands and peoples in Asia, Africa, and—in alternate history—the Americas. The French had never sent many colonists to America, but this would have changed near mid-century when tens of thousands of immigrants from across Europe would have boarded ships for New France and the United Colonies of Britain. The contest for the continent would now be a demographic war, as both France and England would have offered incentives for European immigrants to settle in their American territories. This would have placed the NIC in a peculiar situation. They had long favored the French because of their beneficial trade relationship and the fact that France did not have many of its people in America. In actual history, for instance, New France numbered only 80,000 settlers in 1750, whereas the English colonies consisted of about 1.5 million people. One hundred years later, however, the population of New France would have soared as European immigrants flocked to the fertile lands of the Mississippi River watershed. The Iroquois and their Native allies would have been thus hemmed in by the English to the east and the French to the north and west. The NIC accordingly would begin to rethink its relationship with the French.

The NIC would have remained a powerful multitribal confederacy because of its strength in numbers and because it had a reliable ally in France. When French policies changed to the detriment of this relationship, the NIC would have reinvoked the Grand Settlement and proclaimed its official neutrality. The Iroquois would subsequently have attempted to play both sides off one another to their own advantage. Indeed, the Five Nations of olden times were known for their diplomatic skill in creating room to maneuver between the French and English. This trend would have continued as the NIC held the balance of power between the two rival imperial nations. The French and English in America would eventually have realized that the Iroquois and their Native allies would not sell off their lands and that they had the military and diplomatic muscle to ensure the protection of those lands.

The demographic explosion of Europeans in America would thus have turned in other directions, away from the Ohio Country and the Great Lakes. The population of the United Colonies of Britain would have funneled south below the Appalachian Mountains into present-day Georgia, Alabama, and Mississippi. Displacing the southern tribes, who refused to join the Northern Iroquois Confederacy, the English would have settled all the way to the Mississippi River, where they would have met stiff French resistance in Louisiana. Louisiana would have replaced Quebec as the center of the French Empire in America, for it was at the all-important port city of New Orleans that trade from as far north as Canada flowed. The French therefore would have been determined to stop English expansion at the Mississippi, which they would have done in a series of confrontations that were also tied to imperial conflicts in Africa and Asia. The French Empire in America and its mass of new immigrants would thus have begun to spread to the far west where they would have come into conflict with the Plains Native Americans. Failing to unify in the manner that the NIC had done, the Plains Native Americans would have lost vast amounts of territory to the newcomers, much as they did in actual history to the Americans.

The map of North America in the modern era would thus look very different in alternate history. Britain and its colonies would occupy the east coast and lower south. New France would rival the British in power and extent of territory, as they would hold large sections of Canada, lands along the Mississippi River, and the Plains. Since there would be no United States, no American expansion, and thus no Mexican War and Civil War, the Spanish Empire in the American southwest and California would have remained intact. In the midst of these great European powers would have been the only indigenous confederacy to form on the continent, the NIC. Nearly all other Native American peoples would have been conquered or had their lands swindled from them. They would live on small reservations within the United Colonies of Britain, New France, and Spanish America, much as they do today in actual history in the United States. The NIC, however, would have done what most historians would think impossible; they would have set aside their tribal differences and united into a confederacy that successfully held on to their lands. Because of this, the history of North America and, indeed, the world would never be the same.

Tyler W. Boulware

Discussion Questions

1. Why do you think the Five Nations were unable to incorporate other tribes, besides the Tuscaroras, into their confederacy?

2. Given what you know about the diversity and factionalism of Native Americans, was it within the realm of historical possibility that a successful multitribal confederacy could be formed?

3. Do you agree that a broader Iroquois confederacy, which included Algonquians of the Great Lakes, would have saved France from defeat during the French and Indian War? Why or why not?

4. With the benefit of hindsight, it is often natural to think of historical processes as inevitable. But at the time participants had no idea how things would turn out. With this in mind, do you think that Native

Americans could have successfully resisted the tide of American expansion? Or were differences in technology, population, and political organization too much for the Native peoples to handle?

5. If you had to write an alternate history of the Five Nations, which allowed for its inclusion of non-Iroquoian tribes, how would your account read?

Bibliography and Further Reading

Bjornlund, Lydia. *The Iroquois.* Farmington Hills, MI: Lucent Books, 2001.

Breen, T. H. *America Past and Present.* Chicago: Longman, 2001.

Calloway, Collin G. *First Peoples: A Documentary Survey of American Indian History.* New York: Bedford/St. Martin's, 2004.

Engelbrecht, William. *Iroquoia: The Development of a Native World.* Syracuse, NY: Syracuse University Press, 2003.

Fenton, William. *The Great Law and the Longhouse: A Political History of the Iroquois Confederacy.* Norman, OK: University of Oklahoma Press, 1998.

Jennings, Francis. *The Ambiguous Iroquois Empire: The Covenant Chain Confederation of Indian Tribes with English Colonies from Its Beginning to the Lancaster Treaty of 1744.* New York: W. W. Norton, 1984.

Merritt, Jane T. *At the Crossroads: Indians and Empires on a Mid-Atlantic Frontier, 1700–1763.* Chapel Hill, NC: University of North Carolina Press, 2003.

Mintz, Max M. *Seeds of Empire: The American Revolutionary Conquest of the Iroquois.* New York: New York University Press, 1999.

Morgan, Lewis Henry. *The League of the Iroquois.* Emmaus, PA: JG Press, 1995.

Richter, Daniel K. *The Ordeal of the Longhouse: The Peoples of the Iroquois League in the Era of European Colonization.* Chapel Hill, NC: University of North Carolina Press, 1992.

Richter, Daniel K. "War and Culture: The Iroquois Experience." *William and Mary Quarterly* 40 (1983): 528–559

Snow, Dean R. *The Iroquois.* Malden, MA: Blackwell, 1994.

White, Richard. *The Middle Ground: Indians, Empires, and Republics in the Great Lakes Region, 1650–1815.* New York: Cambridge University Press, 1991.

European diseases took a heavy toll on Native Americans. What if the situation had been reversed and European explorers were decimated by diseases from Native Americans?

INTRODUCTION

In November 1491, the rulers of Grenada, the last Moorish, or Muslim, kingdom of Spain surrendered to their Catholic majesties, Ferdinand and Isabella. It had been nearly eight hundred years since the first Muslim leader, Tariq, had landed in Spain in 711 near the mountain that bears his name: Gibraltar, which in Arabic is Jebel al-Tariq, or "Tariq's mountain." The terms of the surrender between Ferdinand and Isabella, and Boabdil, the last Sultan of Grenada, had been worked out in advance. No bloodshed would mar the sacredness of this event for the Spanish, for the capture of Grenada marked the final end of their Reconquista, the centuries-long struggle to drive the Moors out of Spain. According to historian Hugh Thomas in *Rivers of Gold*, "on November 28, 1491, terms of surrender, the Capitulaciones, were ratified by both sides. They were liberal. They were signed by the two Spanish monarchs and witnessed by the experienced secretary Hernando de Zafra." Yet not everyone at the surrender of Grenada was moved by the solemnity of the event: one of the eyewitnesses was Christopher Columbus.

Columbus, born in Genoa in Italy, had been to sea since 1472 and already by Grenada's surrender had two decades of maritime experience. Yet he had no interest in following the path of most Genoese mariners into the profitable Mediterranean trade, which at this time was constantly endangered by the attacks of the so-called Barbary Pirates of North Africa, who flew under the flag of the Ottoman sultans in Istanbul. In May 1453, Sultan Mehmet II had conquered the Byzantine Empire and renamed its capital of Constantinople. Not until the decisive naval Battle of Lepanto in 1571, a century after Columbus's first voyage, would European sailors have a measure of freedom from Barbary Pirate raids on the Mediterranean.

Instead of sailing the waters of the Mediterranean, Columbus wanted to find a sea route to the Orient, now that the Ottoman Empire blocked much of the land passage to China and the riches of Asia. After King Jao of Portugal turned a deaf ear to Columbus's plans, he decided to plead his case before Ferdinand and Isabella, the monarchs of Spain. In 1484 Jao had rebuffed Columbus, and soon after, Columbus had journeyed to

Spain. "Columbus arrived," Thomas wrote in *Rivers of Gold*, "in Andalusia in the second half of 1485 and made his way to the Franciscan monastery of La Rabida." La Rabida, at the time, had a reputation as a center of maritime learning. Pedro de Velasco, a lay brother, "had been, in his youth, pilot to Diogo de Teive, who had served Prince Henry the Navigator" of Portugal. Prince Henry, above all others, would be the inspiration to those brave captains who would shake off centuries of superstition and eventually circumnavigate the world in their voyages of exploration.

On January 20, 1486, Columbus had his first audience with Ferdinand and Isabella, but he made no progress in convincing them to support his plans to reach Asia by sailing to the west. According to Justin Winsor in *Christopher Columbus*, Columbus entered the service of Ferdinand and Isabella on that day. Winsor, using what he says is Columbus's own journal in *Christopher Columbus*, notes that in an entry made on January 14, 1493, "he [Columbus] says that on the 20th of the same month he would have been in their Highnesses' service just seven years," implying that Columbus was accepted by Ferdinand and Isabella in his first meeting with their Catholic majesties.

The more likely reason that his voyage of discovery was not given royal approval then was that both Ferdinand and Isabella were occupied in the final campaign to conquer Grenada, the last part of what once was the Muslim kingdom of al-Andalus in Spain, from which the province of Andalusia had gained its name. Modern warfare had come to Europe by now, and the conquest of Grenada would have occupied all the manpower and treasure at Ferdinand and Isabella's command. In August 1485, Henry Tudor had defeated Richard III at the Battle of Bosworth Field in England, thus beginning the Tudor Dynasty. As Henry VII, Tudor would make of feudal England a modern, unified country, and his example must have been a spur to the Spanish monarchs as they planned the ultimate campaign in the Reconquista to recover all of Spain from Islam.

Embarkation of Christopher Columbus for the New World. (National Archives)

Subsequent to the fall of Grenada, Ferdinand seemed to have second thoughts about Columbus's undertaking, after the cost and effort of taking Grenada. But, as is well known, his wife Queen Isabella was not as hesitant. Historian Edward Everett Hale recalled a famous scene in *The Life of Christopher Columbus*: "Spain would have lost the honor and the reward of the great discovery, as Portugal and Genoa had lost them, but for Luis de St. Angel, and the queen herself." St. Angel had been the friend of Columbus. He was an important officer, the treasurer of the church revenues of Aragon. He now insisted on an audience with the queen. It would seem that Ferdinand, though King of Aragon, was not present. St. Angel spoke eloquently. The friendly Marchioness of Moya spoke eagerly and persuasively. Isabella was at last fired with zeal. Columbus should go, and the enterprise should be hers.

The sum required for the discovery of a world was only three thousand crowns. Two vessels were all that Columbus asked for, with the pay of their crews. But where were three thousand crowns? The treasury was empty, and the king was now averse to any action to support the voyage of discovery. It was at this moment that Isabella said, according to historian Edward Hale, "The enterprise is mine, for the Crown of Castile. I pledge my jewels for the funds." The funds were in fact advanced by St. Angel, from the ecclesiastical revenues under his control. They were repaid from the gold brought back from the first voyage. But, always afterward, Isabella regarded the Indies as a Castilian possession. The most important officers in its administration, indeed most of the emigrants, were always from Castile.

Columbus gathered his fleet, the *Nina*, the *Pinta*, and the *Santa Maria*, in the port city of Palos. Finally, he was able to write, "Friday, August 3,

A recreation of one of Christopher Columbus's vessels, the *Santa Maria,* at the Chicago Exposition, 1893. (National Archives)

1492. Set sail from the bar of Saltes at 8 o'clock, and proceeded with a strong breeze until sunset 60 miles, or 15 leagues south, afterward southwest and south by west, which is in the direction of the Canaries" (Hale, *The Life of Christopher Columbus*).

As the voyage continued, the crew became dissatisfied and concerned. Most likely, the crews of all three ships were veteran mariners, but none had ever been on a voyage this long and, more important, completely out of sight of land. Those who had voyaged in the Mediterranean, and even up the North Atlantic to Scandinavia or the cod fishing banks off Newfoundland, were used to making "landfalls," charting their passage by landmarks that were familiar to them, like islands, mountains, bays, or the mouths of rivers. Here, for the first time, they were making a transoceanic voyage across the Atlantic Ocean which, after the Azores and Canary Islands were behind them to the east, meant sailing straight across the sea, with no land in sight.

Columbus, becoming concerned about his crew, was forced to falsify the records of the voyage. Historian Edward Hale notes, "Columbus every day announced to his crew a less distance as the result of the day than they had really sailed. For he was afraid of their distrust, and did not dare let them know how far they were from home. The private journal, therefore, has such entries as this, 'Sailed more than 55 leagues, wrote down only 48.' That is, he wrote on the daily log, which was open to inspection, a distance some leagues less than they had really made." But by October 8, land birds were sighted from the decks of the ships, a sure sign that their voyage was coming to an end. "With the 11th of October, came certainty." October 11

The three vessels under command of Christopher Columbus: the *Nina*, the *Pinta*, and the *Santa Maria*. (National Archives)

is sometimes spoken of as the day of discovery, and sometimes October 12, when they landed on the first island of the new world.

The whole original record of the discovery is this: "October 11, course to west and southwest. Heavier sea than they had known, pardelas and a green branch near the caravel of the Admiral. From the *Pinta*, they see a branch of a tree, a stake and a smaller stake, which they draw in, and which appears to have been cut with iron, and a piece of cane. Besides these, there is a land shrub and a little bit of board. The crew of the *Nina* saw other signs of land and a branch covered with thorns and flowers. With these tokens, every one breathes again and is delighted. They sail 27 leagues on this course. The Admiral orders that they shall resume a westerly course at sunset. They make 12 miles each hour; up until two hours after midnight they made 90 miles. The *Pinta*, the best sailer of the three, was ahead. She makes signals, already agreed upon, that she has discovered land. A sailor named Rodrigo de Triana was the first to see this land" (Hale, *The Life of Christopher Columbus*).

The next day, October 12, 1492, Columbus landed on the island of San Salvador, although some sources claim he had set foot on Watling Island instead. Columbus explored the islands of the West Indies, touching Cuba, until December. Then, on December 4, as Winsor writes in *Christopher Columbus*, "he observed, the same day, land in the southeast, which his Indians called Bohio, and this was subsequently named Espanola [Hispaniola]." He found the Native Americans and their chiefs, or *caciques*, to be welcoming and friendly. Near the end of the month, Columbus decided that Hispaniola was the best place to make a permanent camp. Historian

After the first transatlantic crossing, Christopher Columbus lands in the Caribbean. (National Archives)

Edward Hale observed, "On the 19th, after these agreeable hospitalities, the squadron sailed again, and on the 20th arrived at a harbor which Columbus pronounced the finest he had ever seen. The reception he met here and the impressions he formed of Hispaniola determined him to make a colony on that island. It may be said that on this determination, the course of his after life turned. This harbor is now known as the Bay of Azul."

TURNING POINT

The tribe Columbus encountered on Hispaniola was the Taino tribe, and their *cacique* was Guacanagari. According to historian Samuel H. Wilson in an article in *Natural History*, "The Taino Indians of Hispaniola brought the foreigners food and water, parrots, weapons, cotton, ornaments, and

A sixteenth century map of the Caribbean area. (National Archives)

gold. The Spanish sailors would trade what were, to them, less precious objects: old nails, bits of glass, coins of infinitesimal denominations, bits of brightly painted majolica pottery, small copper bells, and glass beads. The Spaniards' interest was clearly in gold; all their questions, as nearly as they could be understood by signs and a few words, concerned the source of the gold. Gold was also important for the Taino. One of their words for gold had the same root as *cacique*, their word for ruler. In a strange parallel—one of many odd similarities between European and Caribbean cultures—gold, kings, and the sun were tied together in the same words and cultural categories."

Yet, along with the exchange of goods, came the mingling of the two peoples. And given human nature, sexual contact came with the association of the Tainos and the Spanish. While some like Columbus may have sensed that a new age of discovery was now opening before them, none, neither Taino nor Spanish, could ever have guessed that a new age of disease was making its debut as well. In actual history, diseases, especially what was thought to be smallpox, carried by Europeans, decimated the Native American populations throughout the Americas. In our alternate history, it is the Europeans who are struck by a disease possibly native to the Americas—syphilis.

ACTUAL HISTORY

While much of history is the record of the achievements of great men and women, whether Julius Caesar of ancient Rome or Catherine the Great of Russia, none of what they did compares to the infinitely small creatures— call them germs or microbes—with which we share this world. Indeed, in the 2005 film *The War of the Worlds*, based on the 1898 novel of the same name by British author H. G. Wells, it is the microbes of the earth that destroy the invaders from Mars, against which the most powerful earthly weapons proved impotent.

As Frederick F. Cartwright wrote in *Disease and History*, "From 1490 onward something which appeared to contemporary writers to be a new disease swept over Europe." And, from much medical research over the past five hundred years, that disease seems to have been syphilis, brought over to Europe by the voyagers from the first voyage of Columbus to the Americas in 1492. There are, of course, other theories as to the origin of syphilis in Europe. There are two schools of thought on its origin: the Columbian and pre-Columbian thesis. There is ongoing debate in anthropological and historical fields about the validity of either theory.

The pre-Columbian theory holds that syphilis symptoms are described by Hippocrates in Classical Greece in its venereal/tertiary form. Some passages in the Bible could refer to syphilis, especially Exodus 20:5, where the sins of the father are visited unto the third and fourth generation. There are other suspected syphilis findings for pre-contact Europe, including accounts at a thirteenth- to fourteenth-century Augustinian friary in the northeastern English port of Kingston upon Hull. The anthropological evidence is contested by those who follow the Columbian theory.

IN CONTEXT   The Impact of Syphilis on European History

If Columbus did indeed bring syphilis back with him from the New World, few events have had such a strong impact on European history. In 1494, King Charles VIII of France was on the verge of conquering Italy and creating a French empire in the land of the ancient Romans. Charles VIII was one of the few monarchs in Europe—Ferdinand and Isabella in Spain among them—who realized the terribly destructive power of artillery. France had had a devastating introduction to the effects of concentrated artillery fire in 1429, when the British had used their artillery, or bombards, in the siege of the French city of Orleans. Fighting for King Charles VII of France, Joan of Arc defeated the British army besieging Orleans on April 29, 1429.

From then on, the French determined to follow the British example and created a large force of artillery. When Charles VIII entered Italy, the castles of the Italian nobles, built during the wars between the Italian cities, had no resistance to the massive artillery pieces that Charles's gunners, or artillerymen, brought up to fire at their walls. The French cannon simply pounded the walls of the castles into rubble. Finally, simply the sight of the French army approaching was enough for an Italian city or nobleman to surrender.

Charles VIII's march of victory was stopped permanently when syphilis, most likely brought to his army by Spanish troops under Gonsalvo de Cordoba, spread as an epidemic in his 50,000-man army. Charles VIII was forced to retreat to France. But his retreat did not mark an end to the Italian Wars. Charles VIII's successor, Louis XII, invaded Italy again in 1499 with a new army, determined again to bring Italy under French rule. Although Louis was defeated at Cerignola and Garigliano in 1503, and forced to give up Naples, the fighting continued. Even Pope Julius II entered the conflict with his army from the Papal States. Francis I of France (himself reputed to be a victim of syphilis) won the

The Columbian theory holds that syphilis was a New World disease brought back by Columbus. Although this evidence has been derided as weak and circumstantial, the first well-recorded outbreak of what we know as syphilis occurred in Naples, Italy, in 1494. There is some documentary evidence to link Columbus's crew to the outbreak. Supporters of the Columbian theory find syphilis lesions on pre-contact Native Americans. Again, all the anthropological evidence is heatedly discussed on both sides of the Columbian/pre-Columbian debate.

Alfred Crosby, writing in *American Anthropologist*, has argued that neither side has the full story. Syphilis is a form of yaws, which had existed in the Old World since time immemorial. Crosby argues that syphilis is a specific form of yaws that had evolved in the New World and was brought back to the old. However, the main point arguing against an earlier European origin is that historical sources are exact that the major outbreak of this disease did not antedate the Columbus expedition. The first main outbreak took place a year after Columbus returned in 1494—the Naples outbreak in the Old World. Crosby's view of yaws, an African disease, can be questioned since African slaves had been introduced into Europe centuries earlier by the Greeks and Romans. Cartwright observes in *Disease and History* that "equatorial African Negroes found their way to Egypt, Arabia, Greece, Rome; they may have brought yaws with them." The theory, as Cartwright explains, holds that yaws, when it was introduced by the naked Africans into the European population wearing clothing, somehow mutated into syphilis.

battle of Marignano in 1515, and this temporarily brought northern Italy under the sway of France and Venice.

Then, however, Charles V of Spain became the Holy Roman Emperor, and the Italian Wars entered an entirely new phase. Charles V's tercios, or infantry battalions, soon became the best foot soldiers in Europe. In 1525, Francis again invaded Italy, only to be defeated by Charles's tercios at Pavia. Francis was taken as a prisoner to Madrid, the Spanish capital, and was not freed until he gave to Charles much of his Italian territory. In 1527, Charles would avenge himself on the Papacy and let his Imperial Army, many of them Protestant mercenaries from Germany, sack Rome.

Once freed, Francis invaded Italy again and fought two more wars against Charles, between 1535 and 1544. Francis was so determined to defeat Charles and the Holy Roman Empire that he made a formal alliance with Suleiman the Magnificent, of the Ottoman Empire, who was then attempting to con-

quer Europe. Even after the death of Francis in 1547, his son, Henry II, declared war on Charles V and continued the fighting in what would be the final war from 1547 to 1559. After Charles V abdicated, his son, Phillip II, continued the war. His wife, Queen Mary of England, entered the fighting, only to lose the port of Calais to Henry II, the last remnant of the once great British lands in France. Finally, at the Treaty of Cateau-Cambresis in 1559, Henry II of France was forced to give up his dreams of an Italian Empire.

When syphilis attacked Charles VIII's army at Naples, the king could not foresee the effects of this new health epidemic. The eruption of syphilis at Naples in 1494 ended what could have been a complete conquest of northern Italy by the technologically superior French army with its artillery. Instead, it saw Italy plunged into over sixty-five years of almost continual warfare, conflict that ravaged the countryside and caused almost as many men to die in battle and from battle wounds as would die from syphilis itself.

The idea that simply wearing clothing could have caused the mutation into syphilis seems hardly credible.

Once again the timeline may be the decisive element: the Naples outbreak took place within a year after Columbus returned in the *Pinta* to Palos, Spain, in 1493. For over sixty years this disease ravaged Europe. The epidemiology of the first syphilis epidemic indicates that the disease was either new or a mutated form of an earlier disease. It swept across Europe from the early epicenter at Naples. The early form was much more virulent than the disease of today, the incubation period was shorter, only a few months, and the symptoms were more severe. In addition, the disease was more frequently fatal than it is at present. By 1546, syphilis had changed into the strain existent today. Three possible reasons for the change could be that those who had not immediately died from the disease acquired a relative immunity to it, that the change to a colder climate mutated the syphilis into a more benign form, or that, with the unique uncertainty that is part of nature itself, the disease simply mutated by itself, much like the HIV/AIDS virus has mutated over the past decades in modern times.

Perhaps some of the most telling evidence for an American origin for syphilis comes from the Native Americans themselves. After Francisco Pizarro had the last Inca Emperor Atahualpa killed in 1533, some of the Roman Catholic priests took it upon themselves to preserve as much as they could of the records of the Incan Empire that the conquistadors had destroyed. The same type of rescue operation had taken place in Mexico

"The Courier du Bois and the Savage," an 1891–1892 illustration in *Harpers New Monthly.* (National Archives)

after Hernando Cortes had crushed the Aztecs in 1521. Although most Catholic priests saw the indigenous culture as barbaric and even demonic in both empires, an enlightened few preserved as much as they could for the generations to come, when hopefully such ignorance and superstition would be no more. In *The World of the Inca,* French writer Bertrand Flornoy described in detail Incan medicine as it had been practiced in the years before Pizarro's conquest. Flornoy writes how "it is believed that sulphate of copper and a powder with a base of sulphuretted arsenic, huaini-hampi, was used to alleviate syphilitic ulcers and sores, or at least superficially."

And again, other scholars believed that Incan surgeons trepanned, or cut holes surgically in the skull, because this was a reasonable treatment applied to fractures of the skull, infectious bone inflammations, and bone lesions caused by syphilis. In the final edition of his work *Disease and History*, which was revised with Michael D. Biddiss, Cartwright gave another indication of the Native American origin of the epidemic. One of the first remedies used by European doctors to treat the malady was "by holy wood or guaiacum, a resin obtained from two evergreen trees, *Guaiacum officinale* and *Guaiacum sanctum*, which are indigenous to South America and the West Indies." The only way that European physicians would have known to import this treatment for syphilis was for it to have already been known as a treatment for the disease in the New World.

The course of actual history, though, progressed with one side of the Columbian Exchange (the meeting of Europeans and Americans), the

ANOTHER VIEW   Cortes and the Aztecs

The story that Hernando Cortes and his conquistadors themselves destroyed the empire of the Aztec Emperor Montezuma II has been disproved. It was because the Aztecs, by their imperialist rule, had alienated so many of their subject peoples that Cortes was able to conquer them. Cortes was driven out of Mexico City, then the Aztec capital of Tenochtitlan, by the Aztecs in July 1520, but the Tlaxcalans received him and his conquistadors well, and became his allies. With them and other allies, Cortes was able to besiege Tenochtitlan. Subjugated kingdoms like Tlaxcala provided the thousands of warriors who finally enabled Cortes and his small army to vanquish the Aztecs by 1521.

Yet something even more deadly than a mass rebellion had struck the Aztecs—and all those in Mexico. An epidemic had broken out in Hispaniola in December 1518, and by September 1520 it was already established in Mexico. The epidemic is commented on in *The Broken Spears: The Aztec Account of the Conquest of Mexico*, which has been edited by Miguel Leon-Portilla from surviving Aztec records. The chronicle reveals that after Cortes's retreat from Tenochtitlan in July 1520, "soon after, an epidemic broke out in Tenochtitlan. Almost the whole population suffered from racking coughs and painful, burning sores." The disease has been identified as smallpox.

According to Cartwright in *Disease and History,* these were also the symptoms of the virulent form of syphilis that had appeared in Naples in 1494. Cited in *Disease and History,* Ulrich von Hutten spoke of "disgusting sores" when the disease first appeared in Germany in 1519, coincidentally the year the mysterious disease had come with Cortes to Mexico.

The pestilence, whether smallpox or a mutated form of syphilis, struck the Aztec capital of Tenochtitlan and did far more damage than did Cortes, when he returned to take the city. Although historians note that the Aztecs fought for eighty days before surrendering to Cortes, the real victor was the microscopic army carried in the bodies of each conquistador.

Hernando Cortes, 1485–1547, vanquished the Aztecs by 1521. (Library of Congress)

"Arcadia in North Carolina" depicts a meeting between settlers and Native Americans, drawn by W. P. Snyder. (National Archives)

Native American, being almost wholly wiped out by disease. But as seen in the alternate history, perhaps both sides suffered from the disease that came to be known as syphilis. Further perhaps, the course of actual history was indeed altered by the disease.

ALTERNATE HISTORY

Given the preceding information, the following theory seems the most likely: One or more of Columbus's crew members, or one of the ten indigenous Americans he brought with them to Europe, carried a highly virulent form of syphilis from the New World. Indeed, historian Winsor writes in *Christopher Columbus* that some disease had already broken out while the *Pinta* was still at sea during the forty-eight days of the return voyage. According to Winsor in *Christopher Columbus*, "of the [ten] native prisoners which he had brought away, one had died at sea, three were too sick to follow him, and were left at Palos, while six accompanied him on his journey" to the Spanish court.

If syphilis was indeed of American origin, much of the terrible virulence of the disease would have a more definitive explanation as well. The Native Americans, having lived with the syphilis disease, would have acquired some immunity to its ravages over the centuries. However, never having been exposed to it before, the Europeans would have never have developed antibodies to the infection—and were thus hit with the medical equivalent of an atomic bomb: a totally new disease unleashed on a completely vulnerable population.

William H. McNeill, in *Plagues and Peoples*, writes that "contemporary evidence therefore amply attests that syphilis was new in the Old World, at least in the sense that the venereal mode of transmission and the symptoms that resulted there from were new." In actual history, the disease exploded in 1494 in Naples, where the army of King Charles VIII of France was fighting for control of Italy. As Peter Brookesmith writes in *Biohazard: The Hot Zone and Beyond*, "when the king discharged his 50,000 mercenary soldiers, they spread the disease across Europe to their homes in Switzerland, Flanders, Spain, France, and Italy." Most likely the disease had been carried to Italy by mercenaries from Spain. By 1498, the disease reached as far as India with the sailors of the Portuguese explorer Vasco da Gama. By the same time, a Persian writer had noted it had spread as far as Azerbaijan. This leads to the critical question of this chapter: suppose the virulent strain that broke out in Naples in 1494 had appeared among the Europeans in the New World at the same time, in the Spanish settlement on the island of Hispaniola?

It was in September 1494 that Columbus returned to the New World on his second voyage. At the time, the Spanish already faced indigenous resistance, centering around the cacique, or chief, Caonabo. By this time, syphilis would have been spreading throughout the Spanish population, causing great weakness but no great "die-off" like some tropical fevers would have done. We know that there had been much sexual contact between the indigenous population and the Spaniards remaining in the New World after Columbus had left for Spain, arriving in Palos on March 1493. To quote Winsor in *Christopher Columbus*, the Spanish commander in Hispaniola, probably Pedro Margarite, had "spent his time despoiling its tribes and squandering the energies of his men in sensual diversions." In the end, Columbus was not able to defeat Caonabo in open battle, but had to rely on stealth. Columbus's captain Alonso de Ojeda kidnapped the cacique and brought him before Columbus in about April 1495.

But already, there would have been signs that something had gone seriously wrong among the troops of the garrison. Winsor writes in *Christopher Columbus* that when Ojeda took the field against a brother of Caonabo who was advancing on Fort St. Thomas, Ojeda "sallied forth with his horsemen and with as many foot [soldiers] as he could muster and attacked the approaching host." Spanish arms and military tactics, notably the light arquebus musket and the use of the horse, won the day for Ojeda, not the numbers of his little army. More ominous events took place in the Spanish colony of Hispaniola. In October 1495, Juan Aguado arrived at the main port of Isabella with direct orders from King Ferdinand: immediately some five hundred of the colony's population of one thousand were to return to Spain. Was this a sign that the colony's provisions were being depleted, or that some unknown disease had progressed to a point that an epidemic "die-off" had begun? The answer appears to already lie in Washington Irving's biography of

Columbus, which Winsor quotes in his book *Christopher Columbus*. Columbus arrived back in Spain on June 11, 1496. When the crews debarked, to quote Irving in *History of the Life and Voyages of Christopher Columbus*, "the wretched men crawled forth, emaciated by the diseases of the colony and the hardships of the voyage."

Based on the available medical history, it appears that something significant had happened with the American syphilis with which the sailors of Columbus may have first been infected on the initial voyage. Coming into contact with a new "host" population, the disease could have mutated by 1518. Quite simply, the American syphilis could have changed within the bodies of the European victims into another variation, or mutation of the disease, which we can call from now on European syphilis. The mutation was likely brought back from Europe among the waves of adventurers who came to the New World seeking easy fame and fortune. Those Native Americans, who had lived in an uneasy relationship with American syphilis for perhaps centuries, were now struck by what—to their bodies—would be virtually an entirely new disease: European syphilis. And, like the Spanish of 1492 and 1493, they had no acquired immunity against it. Instead of simply making them sick, it killed them in the thousands—the epidemic "die-off" of the Native American population would have begun. Indeed, it is possible that between 1494 and 1518 in Europe, the syphilis spirochete had gone through a second mutation, and that was the devastating disease that erupted in Hispaniola in 1518, among those already vulnerable to American syphilis. Indeed, the idea that American syphilis could have mutated into European syphilis, and then have been brought back to the New World in Hispaniola in 1518 is entirely possible, based on the history of HIV, the sexually transmitted virus that causes AIDS.

Now, the Spanish and the Native Americans, who had killed each other in battle, were both victims of an enemy no bravery could deter or defeat. Plans of colonization and empire would have been disrupted. It would take Hernando Cortes until 1525 to conquer the last vestiges of the Mayan kingdoms in the Yucatan. And did Francisco Pizarro sail as far south as what is now Peru not just to subdue the Incas, but to escape the plague that would have been ravaging the population of Central America? Yet wherever the Spanish went, they would have taken syphilis with them, now the extremely lethal European syphilis, as surely as their swords and horses.

When viewed chronologically, the Spanish conquest of the New World was not the steady march of conquest that was portrayed by earlier historians. It was an extremely slow process, especially considering that the Spanish not only had the horse and their war dogs, or mastiffs, but also the most sophisticated military technology of the time, which was pitted against the Neolithic (New Stone Age) weapons of the Native Americans who fought them.

The exploration of Mexico, north of the Valley of Mexico, where Tenochtitlan stood (renamed by the Spanish, Mexico City), is another story of a long, arduous process, as one would expect of men who would have been weakened by a debilitating illness. Twenty years would pass after the conquest before Francisco Vasquez de Coronado, with some three hundred Spanish soldiers and one thousand Tlaxcalan Native allies, marched north in July 1450. Coronado would reach as far north as what is today's Kansas in his historic exploration of the American southwest. To give an impression of the ravages of European syphilis, compared to the one thousand Tlaxcalans who were able to accompany Coronado, Michael Wood, in *Conquistadors*, stated that nearly 250,000 allies were with Cortes to help him besiege Tenochtitlan in 1520–21. This horrible die-off, if the figures are accurate, took place in only twenty years. In 1542, Coronado would return to the Viceroyalty of New Spain, as Mexico was then known. The Spanish authorities were disappointed to learn that instead of finding the fabled Seven Cities of Gold, he had found little more than the adobe pueblos of the Zuni Natives. Yet he had proved that there was no reason for Spain not to extend its colonization up beyond the river that became known as the Rio Grande. Every enemy that he met was decisively defeated.

However, nearly sixty years would pass before the Spanish mounted another expedition to colonize what Coronado had claimed for Spain. Except for desultory warfare against the Chichemecs, who were in no way comparable to the Aztecs or Incas, Spanish exploration north was at a standstill. Enervated by European smallpox themselves and faced with a subject population decimated by the same disease, the Spanish apparently just marked time. It would not be until 1598 that Juan de Oñate was given permission to follow in Coronado's footsteps to the north. Oñate moved north and crossed the Rio Grande in May 1598, fifty-eight years after Coronado. Oñate founded the settlement of El Paso del Norte along the river. Then, marching to the west, by July 1598, he reached the pueblos that Coronado had first visited. At the San Juan Pueblo in New Mexico, he established his headquarters, but it proved only a transitory attempt at colonization. In 1607, Oñate would return to found the town of Santa Fe.

In an alternate history, American syphilis in Europe might have mutated to a less virulent strain, or the population could have acquired some immunity to it. Yet, given the scientific proof of the mutation of the HIV virus, there is nothing to have prevented the syphilis virus from mutating yet again, once it had passed through the Native American population. Thus, it is altogether possible that there could have been a strain or mutation of syphilis that for the purposes of this alternate history can be designated American syphilis II.

A striking sequence of events could have developed from disease mutation if American syphilis II had turned out to be more lethal to Europeans than to Native Americans. If the disease had so thoroughly

Map of Francisco Vasquez de Coronado's 1540 journeys of exploration in North America. (National Archives)

destroyed the early colonies of Columbus that Europeans put an embargo on further exploration and travel to the New World, then the smallpox epidemic that in fact destroyed up to 90 percent of the Native American population might never have had a chance to arrive. If Native Americans had retained a degree of resistance to syphilis and had developed a degree of resistance to smallpox similar to that of the Europeans, the history of the whole Atlantic world, including Europe, North America, and South America, could have been greatly altered. The conquests and explorations of Cortes, Pizarro, and Coronado would simply not have taken place if Spaniards had realized that any explorers, troops, and missionaries would be eliminated by disease. Furthermore, if a devastating plague had swept Europe, beginning in the early 1500s, the personnel, funding, and incentive for such exploration and conquest would all have been lacking.

If, after the first contacts by Columbus and a few follow-on explorers, Europeans had decided to ignore the Western Hemisphere for one hundred years or more, and if Europe had been swept by a virulent disease that eliminated up to 90 percent of its population, what would have been the reaction when the two worlds once again came in contact, perhaps in the late 1600s or early 1700s? When in fact Europeans explored parts of the New World in those years, they found it surprisingly empty, and often encountered whole villages that had been destroyed and abandoned by a disease that had swept through just before their arrival. In actual history, that disease was probably smallpox, or a combination of other European diseases, wiping out vast populations and facilitating the European conquest of the Americas. However, if a similar plague or set of plagues had swept Europe during the 1500s and 1600s, the peoples of Europe, including not only those of Spain but of France and England as well, would not have been in any condition to consider military conquest or overseas colonization. One driver behind British colonization in the 1700s was the surplus population in Britain; with a virulent plague or epidemic sweeping Europe, there would have been no excess or surplus population available to send overseas as colonists.

If by the time Europe recovered or developed sufficient immunity or preventive methods, Native American cultures had gradually acquired horses, agriculture, and some of the technology of the Europeans in metallurgy, water-powered and wind-powered mills, and weaponry, and if Native American empires had evolved into technologically more advanced societies, there would have been no easy conquest of near-empty land in the New World by Europeans. Given this condition, would it have been possible that there would have been no attempt by Christian missionaries to convert the population of the Western Hemisphere? Although members of the clergy took vows of celibacy, records of sexual liaisons between the priests and women of the indigenous population suggest that the vows were often violated. Of course, as soon as it was realized that the disease spread primarily through sexual contact, there would have been a greater incentive for clergy to honor their vows.

Native Americans might very well have been able to resist the military conquest of North America by Europeans if they had possessed horses, agriculture, and some parity in weapons technology. Most important, if the Native American population had met the invaders with some foreknowledge of their culture and with vastly superior numbers, conquest would have been out of the question, at least until Europeans acquired a new level of weapons superiority, developed a level of immunity, or adopted measures for safe sex.

In fact, the circumstances would have resembled those in Equatorial and West Africa, which did, in actual history, resist European conquest until the mid and late nineteenth century. In those regions, malaria and sleeping sickness kept out Europeans, except for isolated trading stations and slave "factories" or stations along the coast. Only when Europeans developed vastly superior weapons, including modern repeating rifles and high-explosives, and after they discovered the preventive value of quinine against malaria, did they penetrate the interior of regions in the Congo, Nigeria, and along the rest of the West Coast of Africa. If the Americas had offered a similar barrier to European conquest with the presence of a disease to which the Europeans had little or no resistance, European attempts at colonization or conquest of the interior lands of the Western Hemisphere might possibly have been delayed until the middle or late nineteenth century. It was about that time that the British, French, Germans, Belgians, and other European countries were establishing the boundaries of their colonies in Africa and sending expeditions into the interior on missions of discovery and conquest.

When one looks back on early American history from Columbus's landing in 1492 to the landing of the Pilgrims in 1620, one can only marvel at the brutal and effective biological warfare that smallpox and other European diseases did in fact represent. In an alternate history, syphilis and its later mutations could have waged an equally effective biological war against the Europeans invading the New World. Seen in this light, the colonization of the Americas might have been greatly delayed. Indeed, the question becomes this: Would the conquest and colonization ever have succeeded at all?

John F. Murphy, Jr.

Discussion Questions

1. What facts in actual history support the theory that syphilis originated in the New World and was transmitted by explorers to Europe?

2. In actual history, the Native American populations were greatly reduced by smallpox and other diseases, making it extremely difficult to resist conquest by the Europeans. If Native American populations had remained at their full strength, would the Europeans still have been able to conquer the lands of the interior? Would full population have delayed or completely prevented such conquest?

3. When Europeans found the interior of Africa too dangerous to explore or conquer because of disease, they restricted their initial conquest to offshore islands and coastal regions. If they had followed a similar

pattern in the lands that in actual history became the United States because they feared a virulent and fatal disease, what specific islands and regions do you believe they would have tried to first colonize?

4. If Europeans had been concerned about contracting a fatal sexually transmitted disease in the sixteenth century, what effect would this concern have had on sexual morality?

5. In actual history, the population of Native Americans nearly vanished from parts of North America to be replaced by peoples mostly from Europe and Africa. If events had turned out in an opposite pattern, with sections of Europe completely devastated by disease and abandoned, what peoples do you believe would have been more likely to have moved in to resettle the abandoned territories there? Would repopulation have come from Africa, from the Middle East, from Asia, or from the Western Hemisphere?

Bibliography and Further Reading

Bolton, Herbert Eugene, ed. *Spanish Exploration in the Southwest, 1542–1706.* New York: Scribner, 1908.

Brookesmith, Peter. *Biohazard: The Hot Zone and Beyond.* New York: Barnes and Noble, 1997.

Cartwright, Frederick F. *Disease and History: The Influence of Disease in Shaping the Great Events of History.* New York: Crowell, 1972.

Cartwright, Frederick F., and Michael D. Biddiss. *Disease and History.* Thrupp, UK: Sutton, 2004.

Crosby, Alfred. "The Early History of Syphilis: A Reappraisal." *American Anthropologist,* 71 (1969).

Exploring Florida. "Pedro Menendez de Aviles Claims Florida for Spain." http://fcit.coedu.usf.edu/florida/lessons/menendz/menendz1.htm (accessed April 27, 2006).

Flornoy, Bertrand. *The World of the Inca.* New York: Anchor Books, 1958.

Hale, Edward Everett. *The Life of Christopher Columbus: From His Own Letters and Journals and Other Documents of His Time.* http://etext.lib.virginia.edu (accessed October 1, 2005).

History of Jamestown. http://www.apva.org/history (accessed April 27, 2006).

"History Net: A Brief History of Jamestown, Virginia." http://www.historian.org/local/jamstwnva.htm (accessed April 27, 2006).

Irving, Washington. *History of the Life and Voyages of Christopher Columbus.* New York: New Library Press, 1928.

Isaacs, Haskell. "European Influences in Islamic Medicine." In *Mashriq: Proceedings of the Eastern Mediterranean Seminar.* Manchester, UK: University of Manchester, 1980.

Leon-Portilla, Miguel, ed. *The Broken Spears: The Aztec Account of the Conquest of Mexico.* New York: Beacon Press, 1992.

McNeill, William H. *Plagues and Peoples.* Garden City, NY: Anchor, 1976.

Oman, Charles. *The Art of War in the Sixteenth Century*. Harrisburg, PA: Stackpole, 1999.

Thomas, Hugh. *Rivers of Gold: The Rise of the Spanish Empire, from Columbus to Magellan*. New York: Random House, 2005.

Tsouras, Peter G. *Warlords of the Ancient Americas: Central America*. London: Arms and Armour Press, 1996.

Wilson, Samuel H. "The Admiral and the Chief," *Natural History* (March 1991).

Winsor, Justin. *Christopher Columbus*. Woodbury, NY: Longmeadow Press, 1991.

Wood, Michael. *Conquistadors*. Berkeley, CA: University of California Press, 2000.

The first settlements by whites often failed from an inability to adapt to the new environment. What if settlers adopted Native lifestyles and the first settlements were peaceful and successful?

INTRODUCTION

When looking over America's growth and accomplishments, the tragedy that befell the Native Americans casts a shadow. The great tragedy is that two cultures, European and Native, met with what one historian has called a "fatal impact." Although there were small European settlements that came into existence very early along the coastline, these were usually very small. And they were never permanent. Not until the end of the sixteenth century was any attempt at a permanent settlement made in the lands north of Florida that became English North America.

After some false starts, a settlement in Virginia at Jamestown was founded in 1607. Europeans coming to America faced many difficulties: finding and growing food, making the enterprise worthwhile for their sponsors in England, and surviving a difficult, different climate. There was one other significant obstacle, however, and this was the Native population. These Native people were already there, well established, and, in many cases, hostile. The Europeans had to find a way to cope with this particular situation. Their choices came down to two: live in peace with the Native peoples and share the land or fight them and conquer.

The pattern we see in most instances is that Europeans made some efforts initially to live in peace with the indigenous people. These efforts sometimes lasted longer or shorter periods of time but always seemed to end in armed conflict. There were several reasons for this but perhaps the central one was that the two cultures were so different that communicating even basic concepts and values to each other was very difficult. Without effective communication coexistence became increasingly problematic. Misunderstanding, compounded by the fear that Native Americans and settlers felt for each other, eventually led to conflicts. To a minor extent, depending on the location they settled in, Europeans took up some elements of the Native American lifestyle. They adopted some aspects of the food or material culture but none of the values or beliefs. Used to particular forms of hierarchy, organization, religion, and technology, the settlers did not absorb very much of what the Native Americans had to teach.

Historic photograph of the Old Church in Jamestown, Virginia, part of the first settlements. (Library of Congress)

For their part, the Native Americans adopted some of the material items the Europeans brought but took only the things and not the means for making them. As a result, the indigenous people eventually adopted firearms and metal tools, but in the seventeenth and eighteenth centuries, they did not know how to make them. They were consumers of goods and technology but they could not develop them. For Native Americans, that gap eventually became part of their undoing, leading to their loss of the continent.

One more thing that the Native Americans did not grasp or adopt was the European view of land and ownership. They never practiced, and could not understand, a system that granted a single individual the right to completely own a piece of property and deny its use to anyone else. The Native Americans believed that land was there to be used by everyone. When they concluded treaties with the early Europeans, they believed that they were granting them the use of the land in the same general way that they used it.

For their part, Europeans could not understand the general idea of use and access and loose ownership that the Native Americans practiced. If they had grasped this concept and then adapted their society and politics to accept and live with it, American history might have been very different.

While the first permanent settlement was established in Virginia, the first major successful colonization took place several hundred miles to the north in what is now Massachusetts. The Separatist Sect we now refer to as the Pilgrims, landed in December 1620. Three years later, a settlement

A Currier & Ives print of landing of the Pilgrims on December 11, 1620. (National Archives)

to the north, in what would be New Hampshire, was established. Seven years later the settlement of Boston was begun. In the next few years, thousands of settlers would arrive in New England from old England. They brought whole communities to settle, and to do this they needed land.

The question of ownership and access to land, a concept so very different to each party, became a very important issue—one that would underlie European-Native American relations not only in colonial America but into the twenty-first century as tribes and the U.S. government continue attempting to resolve old disputes.

Of all the aspects of Native values, perhaps the one of owning and using the land may have been the most important. This chapter looks at how the problem surfaced in the earliest large settlements, those in New England. Although there were some similarities in all of the colonies, there were also some differences. We examine how this problem might have been faced in one area, New England. Then, we speculate how this solution, arrived at with an acceptance of Native values, might have affected colonial settlements in the east with effects lasting centuries later.

TURNING POINT

The early settlements in New England enjoyed substantial growth in their first two decades of existence, and this must have given the Native Americans cause for concern. These were not seasonal encampments

Site of the original 1621 fort in Plymouth, Massachusetts. (National Archives)

sheltering fishermen but permanent towns. In very dramatic fashion, both the towns and the numbers of whites were increasing. In the 1630s, a movement called the Great Migration brought 20,000 people from England. Plymouth Plantation was not the only colony now, as by the early 1630s there were the additional settlements of Massachusetts Bay, Connecticut, and New Haven. Also, there was new pressure on the Native peoples of the northeast as the Dutch established their colony at what is now New York City and spread their farming and trading efforts north and east.

Eventual conflict was inevitable, but for the first seventeen years, there were no serious problems. The differences in general outlook and culture between the Native Americans and the settlers had always been substantial, but other more particular issues began to appear, including different concepts of property, ownership, and exclusive rights over the land. The Europeans believed that when you had title to a piece of land, whether by purchase or inheritance, it was exclusively yours. No one else could use it without your permission. This idea was completely alien to the Native Americans. A tribe could claim an area for the tribe's use, but individuals did not stake out their own lots as the Europeans did.

What one did with the land was a point of potential conflict. The English in New England strictly believed in the biblical command that one had to subdue the land. Often, researchers see in records that the person accepting a grant of land promises that he will "perfect" it. Otherwise, he will lose his claim. To the English in the seventeenth century, the Native Americans had basically forfeited their claim to the land because they had not perfected it by cutting down forests so they could build or sell the timber, and had not put up extensive permanent buildings. Because the Native Americans were not perfecting (developing) their holdings, they should surrender any claim to those who would.

Although not yet a major problem in the 1630s, the legal rights of Native Americans as opposed to Europeans also became a potential source of conflict. As Indians found themselves increasingly in court, they felt that they could not get a fair hearing. Research by some historians tends to show that many of the courts were fairly run, but the perception of the Native peoples must be taken into account when discussing their attitudes toward the Europeans.

Finally, there was religion. Like all Europeans, those who settled in New England believed very strongly that their religion was the one true way to God. They were not enthusiastically tolerant of Native beliefs, which many whites thought was the work of the devil.

With this growing set of issues in the background, the Europeans began to come into conflict with the most powerful Native tribe in the region, one that also had expanded into New England, the Pequots. The Pequots had migrated from the west, then conquered and settled what is now the region along the eastern Connecticut River. Despite their losses from a smallpox epidemic in 1636 (with 4,000 dead out of a population of 8,000), they were still a force to be reckoned with.

Although the Pequots invited the English to live in the area near the Connecticut River in 1633, there were problems from the very beginning. In 1634, an Englishman named John Stone went into the Pequot territory and kidnapped some of the Native Americans. He was caught and killed by the Pequots. Although Stone was a well-known pirate and was acting illegally, the English demanded that his killers be brought to justice. The Pequots would not agree, beginning tensions between them and the English.

A similar situation occurred two years later with the English landing at nearby Block Island to punish the Native Americans there for killing some English. The Indians managed to escape but the English destroyed their villages before going on to the Pequots, demanding that they hand over Stone's killers. Because they refused, the English burned any Pequot settlements they could find as they marched through the countryside. In retaliation, the Pequots attacked Connecticut settlements that fall and winter.

The most dramatic incident of the war could hardly be called a battle but was, instead, a massacre. Just before dawn on May 26, 1637, a combined force from Connecticut and Massachusetts Bay, with help from the Mohegan and Narragansett tribes, attacked a large Pequot settlement near the site of present-day Mystic, Connecticut. There were four hundred to seven hundred people living in the village, and within an hour after the attack began, nearly all of them had been killed.

This massacre was the last major action of this conflict. Other bands of Pequots attempted to avoid the English but were either surrounded or turned over by other tribes. By the end of the summer 1637, most organized resistance was over. In September of the following year (1638), a treaty was signed.

The Pequot war that had just come to an end was the first major conflict between the whites and the Native Americans. The ending was as harsh as the conduct of the war had been. The Pequots, once feared by other tribes as the Destroyers, were now totally defeated. Many had died; survivors were sent into slavery to tribes that had helped the English. Others were sent into slavery in Bermuda. This was not enough, however, for in September 1638, by the treaty that concluded the war even the name "Pequot" was outlawed. Those who survived who had not been enslaved could not resettle in their former homes. Eventually, this punishment was rescinded and they were allowed to reassert their identity but always with limitations. They then were divided into the eastern and western Pequots and settled on the first Native American reservations in America.

In 1643, six years after the war, representatives of Connecticut, New Haven, Massachusetts, and Plymouth met to discuss and act on matters of mutual interest. The most important item, of course, was defense. The New England Confederation, as it was called, established rules that called for six out of eight votes on matters to pass any resolution. In addition to acting on defense, the Confederation would arbitrate disagreements between colonies. Meeting once a year, sometimes more frequently, the Confederation existed for forty years, finally disbanding in 1684. It would see New England through some very perilous issues, many of which the New Englanders brought upon themselves by their relations with the Native Americans.

Suppose, that when the New England Confederation first met, the representatives had discussed the recent war as a horror that must never happen again. In their discussions, they might have seen that misunderstandings on both sides had resulted in losses to the English and the destruction of an entire tribe, and that if steps were not taken to stop possible conflicts all sides would lose. They might have formalized their concerns and written the "New England Declaration," a document that might have contained the following provisions:

- The New England Confederation would include not only representatives from Massachusetts Bay, Plymouth, Connecticut, and New Haven but also from major tribes in the region.

- That the English would review their laws about selling, buying, and holding property and change them to incorporate Native practices and customs. A panel would exist in each colony to inspect every sale to ensure that the terms would meet the laws.

- That all courts, both civil and criminal, would have participation, by equal numbers, of Native Americans and English and that local tribal laws would be reviewed. A joint committee in each colony would incorporate tribal laws into the legal process.

This proposal from the New England Confederation would then have been sent to the legislatures in each colony. In our alternate scenario, we could then suppose that the war had made such a deep impression on the English and the Native Americans that all of the colonies wanted the plan to be adopted. If it had been adopted, New England's interactions with the Native peoples, based in large part on adopting some of their customs and including them in all decision making, might have changed history in New England. It might also have changed the subsequent history of the United States.

ACTUAL HISTORY

The end of the Pequot war removed the most powerful and organized of all the tribes that might have halted English settlement. For the next almost forty years, the settlers moved into the interior and populated New England. In addition to the four colonies of the 1630s, a new one would be established: Rhode Island. With the population growth and increased interaction between the settlers and the Native Americans, disagreements on ownership and use of land as well as matters of criminal justice became more frequent and a source of tension.

In June 1675, Chief Metacomet (known to the English as King Philip) launched an uprising that eventually embraced several of the tribes in New England and resulted in the bloodiest war in American history proportionate to the population. Five percent of New England's European population was killed. Twenty-five towns were abandoned. Over six hundred houses were destroyed, eight thousand cattle slaughtered or stolen, and thousands of bushels of grain lost. More than two thousand people lost their homes and became refugees in eastern towns.

As an example of the effects, we briefly visit a town that had come into existence after the Pequot War and that was destroyed as a result of the conflict with King Philip. It was a case of destruction that an agreement like the New England Declaration might have prevented.

If you were going to visit Marlborough in Massachusetts in June 1675, when King Philip's War started, you would have had to start from Boston. Crossing the Charles River by boat to Cambridge, you would then have journeyed west down the Boston Post Road through Watertown, entered Sudbury, passed the mill on the Sudbury River, and, finally, twenty-five miles from where you had started, you would have entered Marlborough. Along the way you would have noticed that despite the farms carved out by settlers, there were still many trees along the remarkably wide roads. The roads had been made very wide to accommodate the herds of cattle that would be driven into Boston each fall.

Marlborough was now twenty years old and had almost fifty families, with a total population of about two hundred fifty people. In the center of town stood the meeting house where the people met for services or politics (town meetings). From there, one could see the fields of maize tended and owned by the Native Americans of Ockoocangansett, one of the Praying Towns established for Christian Natives by John Eliot. Their village, with its 6,000 acres and a dozen families, was smaller than Marlborough. Many of the English in town resented having Native Americans living so close and occupying land that the townspeople thought should be theirs. However, there was not a great deal of tension

A local leader rallies the men of Hadley in defense of Indian attack during King Philip's War, Hadley, Massachusetts, 1675–1676. (Library of Congress)

KEY CONCEPT   John Eliot and the Praying Indians

While the Massachusetts Puritans were not receptive to adopting any elements of the way Native peoples lived outside of material culture, they were very interested in converting Native Americans to Christianity. The foremost proponent of this movement and person who managed to mobilize political support for his endeavors, while winning the respect of the Indians, was a minister named John Eliot. Eliot was a Puritan, born in Britain in 1604, who arrived in Massachusetts in 1631.

At first, he was very much like the other ministers in that his chief priority was his own church and its members. As time went on, however, Eliot became more interested in the Native Americans and even began to learn their language so he could preach to them. In 1646, he finally achieved his goal and began preaching to and eventually converting Native Americans. With some success in converting Indians to Christianity, Eliot then convinced the General Court (the Massachusetts colonial legislature) to set aside land for the Indians who had converted. The result was a group of settlements known as the Praying Towns in which Indians lived as Christians. The first of what would eventually number eleven communities was established in Natick in 1651.

For the Indians living in the Praying Towns there was a significant trade-off. They were promised protection, were able to have access to the English communities in the areas for commerce, and could learn English trades. At the same time, they were, by adopting Christianity and other aspects of European civilization, cutting themselves off from their heritage and from other Natives in New England. As a result, they were never entirely trusted by either side—other Native Americans or the European settlers. The dangers of this middle ground became very apparent when King Philip's War broke out. The Praying Town Natives were looked on with suspicion by both the Indians and the whites. The Indians living in the Praying Town of Ockoocangansett near Marlborough were rounded up and brought to an open area on Deer Island in Boston Harbor. Here, despite their conversion to Christianity and despite the work of John Eliot to free them, they were kept in captivity. Eventually those who survived were released and allowed to return to their homes in the Praying Towns.

Until his death in 1690, Eliot remained a tireless advocate for the Native Americans. He not only mastered the local language but translated the Bible from English to Algonkian. The very first Bible printed in North America was not in English but in the local language. The experiment of the Praying Towns, while successful in some ways, only underlines the differences between the two cultures and the ultimate refusal of the English in New England to learn and accept lessons the Indians could have taught them in how to conduct life.

or discomfort. All of that changed in June 1675 when King Philip's War began. By October, many of the Native residents were forced off the land and packed off to an open-air prison in Boston Harbor, where they spent the winter of 1675–1676.

Marlborough was not raided until Sunday, March 26, 1676. With that assault, however, the residents fled and went to safer towns in the east. Marlborough now became a fortified camp, no longer a peaceful farming community. Through the winter and into the next year, soldiers were garrisoned in Marlborough. Although the garrison was able to stay in a few buildings, the remaining structures were all destroyed by the Native peoples, who also slaughtered any animals they found. In one respect Marlborough had been fortunate; during the entire war, only four people were killed and one wounded.

It would be two years before Marlborough could be resettled. When it was, things had changed profoundly and in no way more than the relations

---

IN CONTEXT   Violence in North America, Violence in Europe

As Simplicius was returning home from gathering berries, he saw intruders come out of the forest and drag his parents and sister out of their home. From his hiding spot behind some bushes he saw his family tortured and killed before his eyes. Then the raiders went into the home, took what they liked, and set the small house on fire. Simplicius was now an orphan and had to make his way in the world alone.

That scene does not come from an account of a Native attack on a frontier European settlement or of Europeans attacking Native Americans. It comes from the first novel written in German, *The Adventures of Simplicius Simplicissimus*, published in 1668, which describes events during the Thirty Years' War. This conflict, fought in Germany and other parts of Central Europe from 1618 to 1648, started as a war of religion in what was called the Holy Roman Empire. During this period the armies of France, Germany, and Sweden marched across central Europe. Perhaps up to one-third of all of Germany's towns and villages were destroyed. Along with plague and famine that accompanied the armies, there was the fighting and pillaging. Civilians in the path of armies fighting and marching could expect no mercy. In one famous

instance, the city of Magdeburg, Germany, went from a population of over 25,000 before the war to just over 2,000.

At about the same time, the Spanish were fighting in the Low Countries, what later became the Netherlands and Belgium. In this region, Spain strengthened its claim while it imposed Catholicism on a largely Protestant population. Cities were burned, heavy taxes collected, and hostages taken. In the 1560s, when the Dutch artist Pieter Brueghel wanted to portray a biblical scene in which Herod's soldiers killed all of the infants under the age of two, he set the scene in a Flemish village with Spanish soldiers entering the town. Everyone understood both the original meaning and what the painting said about contemporary events.

Although there can be no excuse for the brutal treatment of the Native Americans by Europeans, North America was not the only place this violence and disregard for life existed. Unfortunately in that age, anyone who was different, in terms of religion, language, or nationality, was a potential victim of one army or another. Civilians were not accorded any protection or mercy whether they were German peasants or Pequots in Connecticut.

---

between the Native Americans and their English neighbors. Where there had been a certain degree of distrust, there was now hostility. Eventually the Europeans would get title to all of the Indian Praying Town land.

After King Philip's War, which we can see as the eventual and almost inevitable outcome of the failure to reach an understanding after the Pequot war, the pattern became well established. There were, of course, variations from colony to colony on the east coast, but in general the outcome was always the same. The Europeans and the Native Americans, so very different in culture and outlook, confronted each other over issues of the land and came to blows, with the Native Americans losing everything. That pattern would recur throughout American history.

Pennsylvania, settled after New England, might have become a model for European-Native American relations. William Penn had been very open and honest in all of his transactions to acquire land rights. Additionally, he monitored all sales that he was not involved in to be sure that the rights of the Native American were being preserved or that they were not cheated. The climate in Pennsylvania for Indian-white relations was so good that Native tribes moved into Pennsylvania to become permanent residents. Unfortunately, this policy ended when Penn died and his family took charge.

KEY CONCEPT   The Royal Proclamation of 1763

[Text dealing with Native Americans]

And whereas it is just and reasonable, and essential to our Interest, and the Security of our Colonies, that the several Nations or Tribes of Indians with whom We are connected, and who live under our Protection, should not be molested or disturbed in the Possession of such Parts of Our Dominions and Territories as, not having been ceded to or purchased by Us, are reserved to them, or any of them, as their Hunting Grounds—We do therefore, with the Advice of our Privy Council, declare it to be our Royal Will and Pleasure, that no Governor or Commander in Chief in any of our Colonies of Quebec, East Florida, or West Florida, do presume, upon any Pretence whatever, to grant Warrants of Survey, or pass any Patents for Lands beyond the Bounds of their respective Governments, as described in their Commissions: as also that no Governor or Commander in Chief in any of our other Colonies or Plantations in America do presume for the present, and until our further Pleasure be known, to grant Warrants of Survey, or pass Patents for any Lands beyond the Heads or Sources of any of the Rivers which fall into the Atlantic Ocean from the West and North West, or upon any Lands whatever, which, not having been ceded to or purchased by Us as aforesaid, are reserved to the said Indians, or any of them.

And We do further declare it to be Our Royal Will and Pleasure, for the present as aforesaid, to reserve under our Sovereignty, Protection, and Dominion, for the use of the said Indians, all the Lands and Territories not included within the Limits of Our said Three new Governments, or within the Limits of the Territory granted to the Hudson's Bay Company, as also all the Lands and Territories lying to the Westward of the Sources of the Rivers which fall into the Sea from the West and North West as aforesaid. And We do hereby strictly forbid, on Pain of our Displeasure, all our loving Subjects from making any Purchases or Settlements whatever, or taking Possession of any of the Lands above reserved, without our especial leave and Licence for that Purpose first obtained.

And We do further strictly enjoin and require all Persons whatever who have either wilfully or inadvertently seated themselves upon any Lands within the Countries above described or upon any other Lands which, not having been ceded to or purchased by Us, are still reserved to the said Indians as aforesaid, forthwith to remove themselves from such Settlements.

And whereas great Frauds and Abuses have been committed in purchasing Lands of the Indians, to the great Prejudice of our Interests. and to the great Dissatisfaction of the said Indians: In order,

---

In the southern colonies—Virginia, North and South Carolina, and Georgia—relations were bad almost from the start. The English not only fought the Native peoples but encouraged fighting between the Native American tribes in an effort to divide and conquer.

In the 1750s and 1760s, there was a great deal of conflict with the Native peoples, but much of this was based on alliances that different tribes had formed with either the English or the French. In the northeast, many tribes from what is now Canada or the regions that border Canada were allied with the French. There had been raids into New England from the late seventeenth century onward, but these increased in scale with raids and counter raids, the most famous being the assault by Robert Rogers on the Native American town of Saint Francis, in retaliation for the massacre of British soldiers who had surrendered at Fort William Henry the previous year.

Native Americans, while they saw the differences between the French and the British, regarded all of them as invaders. Part of their concern for what could happen to their tribal lands was addressed (at least legally) by the Seven Years' War in America (also known as the French and Indian

---

KEY CONCEPT   *The Royal Proclamation of 1763 (Continued)*

therefore, to prevent such Irregularities for the future, and to the end that the Indians may be convinced of our Justice and determined Resolution to remove all reasonable Cause of Discontent, We do, with the Advice of our Privy Council strictly enjoin and require, that no private Person do presume to make any purchase from the said Indians of any Lands reserved to the said Indians, within those parts of our Colonies where We have thought proper to allow Settlement: but that, if at any Time any of the Said Indians should be inclined to dispose of the said Lands, the same shall be Purchased only for Us, in our Name, at some public Meeting or Assembly of the said Indians, to be held for that Purpose by the Governor or Commander in Chief of our Colony respectively within which they shall lie: and in case they shall lie within the limits of any Proprietary Government, they shall be purchased only for the Use and in the name of such Proprietaries, conformable to such Directions and Instructions as We or they shall think proper to give for that Purpose: And we do, by the Advice of our Privy Council, declare and enjoin, that the Trade with the said Indians shall be free and open to all our Subjects whatever, provided that every Person who may incline to Trade with the said Indians do take out a Licence for carrying on such Trade from the Governor or Commander in Chief of any of our Colonies respectively where such Person shall reside, and also give Security to observe such

Regulations as We shall at any Time think fit, by ourselves or by our Commissaries to be appointed for this Purpose, to direct and appoint for the Benefit of the said Trade:

And we do hereby authorize, enjoin, and require the Governors and Commanders in Chief of all our Colonies respectively, as well those under Our immediate Government as those under the Government and Direction of Proprietaries, to grant such Licences without Fee or Reward, taking especial Care to insert therein a Condition, that such Licence shall be void, and the Security forfeited in case the Person to whom the same is granted shall refuse or neglect to observe such Regulations as We shall think proper to prescribe as aforesaid.

And we do further expressly conjoin and require all Officers whatever, as well Military as those Employed in the Management and Direction of Indian Affairs, within the Territories reserved as aforesaid for the use of the said Indians, to seize and apprehend all Persons whatever, who standing charged with Treason, Misprisions of Treason, Murders, or other Felonies or Misdemeanors, shall fly from Justice and take Refuge in the said Territory, and to send them under a proper guard to the Colony where the Crime was committed, of which they stand accused, in order to take their Trial for the same.

Given at our Court at St. James's the 7th Day of October 1763, in the Third Year of our Reign.

War), with the Royal Proclamation of 1763. This edict essentially prohibited white settlement beyond the Appalachian Mountains, reserving this area for Native Americans. The restriction enraged the American colonists and is often cited as a reason for the eventual revolution.

In the American Revolution, most tribes allied themselves with the British or stayed neutral. In the northeast, particularly in upstate New York, the tribes actively supported the British and accompanied them in their battles against the Americans. Using Indians against the Americans was a powerful point in rallying American opposition to the British; many Americans might have not become involved otherwise.

With the end of the revolution and the elimination of restrictions by the king's government, the Americans moved west. In the 1780s, they began settling into the area that became Ohio. This influx of whites started what became an eight-year conflict with the local Shawnee and Miami Indians, known as Little Turtle's war. Although the Native Americans defeated the new U.S. Army several times, they were eventually defeated.

In the old Northwest Territory (Ohio, Indiana, and Illinois), land was taken by settlers to an alarming extent. The Native Americans began to resist the seizure of land by the territorial government of Indiana. The result was fighting just before the war of 1812 at the battle of Tippecanoe, where William Henry Harrison defeated the Prophet, the brother of the war chief Tecumseh. In the next few years, until his death in 1813, Tecumseh also resisted the encroachment of the whites and joined the British in the War of 1812.

These victories over the Native peoples in the northwest and the south, combined with the British withdrawal of their garrisons from U.S. territory, led to the next stage of westward development. In addition, the Spanish finally left Florida, allowing Americans to go south and begin fighting with the Seminoles in a conflict that would last into the 1850s.

More and more settlers were pushing westward, and now there was a government plan to displace Native Americans and move them west so they would be out of the way. This effort began with the Indian Removal Act of 1830. It was remarkably successful as it managed to move nearly all the Native Americans living east of the Mississippi out of their homes by 1840 so the land could be taken over by white settlers. The Indians were relocated to land set aside for them in Arkansas and Oklahoma. This resettlement is remarkable, not only for the design and successful execution of a plan to move so large a population over such a great distance, but also for the scope of its disruption and the cruelty with which it was conceived and pursued.

The trip west was very difficult. The Native Americans were not only torn from their homes forever but lost hundreds of their number from sickness and the hardships of the journey. Many died of starvation or illnesses such as cholera. Not all went willingly, and those who protested were often forcibly removed from their homes in chains.

The Cherokee sought to use the court system to have their removal stopped; other tribes, such as the Sac and Fox in the Old Northwest, resisted with force. In this conflict, known as the Black Hawk War, the Indians eventually lost and were forced to depart. As a side note, one of the local militiamen called up to fight the Native Americans was a young Abraham Lincoln.

In the 1840s, settlement beyond the Mississippi River began in earnest. Many settlers went to what is now Oregon and Washington through the 1840s and into the 1850s. The Native peoples in that region did not want them there and attacked many of the settlements.

The federal government battled the Native Americans on two fronts during the Civil War of 1861 to 1865. In the first, they fought the Cherokees who had enlisted and served as volunteers for the Confederate States of America, some of them under a Native Confederate general, Stand Watie. When the Confederacy was defeated, these Cherokees lost much of their land in a punitive action by the Union. In addition, there was fighting of the old type that had always gone on. From 1861 to 1863, the Apaches began and sustained an uprising. The most dramatic of the Indian wars during this time, however, began in 1862, when the Santee branch of the Dakotas attacked settlements in Minnesota and eventually spread the conflict to North Dakota. This uprising was defeated in 1864. There were also territorial wars between settlers and the Navajo, Cheyenne, and Arapaho tribes in this same period.

In the twenty-five years after the conclusion of the Civil War, the pace of expansion in the United States quickened. Many families in the existing population in the east as well as new immigrants from Europe began spreading west, spurring the building of railroads and accelerating the movement to take Native land.

Conflict with the Dakota began the year after the Civil War ended over access to western trails (specifically the Bozeman Trail). With this conflict, there was increased pressure for the Plains Natives to move to reservations in either Oklahoma Indian Territory or North Dakota. Portions of some of the tribes agreed to the move to reservations, but this offer (or rather demand) was not accepted by all. In 1871, a conflict began with the Apaches in the American southwest that would last for fifteen years. Simultaneously, wars were fought in California, Montana, Oregon, Washington and Idaho. In one of the military expeditions, the 7th Cavalry under General George Custer pursued the Native Americans in Montana. Custer and a large number of his soldiers were killed. The final armed confrontation took place

General George Custer pursued the Native Americans in Montana. Custer and a large number of his soldiers were killed. (Library of Congress)

at the Wounded Knee reservation in 1890. It was here that a movement known as the Ghost Dance was ended with soldiers using machine guns to kill over two hundred Natives. From this time on, there was no organized resistance and the Native Americans were now all, or nearly all, consigned to reservations selected, organized, and run by the U.S. government, with no significant decisions being made by the Native Americans themselves about their lives or the land they had once lived on freely.

Native Americans did not prosper on the reservations (eventually there were 322 of these all over the country). The level of unemployment, poverty, illness, and social problems on the reservations was quite severe. Even today, Native American children suffer mortality rates that are more than two-and-a-half those of white children.

In the 1970s, serious efforts to change this situation were begun. Native Americans organized themselves into the National Indian Youth Council, the Indian Historical Society, and the American Indian Movement. These groups and others since have had some success in elevating awareness of problems facing Native Americans as well as improving conditions. Some tribes, by opening gambling casinos, have been able to better their tribes' living conditions.

Regardless of what improvements come, however, they cannot make up for the death of individuals and the death of a culture, a situation that might have been avoided if the Europeans had made an effort to change their worldview and incorporate the way that Native Americans looked at the world around them. That they did not is a great tragedy in American history.

ALTERNATE HISTORY

Earlier we suggested that the New England Confederation might have drafted a document (the New England Declaration) that incorporated the views of the Native Americans toward using and owning land and settling disputes. Realistically, we could not expect the Europeans to have completely adopted all Native practices, but they might have changed their own views significantly in ways that would have been accepted by some of them. Such a set of guidelines could have guided European-Native American relationships in New England in the seventeenth century. If it had worked there, it might not only have changed those relationships but could also have affected the country in other ways.

Although we can't imagine everything that might have changed, there are a few things that might have been very different in the intervening years. A reasonably safe assumption is that the New England Declaration could have prevented King Philip's War. The town of Marlborough described earlier would not have been destroyed, and the tensions existing between the English and their Native American neighbors would have been minimized or entirely eliminated.

As the years went on, a successful adoption of this New England Declaration by New York and the central colonies, strengthened and perhaps modified by William Penn's policies, and then implemented in the southern colonies might have had some of the following results.

Even though it probably would not have prevented all conflicts between the whites and the Native peoples, the New England Declaration would have minimized their number, frequency, and intensity. If there had been a recognized practice of incorporating Native values and outlooks into the laws of the colonies and eventually the states, conflicts would have been resolved more easily and with considerably less bloodshed.

The practices outlined and reinforced as the Declaration would have been implemented over time, and would have started and perpetuated the creation of equitable treaties and agreements, marked by a concern for ensuring that each party's understanding and worldview were defined and respected. Adopting the Declaration would not have stopped all fighting between Native tribes but it would have decreased it. With fewer conflicts among the Native Americans, the Europeans would not have been able to take advantage of these frictions to advance their own ends.

There might not have been reservations, but Native Americans would probably have concentrated in specific settlements and regions of the state, or maybe formed the majority of a particular state. Both whites and Native peoples would have lived in each other's communities and shared the same form of government. With no reservation system based on the desire to take Native American land, Oklahoma would not have become what was called the "Indian Territory" and there would have been no forced removal, no Trail of Tears for the Cherokees or any other tribe.

What could have come out of this non–reservation and removal policy would have been the integration of Europeans and Native

Americans into a diverse but unified political and social fabric. Avoided would have been the practice of treating Native tribes as sovereign but inferior entities. At a much earlier time than actual history, we might have seen Native American senators, representatives, and governors. In 1868, President Ulysses Grant chose one of his staff officers, a Seneca Native named Eli Parker, to head the U.S. Bureau of Indian Affairs. Had the New England Declaration been in effect, the country would have been accustomed to having Native Americans in leadership roles, and Eli Parker might instead have been selected as vice president under Grant in 1868 and then become president himself in the election of 1876.

Europeans would have kept their basic idea of private property but it might have become much changed as a result of the original Declaration, and then legal precedents through the years would have created further changes. Larger areas of land might have been reserved for public or for common use. National Parks might have been adopted earlier than they actually were in the 1870s. The idea of town commons, which the New Englanders used, would have been extended because of the experience with the Native Americans. At the same time, there might very well have been more respect for the country's natural resources. America's Industrial Revolution might not have been so dramatic. The American economy might have been very different although it still would have relied on manufacturing and trade, and agriculture, always a large part of America's economy, might have been even larger.

Those are some general changes that might have taken place. A few specific changes would have happened as well. Although there would have been conflicts in the years before the Revolution with the Indians backed and supplied by the French in Canada, certain events might have happened differently. During the French and Indian War, General Jeffrey Amherst in actual history proposed giving hostile Natives blankets infected with smallpox. If the country had signed the New England Declaration, Americans, conditioned to over one hundred years of treating Native Americans with a more humane set of standards, might very well have opposed this plan.

During the American Revolution and the War of 1812, conflicts with Native tribes in the south or in the New York, Ohio, Indiana, and Kentucky regions might have been much less severe or even eliminated. Because of the precedents set by court cases guided by the New England Declaration, there would have been no question of forcible removal.

At the conclusion of the Mexican-American War in 1848, the Comanche tribes might have started shifting their attacks from Mexicans to Americans as they actually did, but might have been dissuaded from continuing that war because of the work of American envoys who just happened to be Native Americans themselves. Sadly, the Civil War might very well have taken place with Indians participating on both sides rather than primarily in the Confederate service. The great uprisings in Minnesota and the Dakotas or the southwest would not have occurred (there would have been no reservations or bad policy directed at those Indians as actually occurred).

Native American territories in the west would have been protected. The land would have been mined for gold, silver, and other minerals, but under licensing and direction by the tribes who claimed possession of the land. Revenues from this activity would have funded the beginning of a series of tribal colleges and universities making Native Americans a well-educated ethnic group in America.

The values, attitudes, and beliefs of the American public would not have been so receptive to the imperial ideas that emerged in all nations at the end of the nineteenth century. America might have been less interested in an overseas empire: there might never have been a war with Spain. In other instances, developments outside the United States and beyond its control would have created situations in which the United States would have acted the same way as it did in actual history. America might very well have had to participate in both world wars. It is interesting to think, however, that with history having gone as it might have in this alternative universe, perhaps America's large battleships might have been named for tribes and not states. The surrender of Japan might then have been signed on the deck of a ship called U.S.S. Mohawk, instead of U.S.S. Missouri.

It is difficult to say whether atomic weapons would have been developed. Unfortunately, they probably would have been, but America, with its values and reverence for life and the importance of sharing the land, might have become a leader more intent on helping and using diplomacy and less on depending on military might. We cannot say with any certainty what would have happened if the New England Declaration had been written and adopted through American history but it might very well have given us a world much different than the one we now live in.

Robert Stacy

Discussion Questions

1. Although Europeans practiced private landholding, they also had some practices of shared or communal landholding, such as "commons" used as either parks or common grazing land, public roads and rights-of-way, and church lands. Under the alternate history presented here, what other sorts of common uses for property might have developed among European Americans?

2. In what ways are modern federal landholdings, such as national parks, national forests, and bureau of land management lands, similar to the way that Native Americans treated land ownership? In what ways are such modern uses entirely different from Native American practices?

3. The differences in culture and outlook between Europeans and Native Americans extended far beyond their different views of landholding. What differences and failures to understand each other do you think were most important in leading to conflict, wars, and massacres between the two populations?

4. In the alternate history presented here, Native American ideas and values, as well as peoples, become incorporated into the fabric of life in the United States rather than excluded. What impact do you think such incorporation would have on the way people live in the twenty-first century in America?

5. In actual history, what ideas and values prevented the spread of William Penn's Native American policies and the development of the "New England Declaration" presented here?

6. In comparing the conquest of North America by Europeans to the expansion of European colonial systems and conquests in other regions of the world there are many differences. What broad factors account for the different ways the European expansion played out in South America, Africa, Asia, and Australia? What broad factors made the experience in North America take the form that it did, with extermination, removal, and isolation in reservations?

Bibliography and Further Reading

Apess, William. *On Our Own Ground: The Complete Writings of William Apess, a Pequot*. Amherst, MA: University of Massachusetts Press, 1992.

Axtell, James. *The Invasion Within: The Contest of Cultures in Colonial North America*. Oxford: Oxford University Press, 1985.

Bourne, Russell, *The Red King's Rebellion: Racial Politics in New England, 1675–1678*. New York: Atheneum, 1990.

Cave, Alfred A. *The Pequot War*. Amherst, MA: University of Massachusetts Press, 1996.

Cogley, Richard W. *John Eliot's Mission to the Indians before King Philip's War*. Cambridge, MA: Harvard University Press, 1999.

Demos, John. *The Unredeemed Captive: A Family Story from Early America*. New York: Vintage, 1995.

Gallay, Alan. *The Indian Slave Trade: The Rise of the English Empire in the American South, 1670–1717*. New Haven, CT: Yale University Press, 2002.

Jennings, Francis. *The Invasion of America: Indians, Colonialism, and the Cant of Conquest*. New York: W. W. Norton, 1976.

Johnson, Michael G. *American Woodland Indians*. Oxford: Osprey, 1997.

Koning, Hans. *The Conquest of America: How the Indian Nations Lost Their Continent*. New York: Monthly Review Press, 1993.

Milanich, Jerald T. *Laboring in the Fields of the Lord: Spanish Missions and Southeastern Indians*. Washington, DC: Smithsonian Institution Press, 1999.

Oberg, Michael Leroy. *Dominion and Civility: English Imperialism and Native America, 1585–1685*. Ithaca, NY: Cornell University Press, 1999.

Schultz, Eric B. *King Philip's Indian War: The History and Legacy of America's Forgotten Conflict*. Woodstock, VT: Countryman Press, 1999.

Sheehan, Bernard W. *Savagism and Civility: Indians and Englishmen in Colonial Virginia*. New York: Cambridge University Press, 1980.

Vaughan, Alden T. *New England Frontier: Puritans and Indians, 1620–1675*. Norman, OK: University of Oklahoma Press, 1995.

Native American Myths, Narratives, and Songs

Compiled and edited by Kathleen L. Nichols

INTRODUCTION

The small collection of myths, narratives, and songs included in this appendix cannot adequately convey how rich and extensive the Native American tradition of oral "literature" is. Instead, this appendix will provide a few representative Native voices explaining, from their own perspectives, selected aspects of tribal history from its beginnings in prehistory to the end of the nineteenth century. These tribal voices are drawn from four very broad geographical areas of the North American continent: the Northeast and eastern woodlands (Seneca, Iroquois, and Cherokee); the central plains and mountain areas (Sioux, Kiowa, Arapaho, and Paiute); the Southwest (Navajo, Zuni, Hopi, and Jicarilla Apache); and the Northwest/ northern Pacific coast (Lillooet, Chinook, Chippewa, Tsimshian, Haida, and Tlingit).

That said, we are faced with a problem. Myth and legend are not "history," at least not as it is usually defined in terms of verifiable written documents, observable artifacts, and identifiable eye-witnesses. However, to traditional Native Americans, the ancient myths of each tribe are history or, more precisely, a kind of "sacred history." Their oral "records," passed down from one generation to the next, preserve the ancestral explanations of their origins and of the relationship between the supernatural forces and the natural worlds in which Native Americans lived for thousands of years before the first European invasions occurred. That last historical fact—the relentless drive of Euro-Americans to dominate the Americas over the course of approximately four centuries (fifteenth through nineteenth centuries)—constitutes one of the most significant turning points in the destinies of the First Nations. It too left its mark on tribal oral traditions in the form of semi-mythical legends and historical narratives about Native American-European American relations.

Although the texts included in this appendix are arranged according to a rough chronology (i.e., from a vague "in the beginning" to the Wounded Knee Massacre of 1890), the issue of "what constitutes history?"

is most problematic with the myths of origin. Among other considerations, we do not know who created them nor, in creation myths like "The Woman Who Fell from the Sky" (Seneca) or "Jicarilla Genesis" (Jicarilla Apache), what date was intended any more than most people can calculate the era of the Judeo-Christian "genesis." However, if these two Native American creation myths are at all representative, then the ancient tribal belief is that the origins of the earth and the beings who would later inhabit it occurred on the American continent. In the northeastern myths, this event typically happens when "Sky Woman" falls through a hole in the upper world of the earliest spirit-beings. The water animals and birds, which seem to have always existed below, gather from the bottom of the waters, the primeval mud that quickly grows, by some sacred process, into dry land (the earth). Sky Woman then gives birth to a daughter who will later become the first "earth mother" figure by giving birth to the sacred hero twins (or elder brother and younger brother). As the first three stories included here indicate, these hero twins must rid the world of "monsters." (Are these residual memories of woolly mammoths or other extinct creatures?) The sacred brothers must also form the topographical features of the earth such as the mountains and valleys. (Are the twins the glaciers that formed the Grand Canyon?) It would be difficult to say exactly how much early "history" is or is not hidden in these tales that operate primarily in mythic space and time rather than historical time and place.

This movement through mythic time as several generations of first-beings create a habitable earth for the future humans does suggest, however, that the earliest Native Americans believed in a kind of primitive evolutionary process. This possibility is strengthened by the typical southwestern creation myth. In the selection from "Jicarilla Genesis," the early peoples emerge from the center of the earth through four embedded worlds or womb-like "caves" before ending up on the surface of the earth (their "fifth world") where the human-people are soon separated from the animal-people; the myths re-tell the "histories" of what happened in each of those separate worlds or stages of development. Once the fifth world is reached, the hero twins begin a series of adventures as they did in the northeastern myths. Many variations of this overall pattern exist, depending upon which tribal history is consulted, but the southwestern myths tend to agree that a number of migrations or "wanderings," as they are often called, occurred next as each tribe or clan searched for a geographical location it wanted for its home.

Although some myths mention extraordinary journeys through the distant mountains to the western or eastern waters, these journeys have been so mythicized as spiritual journeys (the hero twins, for instance, visiting their father, the sun god, at his beautiful turquoise home somewhere in the ocean) that it would be difficult to find in them any clues to support the popular theory that the ancient ancestors migrated instead from Asia to America via the Bering Strait. Perhaps one could argue that the home of White Bead Woman (mother of the "hero twins") somewhere in the distant west is mythological coding for an almost forgotten place of origin beyond the Pacific Ocean, but traditionalists would probably insist on the American southwest as the ancient place of origin. Better "evidence" in support of a land bridge theory may be found in "The Giants" myth of the Chippewa and related Athapaskan-speaking tribes of northwest Canada.

This myth recounts a fierce struggle between two giants, presumably fighting over territory and fishing rights. The defeated giant falls, we are told, with his head on "this country" and his feet on "another land" (Asia?). In other words, the mud-covered giant's body may be the lost "bridge" over which migratory groups traveled in ancient times from Asia to Alaska. Wherever that connection was located, it evidently became a migratory route for deer and, according to some interpretations, for the Athapaskan-speaking Navajo and Apache as they began their extended journeys to their new homes in the Southwest.

More migratory patterns are mentioned in other myths. The northwestern "Story of the Deluge" (Tsimshian) vividly describes a Native American version of a Noah's-Ark flood that destroys most of the human and animal life in the world of the Tsimshians. The result is that the survivors are "scattered everywhere" and they all end up speaking different languages. While it is not clear how far away "everywhere" is, it would probably take at least hundreds of years for new languages to develop; therefore, a vast geographical scope could also be implied by a mythic conflation of time and space in this story. However, other references in the story seem to set it in the northwest region only. Another northwestern myth, "Story of the Kā´ck!e Qoan" (Tlingit), is very specific about times and places as it recounts the forty-day migration of the inland Athapaskans across frozen glaciers to the British Columbian seacoast town of Yakutat. References to migrations in the southwestern origin myths are often equally specific, with the "wanderings" described in lengthy detail by some storytellers. The "Jicarilla Genesis" included in this appendix severely condenses the wanderings into one paragraph but does carefully note that the ancient peoples travel east, west, and south as far as they can until they are stopped by "oceans" in each direction. Only the ancestors of the Jicarilla Apache, we are told, stay in the Taos area of New Mexico. In like manner, some Iroquois myths (not included here) tell about major migrations over much of the country east of the Mississippi River and, rather intriguingly, mention one tribe crossing over the Mississippi and disappearing into the unknown regions farther west.

Some of the myths note the existence of an older group of Indians who preceded the ancestors of the present-day Native Americans. The cluster of myths listed here under the title "The Age of the Gods, or The Story of the Twins," for instance, seems to refer to the cliff-dwelling Anasazi, called the "Ancient Ones" by the Navajo. The Ancient Ones are characterized as fierce and fearsome warriors who once lived and cultivated crops in the canyon valleys and then either moved on to new places once the canyon soil was depleted of nutrients or eventually moved up into caves and human-made dwellings carved out of the high cliffs surrounding the valleys for their own protection in more dangerous times. Modern readers may misread this story sequence as some kind of ongoing war between various animal groups (i.e., Bear Maiden destroys the cliff-dwelling Swallow People out of revenge for the murder of her Coyote husband), but the animal designations more than likely indicate the historical clans that were created back in post-emergent times when, according to the myths, the animal-spirit known as Grandmother Spider gave an animal emblem to each group of people. Historians today may still argue over what happened to the cliff-dwellers, but the Navajo myths identify the cliff-dwelling Swallow People (i.e., the ancient Indians of the Swallow

Clan) as one of the obstructions destroyed by the sacred twins so that the earth could be made habitable for the Navajo and other tribes that were created later and still exist today.

Many other myths cannot be linked to a particular historical period or event, but they do give some sense of the ongoing problems the tribes historically dealt with. As the next cluster of stories in the appendix shows, finding sufficient food resources was sometimes a major and ongoing problem. In the northwestern story "The Trickster Becomes a Dish" (Lillooet), the brother becomes seriously ill from an inadequate diet because the nutritious salmon are being hoarded by a group of selfish spirit-beings. By freeing the salmon and directing them to the various rivers, trickster ensures a plentiful food supply for his brother and for the future human tribes. Variations on this "release of the animals" motif can be found in many Native American myths. In the important Sioux myth "The White Buffalo Woman," the hunger of the tribe is movingly described; it is alleviated only when the spirit of the buffalo (White Buffalo Woman) brings the buffalo herds to the tribe.

In these myths, as well as the following planting myths and songs, food resources are considered gifts from the spirit world, but the stories also indicate that the renewability or depletion of those resources is dependent upon the attitudes and behaviors of the human beings. Many of the northwestern salmon tales, for instance, carefully specify the proper ways to dispose of salmon bones if the people want the salmon to return in large numbers. Likewise, the Cherokee myth "Origin of Disease and Medicine" insists on the performance of a ritual over a dead deer to indicate that the hunter possesses the proper attitude toward the deer spirits willing to sacrifice their lives for the benefit of the hungry people. On the other hand, in the Sioux tale of "The White Buffalo Woman," the disrespectful attitude of a warrior who crudely accosts the beautiful female spirit of the buffalo is associated with the scarcity of the buffalo. In contrast, the proper attitude of the hunter toward the corn goddess in the Cherokee myth "The Hunter and Selu" changes him from a hungry and lonely failure into "the most successful of all the hunters in the settlements."

In many cases, Native American myths seem to exist less as "history" than as explanations for the various ceremonies and rituals historically practiced by the tribes. Thus, the sacred pipe was (and still is) cherished because, as the myth explains, White Buffalo Woman brought it as a gift (along with many ceremonial instructions) to the people who honored her; she wanted them to have a way to communicate with the spirit world after she departed. Likewise, many corn mother or corn maiden myths function as explanations of the corn-planting ceremonies used by the tribes to attract rain for the crops. This active participation in the growth of their crops through invocations of the spirits that activate the natural processes is succinctly captured in the Navajo "Songs in the Garden of the House God," which form a small part of an elaborate ceremony called "Night Chant." Like most Native American song chants, these songs do not describe a present or past event, but rather the future result hoped for, as taught by the Harvest God. They are prayers for adequate moisture ("The corn grows up. The Waters of the dark mist drop, drop") and for a plentiful harvest, an exciting event in which everyone in the tribe is eager to be involved ("Shall I? Shall you?"). If the tribe assists in creating the proper alignment of human, natural, and supernatural worlds, everyone will have plenty to eat.

Because the thoughts and actions of the earlier spirit-beings often determined the conditions of later human life, it should come as no surprise that disease was also created by those same spirit-beings, although the reason might not be anticipated—to make sure the world does not become overpopulated, according to the earlier Navajo myth "The Story of the Four Last Ills." In an interesting variation, the Cherokee "Origin of Disease and Medicine" explains that the prehistoric animal-people were also advocating population control—in this case, because the thriving human population was endangering animal life. However, once the animal-people create diseases to keep humans in check, the plant-people agree to provide the cures, thereby ensuring an appropriate balance in the universe. That same balance is maintained in the unusual courtship myth "The Story of San´hode´di's Medicine" (Navajo) in which the spirit-being San´hode´di creates "dreadful sores" all over his body and then cures himself, thus making possible the medicines the tribes can use later. One of the most famous cures of all is the Navajo "Night Chant," an elaborate ceremony accompanied by sacred sandpaintings; it is performed over a period of nine days during which the patient prays not just for physical health, but also for spiritual well-being and a life surrounded by beauty and harmony (see "Night Chant Prayer"). What is notable about these myths and songs is their positive, sometimes even humorous, tone as they assure the listeners that they have access to supernatural healing powers and resources.

If beliefs such as these gave meaning and hope to many Native Americans over the centuries, they were also responsible for the identity crisis experienced later when the tribes saw their way of life and their sense of who they were in relation to the universe eroding and finally being destroyed by the coming of the Euro-Americans. This problem is apparent in Native American accounts of their first encounters with new European diseases like the deadly smallpox. As they discovered, their traditional medicines could not cure it. In the selection from the Tsimshian myth "TsEgu´ksk^u," a shaman of the older school undergoes several death experiences followed by an equal number of miraculous resurrections, but that cyclic pattern is disrupted in what appears to be a second and later ending in which the shaman suddenly loses his supernatural powers and dies for the last time. Abruptly and with curt understatement, the myth informs us that "the epidemic continued for some time, and all the people died. This was the first visitation of smallpox." The shock of this ending drives home the point that the deaths of the shaman and of the entire tribe symbolically mark the death of the old beliefs that were powerless before the destructive force of the Euro-American diseases.

This sense of a myth evolving over time until it reaches a cultural deadend is even stronger in the Haida myth "Story of the Shaman, G.A´ndox's-Father." Although this myth suffers from an awkward translation (or perhaps a less talented storyteller), the selection included here opens with a dramatic image of the supernatural origins of disease. The moon god's son, Wu´ltc!ixaiya, batters down the door to the "House of Pestilence" in order to rescue his sister (save her from disease?). Unfortunately, opening that door also releases sickness into the world, but Wu´ltc!ixaiya has another spirit perform a ceremonial dance and chant that bring about a cure. At this point, the myth moves over to the human realm where spirit-inspired shamans base their curing methods on the supernatural model. However, the last portion of this myth, which shows the later influence of white beliefs, proposes an alternate theory of illness in a strange and vaguely Christianized dream-vision. It includes an odd kind of triune God (with "three sets of clothing"), a rather garbled reference to the crucifixion, and a devil-like being "with a black skin" who sends sickness into the world to punish those who behave badly. The idea of disease as divine punishment can be found occasionally in Native myths, as in "The People of the Stone Houses" (Navajo), but it is here being reinterpreted as the punishment administered by the white man's divinity for Indian wrong-doings, and no cure or "balance" is mentioned. Instead, once again, an abrupt ending marks the end of the old ways. The shaman dies and, as we are informed, there is nothing left to say. Unfortunately, this stunned response may have been common among disillusioned Native Americans who had lost the reassuring explanatory power of their centuries-old beliefs.

Not all "first encounter" tales employ the mythic method, yet even relatively straightforward oral histories about early Native-white relations can pose some problems in interpretation for a modern reader who views them through the lens of historical hindsight. As "literary" creations, some of these tales may gain a certain poignancy and even richly suggestive ambiguity from our modern readings, but it is hard to determine how they would have been transmitted or received in a traditional Native American setting. Take, for instance, the short Chinook narrative "First Ship Seen by the Clatsop." One might view the death of the old woman's son followed by the sudden appearance of the first European ship as ominously foreshadowing the end of Native American culture and the arrival of the new (white) culture that will replace it. However, the old woman's fears about the "monster" ship are ignored by the alternately frightened and curious tribe that burns the ship, enslaves the white men, and then celebrates its newfound wealth (copper, iron, and brass goods taken from the ship). Should this simple story be viewed as an ironic moral tale about how the tribe's greediness deafened them to the warnings about the "monstrous" new era that had begun and would sooner or later destroy the traditional Native American way of life? Or is it a straightforward "history" of how an enterprising tribe took advantage of and thrived for a time in the new circumstances?

At first glance, there seems to be no problem deciding how to interpret an oral narrative like "How the Spaniards Came to Shung-opovi. . . ." It gives the Hopi version of the events leading up to the Pueblo Revolt on August 13, 1680, an event the Pueblo Indians of today still look back to with some pride. According to this narrative, in the seventeenth century some of the southwestern Hopi villages welcomed with open arms the first Spanish explorers and missionaries because the Hopi believed the newcomers were the "Bahana" or the white-spirit savior who would bring some future blessing to them, as predicted in some of their own myths. We can almost imagine them anticipating a kind of White Buffalo Woman experience and revelation. Instead, the rest of the narrative recounts the ways the Spanish priests used fear and intimidation to gain ascendancy over the Indians while those same corrupt priests repeatedly engaged in sexual exploitation of the Hopi wives and especially of the younger teenage girls. It is clear that this narrative was carefully constructed as a persuasive argument justifying the uprising of the pueblos. On the other hand, if the narrative is read as part of the related cycle of historical tales (not included here) about the later return of the Spanish with their armies and their negative impact on pueblo life, that sense of victory gives way rather quickly to a kind of fatalistic pessimism.

The Pueblo Revolt is a good example of a successful defensive alliance being formed among disparate tribes to achieve a larger common goal, but hostilities were not always the norm in everyday Native American life. True, the code of revenge did motivate the hostile actions in the earlier "The Story of the Twins" (Navajo), and it was an important imperative in the early life of Charles Eastman in "First Impressions of Civilization" (Sioux). An even worse picture of intertribal hostilities is provided by the Iroquois "Legend of the Peacemakers," which describes the revenge tradition as out of control and producing near anarchy:

> In those same days the Onondagas had no peace. A man's life was valued as nothing. For any slight offence a man or woman was killed by his enemy and in this manner feuds started between families and clans. At night none dared leave their doorways lest they be struck down by an enemy's war club.

On the other hand, many myths like the "Story of the Kã´ck!e Qoan" (Tlingit) testify to the lengths some tribes were willing to go to avoid violent conflict. In this northwestern myth, when the Athapaskan inlanders experience serious internal conflict, the dissatisfied part of the tribe simply leaves to go find a better place to live. And when the seacoast town of Yakutat decides it does not want the inlander newcomers living there, the wealthy Athapaskans quickly solve the problem by buying the entire town. And "First Ship Seen by the Clatsop" (Chinook) ends with the excitement of the Clatsop town developing into a rich trading center for the entire region. These myths should remind us that many tribes, on a daily basis, were actively involved in trading networks (business enterprises, in modern parlance) and accumulating disposable wealth (copper and iron as money in these tales).

One of the most remarkable examples of a peaceful alliance among formerly warring tribes is the Iroquois Confederacy, also called the League of the Five Nations (later, Six Nations) or the Hodenosaunee by the Native Americans themselves. The world's oldest democracy (still functioning on Iroquois reservations today), this confederacy dominated the eastern half of the United States for at least four centuries from the fourteenth century (or much earlier, according to Native American sources) to the period of the American Revolutionary War (1775–1783). As indicated by the passage quoted earlier, these northeastern nations had a long history of hostilities, but what the "Legend of the Peacemakers" recounts is the formation of a political alliance promoting peaceful interactions among the member tribes and the development of a ritual called the "Condolence Ceremony" to replace the earlier revenge code. This legend celebrates the architects of this Great Peace, namely, the prophet-visionary Deganawida who was idealized into a semi-divine incarnation of the beneficent hero-twin of their creation myth (see "The Woman Who Fell from the Sky"), his historical co-worker and spokesman Ayonhwatha (popularly known, somewhat erroneously, as "Hiawatha"), and the powerful clanswoman Ji-kon-sah-seh who is honored in some versions with the title of "Mother of Nations" or "Peace Queen."

An explanation is needed about the version of the "Peacemakers" legend included in this appendix. Of the many versions that exist, most are rather long and some can take several days for a complete oral recitation; others are too short, omitting many key incidents. Given the space and time constraints involved here, one of the longer versions authorized by the late-nineteenth-century "Keepers" of the Iroquois oral tradition has been condensed, but also supplemented by several selections (indicated in italics) from a second nineteenth-century Native source. The condensed composite tale retains most of the significant episodes most sources agree on and should provide an easy-to-read story that captures the flavor of the longer versions.

One element missing from this composite version is an early reference to the alleged cannibalism of the hero Ayonhwatha before he converts to the Peacemaker's cause. Many earlier myths do refer to cannibal giants existing in ancient times, but no one knows for sure whether those references are to extinct animals like mastodons or saber-toothed tigers that devoured humans, or to an earlier generation of primitive Indians who may have been taller and actually practiced ritual or literal cannibalism, or to the linguistic custom of degrading a tribe's feared enemies by labeling them metaphorically as uncivilized cannibals, to mention a few possibilities. At any rate, the cannibalism motif effectively sets up the legend's central conflict between two opposing ways of relating to others—through violent cannibalism (war) or through persuasive and reasonable conversion (peace)—evidently a central issue in the development of the Iroquois civilization, according to this legend. The Peacemakers' opponent is the terrifying Adodarhoh whose reputation for cannibalistic and other "crazy" behavior is metaphorically and vividly represented in the tale by his twisted shape and his "long tangled locks . . . adorned by writhing living snakes." He forms an appropriate contrast to the peace-loving Deganawida elevated up to demigod status by his miraculous birth and magical white stone canoe, as well as other supernatural powers.

A recognized power player during the period of white colonial conquest, the Iroquois proved to be a crucial factor in helping the English win the French and Indian War (1754–1763), but the Iroquois alliance with England also put the Indians on the losing side during and after the American Revolutionary War. However, the historical anecdote titled "Cornplanter and Washington" about the negotiations between the Seneca Chief Cornplanter and George Washington reveals a still-confident Native confederacy. Based on their past experiences, the Iroquois are sure they are more than equal to whatever forces, Indian or White, they must deal with. In stark contrast is the brilliant but bitter satire "How the White Race Came to America" by Handsome Lake (1735–1815). To this Seneca prophet-reformer, the negative impact of Euro-American imperialistic ambitions could only be explained as the work of the Christian devil bent on destroying the Indian nations. Handsome Lake's code of temperance, tradition, and adaptation (called Gai'wiio' or "Good Message") was his attempt to restore moral dignity to the rapidly declining Iroquois.

The last three selections in this appendix bring us to the end of the nineteenth century and to the end of Native American resistance to the westward expansion of white civilization. Yet, according to Charles Eastman (1858–1939) in his autobiography *Indian Boyhood* (1902), that end was relatively painless for some. In his chapter "First Impressions of Civilization," Eastman, or Ohiyesa, as he was called in his youth, is raised to be a warrior who will take honorable revenge on the whites who supposedly killed his father in the 1862 Minnesota uprising, but he also records his fascination with white inventions like the great trains roaring across the plains. When his father, who was captured and imprisoned rather than killed, shows up later, the teenage boy is introduced to a very different lifestyle; his father had become a Christian convert living and working among the whites in Flandreau, South Dakota. Educated in white schools, the younger Eastman would later earn a medical degree. Both father and son are good examples of Indians who successfully adapted to the changing times, but it must have been an ironic twist of fate that brought Dr. Eastman to the Pine Ridge Reservation Agency, not far from Wounded Knee Creek, in the tragic year of 1890.

For Native Americans, December 29, 1890, is one of those dates that will go down in infamy. That was the day of the Wounded Knee Massacre perpetrated by five hundred U.S. soldiers who surrounded and opened fire on the Chief Big Foot encampment, which consisted of approximately three hundred fifty women, children, and mostly old men. Nearly all the western tribes had been subdued by that time, but the rapid spread of the new Ghost Dance religion among Native Americans during the previous year or two had aroused white fears of renewed militancy among the Indians even though Wovoka (1856–1932), the Northern Paiute messianic leader, preached pacifism. As can be seen in the moving "Songs of the Ghost Dance" included here, Wovoka's followers were desperately trying to invoke a mystically transformed world that would restore to them their dead loved ones as well as the missing great buffalo herds. The images in the songs create a vision of a renewed world coming into view, accompanied by fog, lightning, and whirlwinds, and mysteriously eliminating the whites without any action on the part of Native Americans except ritual dancing and praying. The Wounded Knee Massacre was the last "battle" of the Indian wars.

Although modern literature and myths are beyond the scope of this appendix, it is worthwhile for readers to remember that Native American "history" did not end with the passing of the nineteenth century. In fact, the twentieth century witnessed a Native American "renaissance" of sorts as modern writers attempted to negotiate the gap between past and present by creating written records preserving the meaning and significance of their oral traditions. One cannot help but think of Pulitzer Prize winner N. Scott Momaday writing about his personal rediscovery of the oral myths and histories of his Kiowa past and their meanings to him in his autobiographical *The Way to Rainy Mountain* (1969), or of Leslie Marmon Silko's remarkable Laguna Pueblo novel *Ceremony* (1977) about the relevance of traditional Native American wisdom to the post-modern dilemmas of our own times, or of the post-modern resurrection of the traditional Chippewa trickster in Gerald Vizenor's *Bearheart* (1990).

The technologies of the printed word introduced by white culture may have largely superseded the venerable Native American traditions of oral myth and history, yet, as was discovered by Charles Eastman and Nicholas Black Elk whose Native autobiographies were intended for publication, the newer modes of expression and communication can also play a significant role in preserving Native American oral traditions and perspectives on the past. It is hoped that the collection of myths, narratives, and songs in this appendix will contribute in its own small way to that larger goal.

Kathleen L. Nichols

Note: *Any bracketed information in the following texts indicates brief identifications inserted by the present editor. Information in parenthesis was already part of the original source.*

THE WOMAN WHO FELL FROM THE SKY (*Seneca*)

The "falling woman" or "earth diver" motif is typical of northeastern origin myths. The daughter of Falling Woman is the mother of the "hero-twins" and often considered the corn mother goddess and the mother of the human tribes as well. The twins' rivalries may represent the balance between extremes, the struggle between summer and winter, or the victory of farming cultures over hunting cultures, depending on the myth consulted.

A long time ago human beings lived high up in what is now called heaven. They had a great and illustrious chief.

It so happened that this chief's daughter was taken very ill with a strange affection. All the people were very anxious as to the outcome of her illness. Every known remedy was tried in an attempt to cure her, but none had any effect.

Near the lodge of this chief stood a great tree, which every year bore corn used for food. One of the friends of the chief had a dream, in which he was advised to tell the chief that in order to cure his daughter he must lay her beside this tree, and that he must have the tree dug up. This advice was carried out to the letter. While the people were at work and the young woman lay there, a young man came along. He was very angry and said: "It is not at all right to destroy this tree. Its fruit is all that we have to live on." With this remark he gave the young woman who lay there ill a shove with his foot, causing her to fall into the hole that had been dug.

Now, that hole opened into this world, which was then all water, on which floated waterfowl of many kinds. There was no land at that time. It came to pass that as these waterfowl saw this young woman falling they shouted, "Let us receive her," whereupon they, at least some of them, joined their bodies together, and the young woman fell on this platform of bodies. When these were wearied they asked, "Who will volunteer to care for this woman?" The great Turtle then took her, and when he got tired of holding her, he in turn asked who would take his place. At last the question arose as to what they should do to provide her with a permanent resting place in this world. Finally it was decided to prepare the earth, on which she would live in the future. To do this it was determined that soil from the bottom of the primal sea should be brought up and placed on the broad, firm carapace of the Turtle, where it would increase in size to such an extent that it would accommodate all the creatures that should be produced thereafter. After much discussion the toad was finally persuaded to dive to the bottom of the waters in search of soil. Bravely making the attempt, he succeeded in bringing up soil from the depths of the sea. This was carefully spread over the carapace of the Turtle, and at once both began to grow in size and depth.

After the young woman recovered from the illness from which she suffered when she was cast down from the upper world, she built herself a shelter, in which she lived quite contentedly. In the course of time she brought forth a girl baby, who grew rapidly in size and intelligence.

When the daughter had grown to young womanhood, the mother and she were accustomed to go out to dig wild potatoes. Her mother had said to her that in doing this she must face the West at all times. Before long the young daughter gave signs that she was about to become a mother. Her mother reproved her, saying that she had violated the injunction not to face the east, as her condition showed that she had faced the wrong way while digging potatoes. It is said that the breath of the West Wind had entered her person, causing conception. When the days of her delivery were at hand, she overheard twins within her body in a hot debate as to which should be born first and as to the proper place of exit, one declaring that he was going to emerge through the armpit of his mother, the other saying that he would emerge in the natural way. The first one born, who was of a reddish color, was called Othagwenda; that is, Flint. The other, who was light in color, was called Djuskaha; that is, the Little Sprout.

The grandmother of the twins liked Djuskaha and hated the other; so they cast Othagwenda into a hollow tree some distance from the lodge.

The boy that remained in the lodge grew very rapidly, and soon was able to make himself bows and arrows and to go out to hunt in the vicinity. Finally, for several days he returned home without his bow and arrows. At last he was asked why he had to have a new bow and arrows every morning. He replied that there was a young boy in a hollow tree in the neighborhood who used them. The grandmother inquired where the tree stood, and he told her; whereupon then they went there and brought the other boy home again.

When the boys had grown to man's estate, they decided that it was necessary for them to increase the size of their island, so they agreed to start out together, afterward separating to create forests and lakes and other things. They parted as agreed, Othagwenda going westward and Djuskaha eastward. In the course of time, on returning, they met in their shelter or lodge at night, then agreeing to go the next day to see what each had made. First they went west to see what Othagwenda had made. It was found that he had made the country all rocks and full of ledges, and also a mosquito which was very large. Djuskaha asked the mosquito to run, in

order that he might see whether the insect could fight. The mosquito ran, and sticking his bill through a sapling, thereby made it fall, at which Djuskaha said, "That will not be right, for you would kill the people who are about to come." So, seizing him, he rubbed him down in his hands, causing him to become very small; then he blew on the mosquito, whereupon he flew away. He also modified some of the other animals which his brother had made. After returning to their lodge, they agreed to go the next day to see what Djuskaha had fashioned. On visiting the east the next day, they found that Djuskaha had made a large number of animals which were so fat that they could hardly move; that he had made the sugar-maple trees to drop syrup; that he had made the sycamore tree to bear fine fruit; that the rivers were so formed that half the water flowed upstream and the other half downstream. Then the reddish-colored brother, Othagwenda, was greatly displeased with what his brother had made, saying that the people who were about to come would live too easily and be too happy. So he shook violently the various animals—the bears, deer, and turkeys—causing them to become small at once, a characteristic which attached itself to their descendants. He also caused the sugar maple to drop sweetened water only, and the fruit of the sycamore to become small and useless; and lastly he caused the water of the rivers to flow in only one direction, because the original plan would make it too easy for the human beings who were about to come to navigate the streams.

The inspection of each other's work resulted in a deadly disagreement between the brothers, who finally came to grips and blows, and Othagwenda was killed in the fierce struggle.

Source: Curtin, Jeremiah, and J. N. B. Hewitt. *Report of the Bureau of American Ethnology* 32 (1918); repr. Stith Thompson, *Tales of the North American Indians* (1929; Bloomington, IN: Indiana University Press, 1966).

THE JICARILLA GENESIS *(Selection: Jicarilla Apache)*

Southwestern origin myths typically begin with an "emergence" out of several cave-like inner worlds within the earth, followed by a series of "migrations" once the tribes reach the earth's surface and search for places to settle. The distinctions between insect-

people, animal-people, and human-people are not always clear among these earliest beings who existed long before the later creation of the Jicarilla Apache.

In the beginning the earth was covered with water, and all living things were below in the underworld. Then people could talk, the animals could talk, the trees could talk, and the rocks could talk.

It was dark in the underworld, and they used eagle plumes for torches. The people and the animals that go about by day wanted more light, but the night animals—the Bear, the Panther, and the Owl—wanted darkness. They disputed long, and at last agreed to play the *käyoñ´ti* game to decide the matter. It was agreed that if the day animals won there should be light, but if the night animals won it should be always dark.

The game began, but the Magpie and the Quail, which love the light and have sharp eyes, watched until they could see the button through the thin wood of the hollow stick, and they told the people under which one it was. They played once, and the people won. The morning star came out and the Black-bear ran and hid in the darkness. They played again, and the people won. It grew bright in the east and the Brown-bear ran and hid himself in a dark place. They played a third time, and the people won. It grew brighter in the east and the Mountain-lion slunk away into the darkness. They played a fourth time, and again the people won. The Sun came up in the east, and it was day, and the Owl flew away and hid himself.

Still the people were below and did not see many things, but the Sun staid higher up and saw more. The Sun looked through a hole and saw that there was another world, this earth above. He told the people and they wanted to go there; so they built four mounds by which to reach the upper world. In the east they built a mound and planted it with all kinds of fruits and berries that were black in color. In the south they built another mound and planted on it all kinds of fruits that were blue. In the west they built another mound and planted upon it fruits that were yellow; and in the north they built a mound, and on it they planted all fruits of variegated colors.

The mounds grew into mountains and the bushes went from blossom to ripened berries, and one day two girls climbed up to pick berries and to gather flowers to tie in their hair. Then the mountains stopped growing. The people wondered, and they sent Tornado to learn the cause. Tornado goes everywhere and searches into every corner, and he found the two girls picking berries on the mountain, and he came back and told the people. Then they sent Tornado again to bring the girls home, and he brought them back to their people, but the mountains did not grow any more. This is why a boy stops growing when he goes for the first time with a woman. If he did not go with a woman he would continue to grow constantly taller.

The mountains had stopped growing while their tops were yet a long way from the upper world, and the people debated how they could get up to the earth. They laid feathers crosswise for a ladder, but the feathers were too weak and they broke. They made a second ladder of larger feathers, but again they were too weak. They made a third ladder, of eagle feathers, but even these were not strong enough to bear their weight. Then the Buffalo came and offered his right horn to make a ladder, and three others came and offered their right horns also. The Buffalo horns were strong, and by their help the people were able to climb up through the hole to the surface of the earth; but their weight bent the Buffalo horns, which before were straight, so that they have been curved ever since.

When the people had come up from under the earth they fastened the Sun and Moon with spider threads, so that they could not get away, and sent them up into the sky to give light. But water covered the whole earth, so four Storms went to roll the waters away. The Black-storm blew to the east and rolled up the waters into the eastern ocean. The Blue-storm blew to the south and rolled up the waters in that direction. The Yellow storm rolled up the waters in the west, and the Varicolored-storm went to the north and rolled up the waters there. So were formed the four oceans—in the east, the south, the west, and the north. Having rolled up the waters, the Storms returned to where the people were waiting at the mouth of the hole.

First went out the Polecat, but the ground was still soft, and his legs sank in the black mud and remain black ever since. They sent the Tornado to bring him back, for the time was not yet. The Badger went out, but he, too, sank in the mud, and his legs were blackened, so they sent the Tornado to call him back. The Beaver went out, wading through the mud and swimming through the water. He began at once to build a dam to save the water still remaining in pools, and he did not return. The Tornado was sent after him and found him at work, and asked him why he had not come back. "Because I wanted to save the water for the people to drink," said the Beaver. "Good," said Tornado, and they went back together. They waited again, and then sent out the Crow to see if it was yet time. The Crow found the earth dry, and many dead frogs, fish, and reptiles lying on the ground. He began picking out their eyes, and did not return until Tornado was sent after him. The people were angry when they found he had been eating carrion, and they changed his color to black, which before was gray.

The earth was now all dry, excepting the four oceans around it and the lake in the center, where the Beaver had dammed up the waters. All the people came up. They went east until they came to the ocean; then they turned south until they came again to the ocean; then they turned west until they came again to the ocean, and then they turned north, and as they went each tribe stopped where it would. But the Jicarillas continued to circle around the place where they had come up from the underworld. Three times they went around, when the Ruler became displeased, and asked them where they wished to stop. They said, "In the middle of the earth;" so he led them to a place very near to Taos and left them there, and the Taos Indians lived near them.

Then he laid down the great mountains—the mountain beyond Durango, west of the Rio Grande; the Sierra Blanca, east of the Rio Grande, and the other mountain to the southeast of Taos. He made also the four great rivers and gave them their names—in the north the *Napĕshtĭ*, the "flint arrow" river (the Arkansas); in the east the Canadian; in the south the Rio Grande, and in the west the Chama, and he gave the country to the Jicarillas. He made other rivers, but did not give them names.

While the Jicarillas were moving about they by accident left a girl behind them near the place where they had come up from the underworld. The girl's name was *Yo'lkai'-ĭstsû'n*, the "White-bead woman." The Sun shone upon her as she sat and she bore a boy child, and the Moon beamed upon her as she slept and she bore another boy child. The first born was stronger than the second, as the Sun is stronger than the Moon. When the boys were large enough to walk the Sun told her where to find her people, and she went to them. . . .

Soon afterward the Sun sent word to the woman to send his son to him. The Moon-boy staid at home with his mother, but the Sun-boy went and found his father at home. His father received him kindly and gave him a bow and arrows and a dress of turquois, with turquois bracelets and wristguard and a necklace of turquois beads for his neck. Then the Sun said to him, "Now you shall be called *Nayé-nayesxû'ni,* 'The destroyer-of-dangerous-things,' because I shall send you to destroy many dangerous things which annoy the people."

[The boys have many adventures while destroying all the dangerous things.]

• • •

When their work was done and the world was made safe, the boys said their last words to the people and started after the Sun along the trail to the west. Twelve men went with them. As they journeyed they came to twelve mountains, one after another, and inside of each mountain the brothers placed a man to wait forever until their return. They went on and on until they went into the western ocean, where they are living now in a house of turquois under the green water.

Source: Mooney, James. "The Jicarilla Genesis." *American Anthropologist* 11, no. 7 (July 1898): 197–209.

THE AGE OF THE GODS, OR THE STORY OF THE TWINS
(Selections: Navajo)

A. The People of the Stone Houses

B. When the Coyote Married the Maiden

C. The Maiden Who Became a Bear

D. The Story of the Last Great Grief, the Swallow People of Mesa Verde

E. The Story of the Four Last Ills

This selection of tales about the "cliff-dwellers" explains, mythologically speaking, what happened to the earliest inhabitants often known as the Anasazi, but called "The Ancient Ones" by the Navajo who are depicted as being a later generation of Native Americans. The creator gods in this series are First Man and First Woman, along with the goddess White Bead Woman who is the mother of the "hero-twins" ("Elder Brother" and "Younger Brother") and of the Navajo people. The hero-twins' adventures involve many more episodes than are presented here.

A. The People of the Stone Houses

Now a certain group of people had already built their houses of stone. They were known as the Blue Bird Clan People. The person at the head of this clan was a woman. She had in her keeping the rock with the 12 months and the seasons marked on it. This rock had been given to her; and by it she was able to know the seasons, the months and the days of the year. Having this rock gave her the knowledge of what is beyond the blue sky, what is under the earth, and what is in the air and the water.

First Man spoke to this woman to whom had been given the Calendar Stone. "I shall go now," he said, "but my work is not yet finished. You will hear of me later." He was thinking that later he would form another tribe which would be called the Dîné [the Navajo].

At this time all the people lived in peace; and all the work that First Man had done was good. He told the different peoples to go over the world and to live as each had been directed. Then he left them.

So it came about that people, human beings, went to the mesa country and built their homes in the caves in the cliffs. They grew to a great number. These people knew how to plant and to care for corn. They learned how to build great houses. They had all that they wanted on the earth. There was plenty, and there was no need to travel afar. It was because of this that they built their houses of stone.

At this time they grew in great numbers and they became a very strong people. But many of them practiced black magic; when they left their homes they traveled in the forms of the coyote, the bird, or the wildcat. It was while in these forms that they began to kill each other. Evil grew among them. They planned to kill First Man.

They learned to build ceremonial rooms, round in form and covered, with the entrance in the roof. They made a ventilator shaft to admit air. These round rooms or kivas were their meeting places, their places of prayer, and also, where some practiced black magic. They set a time when they would go into the kivas and hold meetings. This was the plan of First Man, but they did not know it. Now many of these people did not practice black magic; they were good people. These good men gathered together and formed a plan. They ground a lot of chili, and they dried and ground bile from eagles, hawks, mountain sheep, and mountain lions. This they mixed together to use as a poison. When the time came to go into the kivas, they, the good people, threw the mixture into the fire, and their relatives closed the smoke hole outside. The bad people were killed and the good ones remained unharmed. Now when the relatives of the bad people found

what had happened they turned against First Man. They said that it had been his plan. "Now kill us," they said, "for we have lost our brothers and sisters." First Man heard them and he sent diseases which killed still more of the wicked ones. After the fourth plague was sent among them almost all who practiced black magic were destroyed. The good people went south and grew their corn in other canyons; but after these evil things passed away many of the good people returned to the mesas to live.

B. When the Coyote Married the Maiden

... [The] people lived peacefully for about half a century. Then these strange creatures that were born began to eat the people. There is a little hill called tqnts´i´se ko just across the Mancos Canyon, which used to be a house. It was the home of 12 brothers. (On the top of this hill you can see a ruin.) The brothers were great hunters and hunted all over the mesas. They had one sister. The girl grew to be a beautiful maiden, and the holy men came from far and wide to ask her to marry them.

The maiden's name was Ataed´diy ini. When her brothers were away hunting she stayed at home alone. Now the Coyote came to the brothers and called out: "Brothers-in-law." He wanted this maiden to become his wife.

... But the maiden said that before she would marry him she would have to kill him; and if he could return to life, then he could be her husband. The Coyote hung his head and covered his eyes with his hand for a moment. "Very well," he said, and he went away.

He went a short distance to the east side of the dwelling, and there he formed a little black mountain. He put a tunnel through the mountain, and he traveled still farther to the east. He then took out his lungs and heart and wrapped them in the Black Wind. He returned through the tunnel to the maiden's home. He said: "Now you can do as you wish with me." She got a club and killed him and threw his body on the ash dump. She went into her house, but he followed her. "Are you my wife now?" he asked her.... [This ritual testing is repeated four times.] The maiden asked him how he could do these things. He told her that after she became his wife he would show her his magic. She let the Coyote come. He became her husband and she became his wife....

The following morning when the brothers went out to hunt, the Coyote said that he would go with them. The eldest brother told the others that from then on they could only expect trouble. . . .

They were on a mesa north of the Mancos Canyon when the Coyote came chasing a big ram. (There were many mountain sheep there at that time.) One of the brothers pulled his bow and aimed his arrow at the ram. He shot the arrow and killed the ram. . . .

The brothers dressed the sheep and rolled the meat into a little ball. They told the Coyote to take the meat to his wife and to tell her to have it ready for them when they returned. . . . But no sooner had the [brothers] departed than he put down the meat ball. . . . He walked over to the canyon's edge and he saw that way down in the bottom of the canyon a big game was going on. There were people in the canyon playing this game. They were the Swallow People or cliff dwellers. The Coyote called down to them; he said that they were certainly an ugly people—the men and their wives alike. He said that his wife was beautiful and light of skin.

All this made the cliff people very angry, and they decided to get rid of him, to kill him. . . .

C.   The Maiden Who Became a Bear

When the brothers returned that night they entered the house. Not seeing the Coyote among them their sister . . . asked her eldest brother what they had done with her husband. The eldest brother said: "We sent him back with the meat a long time ago. We thought that you would have the meat cooked for us by now."

. . . Then she went to the rainbow path and there she found the meat. From there she tracked the Coyote to the canyon's edge and she found where he had been killed by the Swallow People. . . .

When the woman returned to the house she told her brothers that the people in the canyon had killed her husband. She would not sit down in the home. She prepared herself to go against the cliff people. First, she took her sewing awls and sharpened them; then she hid her heart and lungs as the Coyote had taught her, and turned herself into a great bear with sharp teeth and claws, and she went forth against the people of the canyon. When she came among them they shot at her with their arrows, but they did not harm her. When she returned home she turned back into her woman form. But every night she went out in her bear form and killed the cliff people with her teeth and claws; however, she did not eat them as a wolf or bear would have done.

It was then that the people moved into the caves in the cliff walls. The Rainbow's strength was their strength. The people, in those days, used a rainbow for their ladder as well as for their bridge. They used it and it was not difficult for them to carry up their goods and to build houses in the caves. For a long time the people abandoned their homes on the floor of the canyon; but the bear woman followed them. She would dig up through the earth and kill them. After that they built their homes of rock in the caves.

. . . After these things happened many people planned to leave the mesas. They were afraid of the Woman who became a bear. They buried the Calendar Stone; they wrapped their dead; and leaving their belongings, they went away. But before they left they drew pictures [pictographs] on the rocks of all the things that trouble came from.

Now only the Swallow People and the Lizard, Snake, and Spider People remained. All the others said that they would never return to make the mesa country their home. They moved into Montezuma Valley and built their homes around Ute Mountain. Their main dwellings were Yucca House and a place near a spring east of Ute Mountain. They multiplied and their homes covered quite a lot of territory. They moved to places where they found good water, good building material, and where their plants would grow. . . .

D.   The Story of the Last Great Grief, the Swallow People of Mesa Verde

There remained the great Swallow People in the Mancos Canyon and beyond. They had been at war ever since the killing of the Coyote.

The Elder Brother said: "Mother, Grandmother, Grandfather, where are the Swallow People to be found?" They told him that they were to be found at a place called Tqo tzosko, Water in the Narrow Canyon. So he started out and traveled to Jackson Canyon.

There were thousands and thousands of Swallow People and he killed them right and left. He killed and killed, and he worked his way to the mouth of Mancos Canyon. Then he began running. He was tired and there were still thousands to be killed. When he reached the second rock near the San Juan River he was very tired. At home, in the hogan, all the medicine sticks were seen burning. The Younger Brother said: "Look, Grandmother, all the medicine sticks are burning." First Woman said: "Hurry and do as your brother told you to do." So the Younger Brother took the smoke from the first stick and blew it on the hailstone next to it, and so on for all four. Then he blew the smoke in the four directions.

A big, black cloud shot out of the sky over the place where the Elder Brother was resting. A great storm broke, thunder, lightning, rain, and hail. This hail destroyed the remaining Swallow People and all the lesser giants who lived in the mesa country.

The Elder Brother caught just one of the Swallow People and he told him that from now on he would be of very little use. "You will be harmless from now on," he said. And he let him go. But he took the scalp of one of the dead Swallow People and started for his home.

On his way someone ran after him. It was Mother Earth, herself. She said: "Grandson, you suffered greatly that time, didn't you?" He said: "Yes, Grandmother, I surely did." And she said: "You are in a hurry; but let me sing you this chant." She sang the two chants for the Twin Brothers.

When the Elder Brother returned to his home with the scalp, the Grandmother danced and chanted four times as before.

E. The Story of the Four Last Ills

The White Bead Woman and First Woman told the Eldest Brother that the four last ills could be found south of their home.

He traveled southward and he found a ragged old man. He was just a bundle of rags. The Elder Brother was about to kill him when he said: "No, my Grandson, you must not kill me, even though I am Tie en, Poverty, for in six months people will have good clothing, and at the end of that time, called autumn, they will use it for the winter, in order to keep themselves warm." The Elder Brother, knowing that the virtue accompanying poverty is appreciation, let him live.

He walked on and he found an old, old woman. He was about to kill her for she was San, Old Age, but she stopped him and said: "No, no, my Grandson, do not kill me. People will grow old. Know that it will be the old people who will tell the young people what happened in years past. It would not be well if there were only young people on the earth. Every growing thing, including human beings will grow old." The Elder Brother knew that wisdom walked with old age, and he let her live.

Then he traveled on and he found the two E ya a´, lice, and he was about to kill them when they said: "No, don't kill us. We shall be seen on animals at different times. When we get on people they will say: 'Sister, there is something on me. Look for it.' Let us live." The Elder Brother let them live, for although they were evils they brought with them compassion.

The fourth ill that the Elder Brother met was a creature of bluish color. "Do not kill me," he said. "I am death, Grandson. Spare me, for if every creature lived there would be no place on earth for youth and laughter." The Elder Brother left him with the others.

He thought great thoughts of the earth and the waters and the sky. If there was no death there could be no new life. . . .

The Twins said that now their work was finished. All the monsters who harmed the people of the earth had been slain. . . . Then the Sun came and said: . . . "I want the White Bead Woman, your mother, to live in a beautiful white shell house in the West. A house like the turquoise house in the East." So the White Bead Woman went to the top of Chol´i´i. . . . With [her] power she was able to make her people, the tribe called Dîné [the Navajo]. This tribe looks upon her as their mother. . . . So it is partly with the power of Wyol gie san, the White Bead Woman, that the monsters were destroyed, and that the tribe called Dîné came to this country and multiplied.

Source: O'Bryan, Aileen. *The Dîné: Origin Myths of the Navaho Indians.* Smithsonian Institution, Bureau of American Ethnology, bulletin 163 (1956).

STORY OF THE DELUGE *(Selection: Tsimshian)*

This northwestern myth is the Native American version of the Noah's Ark Flood, but it is caused, in this case, by youths wantonly destroying nature. The "great deluge" motif is found in many cultures and is combined here with the division of the people into different geographical areas and into different language groups.

There was a town, I might say, on the upper course of Skeena River. This was Prairie Town, and there were very many people—many chiefs, old women, young men, young women, and really many children. They were very foolish, because there were a great many, and the old people did not take care what the children and the youths were doing.

They were almost always happy, and their hearts were glad because they had no enemies to attack them. Therefore they did whatever they pleased. Sometimes a chief made a great feast, and he would kill many slaves; and they did many bad, wicked things.

Then one morning the young men arose to play camping on the other side of Skeena River. There were many youths. After they had finished eating, they went up a little brook up river in order to drink. When they got up there, behold! many trout were jumping in the river. Then they began to fish for trout.

When they had caught a trout, some very bad youths took the trout and opened its mouth and poured urine into the fish's mouth. Then they threw it back into the water. Then it swam about, belly up. Then they all shouted together, and laughed at what the youths had been doing.

Many trout were floating on the water. It was spring when they were doing this, and every day was fine. And while they were doing this, they had a good time. They had been doing this a long time, then the day was at an end.

Suddenly they saw a black fog on the sky; however, the youths did not mind it. They did not mind it when a strong wind and black clouds arrived. Then heavy rain came down to the ground, and the brook where they had been playing with the trout began to rise. The young men did not reach their houses on the other side, but they were all first drowned in the water.

Then a strong wind and rain came. Then the people took up their anchor-stones and put them into the canoes. They used large canoes in those times. All the people of Prairie Town were ready for the Deluge. They took provisions with them, elk-skins, coppers, and every kind of property, and their crests and everything. The people knew that their children had been drowned in the water, therefore they did so.

Now their houses were submerged. The rain lasted for twenty days, and the water was rising. They went farther up every day. The water was rising, and went farther up every day. Then all the people went aboard their canoes. They made houses of elk-skin in their canoes. Now the water passed over

the place where it had been at the former flood. Therefore the people knew that this was going to be a real Deluge.

When the water continued to rise, all the people were in their canoes, and their town was submerged. The very old and the poor people were drowned. All the valleys were flooded, but the canoes floated on the water. The houses of elk-skin were in the canoes, therefore they did not get wet with the rain. Then all the hills were covered by the water; and the canoes were full of foam, because the waters were boiling; while the rain lasted a long time, and the wind was strong.

When the water reached the middle of the mountain, several canoes drifted away one by one, because their anchor-lines broke, and some of their anchor-lines were too short, and they drifted away with their anchor-stones. Then many just went up to the top of the mountain. However, they really died because there was much rain and strong wind.

Then, when all the large canoes were swept away by the wind and the boiling waters, the water stopped and staid there. Then the people of Prairie Town were scattered over the whole earth as far as Alaska and Bella Bella. . . .

Two people were saved on top of the great mountain inland from Prairie Town—one young woman and also one young man. Then the water went down and they walked down. Then they saw that not one tree was left. They were destroyed by the great currents of water. Only clay remained in the whole country.

All the high mountains were not covered by the water. The animals had run up to the tops of the high mountains, and all kinds of animals were saved. . . .

For twenty days the earth was submerged. Then it stopped, and the water began to sink again and went down from the ground. The water went down continually, and all kinds of trees were swallowed by the whirlpool of the sea; and also the corpses of the people and the dead animals and the dead birds, and all the dead snakes—everything was swallowed by the whirlpool of the sea.

Some people did not perish at this time, yet they were scattered around along here. That was when their tongues were mixed. Before the Flood they had one language; after the Flood, when they were scattered everywhere, their languages were different. Therefore the people along here know that they are relatives, although their languages are different; and they know their crests, Eagle, Bear,

Wolf, or Raven—even if they are Tlingit, or from the south as far as Rivers Inlet, and out West as far as the Haida—because they really came from one town before the Deluge, and they were scattered after the Deluge. Although they do not understand their lan-guages, yet they know by their crests that they are relatives. . . .

Source: Boas, Franz. *Tsimshian Texts.* Publications of the American Ethnological Society, vol. 3, part 2 (1912).

THE GIANTS *(Chippewa)*

An older race of giants is often mentioned in Native American myths, but no one knows exactly who or what they were. This fighting giant myth is unique in that it may indicate the presence at some ancient time of a "land bridge" existing between Asia and Alaska, via the Bering Strait.

A giant used to hunt beaver along Lake Athabaska, going about half way to Fond du Lac. He was bringing up a little Indian boy, whom he called his grandchild, and whom he kept alive after killing all the other Indians. In hunting beavers he broke the beavers' lodge, and they all escaped. He broke another lodge. One beaver went across the lake, another up the river. The giant looked around for the former, found a little hole and saw the beaver's head popping out. He struck it with a stick, so hard that blood was sprinkled all over, hence the reddish appearance of the rocks there. The beaver that went up the river escaped, that is why there are many beavers there.

The giant cut off the beaver's tail. Seeing the scales he said, "This is not good to eat," and threw the beaver's tail away. The Indian boy picked it up and put it in the fire. The scales fell off, and the inside was found good to eat. This was the first time the giant ever ate a beaver tail. When through eating, he put his grandson in his mitten, and walked off. He found moose tracks, but said, "These are rabbit tracks." His grandson said to him, "These are not rabbit tracks but

moose tracks." They got a moose, and Hotcowᴇ, the giant, put it in his belt as one would a rabbit. Then he went to the Barren Grounds, and thence to the sea, where he met another giant, named Djéneta. Djéneta was fishing in the ocean with a hook.

Before reaching Djéneta, Hotcowᴇ took his grandson out of his mitten, and bade him approach the fisherman half way and deliver him a challenge to fight. The boy did as he was bidden, and when near enough shouted, "Grandfather!" Djéneta asked, "What do you want?" The boy delivered his message, and ran back, but by that time the giants had already each made a step forward and were already fighting above him. The fisherman was getting the best of the contest, when Hotcowᴇ called to his grandchild, who always carried a beaver tooth, to cut the giant's ankle. The boy obeyed, causing the giant to fall down so that Hotcowᴇ could easily dispatch him.

The fisherman's head fell on this island while his feet reached another land. Mud gathered on his corpse, connecting the island and the other country, and then deer for the first time ran from the new land into this country.

Source: Lowie, Robert Harry. "Chipewyan Tales." *Anthropological Papers of the American Museum of Natural History* 10 (1912): 188–189.

STORY OF THE KÂ´CKǃE QOAN *(Selection: Tlingit)*

The main interests in this myth are the migration of the northern Athapaskan-speaking inlanders travel-ing across large glaciers to their new home by the northwestern seacoast and the importance of copper as a source of wealth in their culture.

Łtᴀxdá´x was dead. He had a valuable copper, and he also had a dish named Tsǃᴀɴᴀtǃû´kǃ. When he was dead they took his property out. Those of the house in which these people lived who obtained the

dish got into trouble over it. Whoever had a sister told her to go with him. "Let us go to some other place," he said. The people that went away were from that side of the house from which the dish was taken away. They were sad on that account. Probably they numbered about forty. They said, "Let us go straight for that mountain." Whoever had three brothers took them along to carry things for him. After that they came out under the brow of the big mountain. On the way they dressed themselves in their fine clothing, some in weasel-skin coats, some in marten-skin coats, and they wore hats also because they wanted to die wearing them. Not very many came away. Many more stayed up there than came out. When they got up to the foot of the mountain they came together to talk over where they should pass through. They came to a place where there were many ground squirrels, which they clubbed. This is why it became foggy. They lost one another in it, and some of them disappeared. It was the fog that they got lost in. Then they let them (those who had disappeared) go. After that they made good headway toward the place whither they were bound. There appeared no place to get through. The mountain seemed to be very close to them.

By and by they came to the very foot of the mountain. There was no place where they could get through. But through the northern part of the mountain passed a glacier, and they went up that way toward the top. They thought that they were all going to die off when they reached the top. They did not come to the highest summit of the mountain, however. Then they put on all of their best clothing for good. They stayed there perhaps five days. They were now going to start on singing the song that they had sung when they left home. The morning of the day after they started away. And they started the song they used to sing up on Copper river. At that time they wore nose pins. When they were about to start from that place they put on weasel hats and coats. All mourned together over the friends they had left behind and over those who had been lost in the fog. When they were through mourning they arose and started off.

The Athapascans did not know about the sea, and they called one another together. They said, "What is that so very blue?" They said, "Let us go down to it. We have saved ourselves," they said. Coming to the lower end of the glacier, they traveled very fast down to the sea. They crossed a river boiling out from under the mountain and almost as large as Copper river. They went down to the sea alongside of the big river. Afterward they stayed down there at the mouth of that river. The first thing they did there was to claim the big mountain (as a crest), because they were the first to pass through it. When winter began to come on they built a house beside the river. They named it Mountain house because they had nearly lost their lives on that mountain. This is why they so named it. They stayed

right there in that house, and the settlement grew into a town.

Then the Cã′dAdūx grew strong. They were the ones who built Mountain house. After they had been there ten years one person began living away from town in order to make the frame of a skin boat....

Then the man sent off six of his nephews. He told them to go along shore in the canoe he had made, to search for people. When the weather was very good they started off. They came down this way to a place opposite Yakutat. There they discovered eulachon and a fish called k!ā′gAn. These were in a creek. They put a small net into it to catch the eulachon, and they put the k!ā′gAn into a small cooking basket while they were still alive. They offended them, however, by laughing at them. Just as day broke they started off. When they got out on the sea there came up a south wind, so that they could not go anywhere. They came right back to their starting point, and their skin canoe was broken. One of them went under it and was killed. They stayed there. Probably they were there for twenty-one days. Then the weather became fair. Meanwhile they lived upon k!ā′gAn and eulachon. When it was good weather they again started off.

At that time the people got over to Yakutat. There were many people in the town, some called Kosk!ē′dî, some L!uq!oe′dî, who refused to let them remain, though they told them truly how they had come out from behind the mountain. They were there for some time. Then they started back to their own place. They came again to the place where their canoe had been broken and remained there for one night. Again they went out. They spent the night in their canoe. Then they came ashore. When they reached the foot of the big mountain they were told that a little girl had been given the name of the woman who followed the sea gull out.

This little girl went out to dig roots and dug up a red [copper?] thing. The thing she dug up was quite long. So they made this into a dish like the one that had been taken away from them. After this dish had been finished they beat the drums for the girl who had followed out the sea gull. At that time a song was composed in remembrance of her. The people remained there one year after the six men had gotten back. Then the ninth month was beginning to come on. At that time a skin canoe came in sight from the direction of Copper river. It was bound southward. The people were called in, and they came, ashore there. These were Kā′gwAntān from the mouth of Copper river. They called them into the house and gave them food. . . .

Now the six brothers started on a journey for the place whence they had all come out. Their uncle told them to go back for a copper plate which was in a valley called Łtaxēn, leading down to Copper river. They did not want to leave it there because it was valuable. When the people first came out, it took them forty days and nights, but the young men took only twenty days and nights. They got back among their friends. When they came among their friends again these wept with them and did not want them to return. But after they had stayed there for some time they went to the valley where was the copper plate. Since they had left their friends no one had been to the valley. The real owner of it, too, was dead. They reached the opposite side of that valley. When they got there they saw the copper, which was very long. It also had eyes and hands. The copper was pointing its hands in the direction whither its friends had gone. They cut it in two in the middle and took it apart. Then all six of them carried it. Their friends did not bother them about it at all. They started back. Again they traveled for twenty days, and came down to the ocean once more.

At that time all the people started for Yakutat. They started off with the copper that the six men had brought out. Again they came out to the place where their canoe had been broken up. They camped there one night. From there they started across to Yakutat. They came ashore there. Then the people did not want to have them there. The Kosk!ē´dî did not want to let them stay. They discovered Duqdanē´kᵘ (one of the new arrivals) coming from a small stream called Kâck! with some humpbacks he had speared. When the Kosk!ē´dî saw him coming with a string of humpbacks they cut the string on which they were hung. They also broke his spear. Then the people were grieved over what had been done to him. They called one another together about it and thought it best to buy the place and pay for it once and for all. So they bought the place. The six brothers were the ones who got it. They bought it for the copper plate, which was worth ten slaves, and sent the Kosk!ē´dî away. Afterward things were compared to the six Athapascan brothers (because they were very fast runners). They stayed here probably twenty years. . . .

Source: Swanton, John R. *Tlingit Myths and Texts.* Smithsonian Institution, Bureau of American Ethnology, bulletin 39 (1909).

THE TRICKSTER BECOMES A DISH *(Lillooet)*

The various "tricksters" that populate Native American tales can also function as benefactors, as in this northwestern myth of the release of the salmon. The "release of the animals" is a common theme in many tribal myths.

Two brothers lived at the very head waters of the Upper Lillooet River, and spent most of their time training themselves in the neighboring mountains, for they wished to become great. One of them became ill, and had to remain at home. After four years' illness, he became weak, and so thin that he seemed nothing but skin and bones. His brother grew anxious about him, and stopped his training. He hunted, and brought in rabbits, squirrel, and all kinds of meat, for his sick brother. He also threw small pieces of stick into the water, making them turn into fish. Then he caught them and gave them to his brother to eat. But no kind of food seemed to agree with the invalid, for he rapidly grew weaker and thinner.

When the youth saw that no food did his brother good, he made up his mind to take him away to some other place to be cured. They embarked in a canoe, and proceeded down the Lillooet River, giving names to all the places as they passed along. They came to a place they called Ilamux. Here there was a rock which dammed the river. They made a hole through it to allow their canoe to pass. Even at the present day it appears like a stone bridge across the river. Proceeding, they came to a place they called Komelux. Here two creeks, running from opposite directions, met each other with very great force. They made the water smooth enough to be safe for a canoe to pass. Proceeding, they came to a place they named Kulexwin. Here there was a steep, rocky mountain close to the river. They threw their medicine-mat at it, and it became flat like a mat.

Thus they proceeded down to Big and Little Lillooet Lakes and the Lower Lillooet River, until they reached Harrison Lake. All the way along they gave names to the places, made the waters navigable, and changed many features of the country. They reached Fraser River, went down to its mouth, and proceeded out to sea to the land of the salmon. When they arrived there, the strong brother hid himself, while the sick man transformed himself into a wooden dish, nicely painted and carved; and in this form he floated against the dam inside of which the people kept the salmon. A man found the dish, and took it to his daughter, who admired it very much, and used it to eat from. Whatever salmon she left in the dish over night always disappeared; but she did not care, because salmon were plentiful.

The dish ate the salmon, or, rather, the sick brother in dish form; and soon he became fat and well again. The other brother left his hiding-place every night to see the invalid, and to eat salmon out of the basket into which the people threw their leavings. He was glad to see his brother getting well so rapidly. When he had become very fat, his brother told him it was time they departed: so one night he broke the dam, and let the salmon out. Then they embarked in their canoe, and led the salmon toward the mouth of the Fraser River.

The salmon traveled very fast, and by the next morning they had reached the river. As they ascended, they took pieces of salmon from their basket, and threw them into the different creeks and rivers. Wherever they threw pieces of salmon, some of the fish followed. Thus they introduced the salmon into the streams of the interior. "Henceforth," said they, "salmon shall run at this time each year, and the people shall become acquainted with them and eat them." Then the brothers returned to their home at the head of the Upper Lillooet River, and they made near their house the hot springs called Tcîq, which they used for cooking their food.

Source: Teit, James A. "Traditions of the Lillooet Indians." *Journal of American Folk-Lore* 25, no. 7; repr. Stith Thompson, *Tales of the North American Indians* (1929; Bloomington, IN: Indiana University Press, 1966).

MYTH OF THE WHITE BUFFALO WOMAN *(Selection: Sioux)*

White Buffalo Woman is one of the most cherished animal-people spirits in Sioux culture and her gift of the sacred pipe is still carefully protected today. Contemporary Native Americans also associate white buffalo with messages from the spirit-world.

Many generations ago, when the Lakota still dwelt beside the lake far away in the east, they experienced a winter of terrible severity. The snow lay deep on the ground, and the streams were frozen to their very beds. Every day could be heard the sharp crack of trees as the frost gnawed at their hearts; and at night the piles of skins and the blazing fires in the tipis scarcely sufficed to keep the blood coursing through the veins. Game seemed to have deserted the country, for though the hunters often faced the hardships of the winter chase, they returned empty-handed, and the wail of hungry women and children joined with the moan of the forest. When finally a tardy spring arrived, it was decided to leave a country so exposed to the anger of Wazíya, Spirit of the North, and seek a better homeland in the direction of the sunset, where ruled the Wing Flappers, who existed from the beginning.

There was little enough to pack besides tipis and fur robes, and what few dogs had not been eaten were soon harnessed to the laden travaux. Two young men were sent in advance. No pair could have been more different in their nature than these two, for while one was brave, chivalrous, unselfish, and kind, the other's heart was bad, and he thought only of the sensuous and vicious.

Unencumbered as they were, the scouts were soon far ahead of the wearily dragging line of haggard men, women bent under burdens that dogs should have been drawing, straggling children, and a few gaunt dogs tugging at the overladen travaux. Late in the day the scouts succeeded in shooting a deer, and thinking their people would reach that point for the night's camp, they left it where it had fallen and were turning away to seek other game when one of them felt a sudden impulse to look back. Wonderful sight! There in a mist that rose above a little hill appeared the outline of a woman. As they gazed in astonishment, the cloud slowly lifted, and the young men saw that she was a maiden fair and beautiful. Her only dress was a short skirt, wristlets, and anklets, all of sage. In the crook of her left arm she carried a bundle wrapped closely in a red buffalo-skin; on her back was a quiver, and in her left hand she held a bunch of herbs. Straightway the young man whose heart was evil was overpowered by a desire to possess the beautiful woman, but his companion endeavored to dissuade him with the caution that she might be *wakán* and a messenger from the Great Mystery.

"No, no!" he cried vehemently, "she is not holy, but a woman, human like ourselves, and I will have her!"

Without waiting he ran toward the woman, who forthwith warned him that she was a sacred being. When he persisted and went closer, she commanded him sternly to stop, for his heart was evil and he was unworthy to come near to the holy things she bore. As he still advanced, she retreated, laid her burden on the ground, and then came toward him. Suddenly it appeared to the waiting youth that the mist descended and enveloped the mysterious woman and his companion. Then followed a fearful sound of rattling and hissing as of thousands of angered rattlesnakes. The terrified observer was about to flee from the dreadful place when the cloud lifted as suddenly as it had descended, disclosing the bleached bones of his former comrade, and the beautiful virgin standing calmly beside them. She spoke to him gently, bidding him have no fear, for he was chosen to be priest of his nation.

"I have many things to impart to your people," she said. "Go now to the place where they are encamped, and bid them prepare for my coming. Build a great circle of green boughs, leaving an opening at the east. In the centre erect a council tipi, and over the ground inside spread sage thickly. In the morning I shall come."

Filled with awe, the young man hastened back and delivered to his people the message of the holy woman. Under his direction her commands were reverently obeyed, for were they not a message from the Great Mystery? In the morning, gathered within the circle of green boughs, they waited in great expectancy, looking for the messenger of the Mystery to enter through the opening left at the east. Suddenly, obeying a common impulse, they turned and looked in the opposite direction, and behold! she stood before them.

Entering the tipi with a number of just and upright men selected by the youth whom she had chosen to receive the sacred rites, she at once spread open the red buffalo-skin, exposing its contents—tobacco, the feather of a spotted eagle, the skin of a red-headed woodpecker, a roll of buffalo-hair, a few braids of sweet-grass, and, chief of all, a red stone pipe with the carved image of a buffalo calf surmounting its wooden stem. At the same time she explained that the Great Mystery had sent her to reveal to them his laws, and teach them how to worship, that they might become a great and powerful people.

During the four days she remained with them in the tipi she instructed them in the customs they were to observe—how the man who would have great *wakán* power should go into the high places and fast for many days, when he would see visions and obtain strength from the Mysteries; how to punish him of evil heart who sinned against the rights of his brother; how to instruct girls at maturity, and to care for the sick. She taught them also how to worship the Great Mystery. . . .

Then she taught them carefully the five great ceremonies they were to observe: . . . the Foster-parent Chant, the Sun Dance, the Vision Cry, the Buffalo Chant, and the Ghost Keeper. The sacred pipe she gave into the keeping of the chosen young man, with the admonition that its wrapping should be removed only in cases of direst tribal necessity. From the quiver on her back she took six bows and six arrows, and distributed them among as many young men, renowned for their bravery, hospitality, and truthfulness. These weapons she bade them take, after her departure, to the summit of a certain hill, where they would find a herd of six hundred buffalo, all of which they were to kill. In the midst of the herd would be found six men. These also they were to kill, then cut off their ears and attach them to the stem of the sacred pipe. Her last words were these:

"So long as you believe in this pipe and worship the Mystery as I have taught you, so long will you prosper; you will have food in plenty; you will increase and be powerful as a nation. But when you, as a people, cease to reverence the pipe, then will you cease to be a nation."

With these words she left the tipi and went to the opening at the eastern side of the camp-circle. Suddenly she disappeared, and the people, crowding forward to see what had become of her, beheld only a white buffalo cow trotting over the prairie.

Source: Curtis, Edward S. *The North American Indian* 3 (1908): 56–60.

THE HUNTER AND SELU *(Cherokee)*

Selu is the Cherokee corn goddess. Beautiful spirit-beings known as corn mothers and corn maidens were associated with planting rituals and ceremonies in many different tribes.

A hunter had been tramping over the mountains all day long without finding any game and when the sun went down, he built a fire in a hollow stump, swallowed a few mouthfuls of corn gruel and lay down to sleep, tired out and completely discouraged. About the middle of the night he dreamed and seemed to hear the sound of beautiful singing, which continued until near daybreak and then appeared to die away into the upper air.

All next day he hunted with the same poor success, and at night made his lonely camp again, in the woods. He slept and the strange dream came to him again, but so vividly that it seemed to him like an actual happening. Rousing himself before daylight, he still heard the song, and feeling sure now that it was real, he went in the direction of the sound and found that it came from a single green stalk of corn (*selu*). The plant spoke to him, and told him to cut off some of its roots and take them to his home in the settlement, and the next morning to chew them and "go to water" before anyone else was awake, and then to go out again into the woods, and he would kill many deer and from that time on would always be successful in the hunt. The corn plant continued to talk, teaching him hunting secrets and telling him always to be generous with the game he took, until it was noon and the sun was high, when it suddenly took the form of a woman and rose gracefully into the air and was gone from sight, leaving the hunter alone in the woods.

He returned home and told his story, and all the people knew that he had seen Selu, the wife of Kana'tǐ. He did as the spirit had directed, and from that time was noted as the most successful of all the hunters in the settlement.

Source: Mooney, James. "Myths of the Cherokee." *Nineteenth Annual Report of the Bureau of American Ethnology 1897–1898*, part 1 (1900): 323–324.

SONGS IN THE GARDEN OF THE HOUSE GOD *(Selections: Navajo)*

These songs were sung to promote, through the assistance of Hastshehogan ("House God"), the healthy growth and plentiful harvest of the bean, corn, and squash crops. As with most Native American song-chants, planting and rain songs are not descriptions of past or present conditions, but prayers for the realization of a future event. In the dry Southwest, the coming of the rain was crucial to a successful harvest.

I
Truly in the East
The white bean
And the great corn-plant
Are tied with the white lightning.
Listen! [rain] approaches!
The voice of the bluebird is heard.
Truly in the East
The white bean
And the great squash
Are tied with the rainbow.
Listen! [rain] approaches!
The voice of the bluebird is heard.

II
From the top of the great corn-plant the water gurgles, I hear it;
Around the roots the water foams, I hear it;
Around the roots of the plants it foams, I hear it;
From their tops the water foams, I hear it.

III
The corn grows up. The waters of the dark clouds drop, drop.
The rain descends. The waters from the corn leaves drop, drop.
The rain descends. The waters from the plants drop, drop.
The corn grows up. The waters of the dark mists drop, drop.

IV
Shall I cull this fruit
Of the great corn-plant?
Shall you break it? Shall I break it?

Shall I break it? Shall you break it?
Shall I? Shall you?
Shall I cull this fruit
Of the great squash vine?
Shall you pick it up? Shall I pick it up?

Shall I pick it up? Shall you pick it up?
Shall I? Shall you?

Source: Matthews, Washington. "Songs of Sequence of the Navajos." *Journal of American Folklore* 7 (1894): 185–194.

ORIGIN OF DISEASE AND MEDICINE *(Cherokee)*

Traditional Cherokee medicine was usually based on the theory that disease is caused by animal spirits, ghosts, or witchcraft. The location of this somewhat humorous tale is the Smoky Mountains on the Tennessee line.

In the old days the beasts, birds, fishes, insects, and plants could all talk, and they and the people lived together in peace and friendship. But as time went on the people increased so rapidly that their settlements spread over the whole earth, and the poor animals found themselves beginning to be cramped for room. This was bad enough, but to make it worse Man invented bows, knives, blowguns, spears, and hooks, and began to slaughter the larger animals, birds, and fishes for their flesh or their skins, while the smaller creatures, such as the frogs and worms, were crushed and trodden upon without thought, out of pure carelessness or contempt. So the animals resolved to consult upon measures for their common safety.

The Bears were the first to meet in council in their townhouse under Kuwâ'hǐ mountain, the "Mulberry place," and the old White Bear chief presided. After each in turn had complained of the way in which Man killed their friends, ate their flesh, and used their skins for his own purposes, it was decided to begin war at once against him. Some one asked what weapons Man used to destroy them. "Bows and arrows, of course," cried all the Bears in chorus. "And what are they made of?" was the next question. "The bow of wood, and the string of our entrails," replied one of the Bears. It was then proposed that they make a bow and some arrows and see if they could not use the same weapons against Man himself. So one Bear got a nice piece of locust wood and another sacrificed himself for the good of the rest in order to furnish a piece of his entrails for the string. But when everything was ready and the first Bear stepped up to make the trial, it was found that in letting the arrow fly after drawing back the bow, his long claws caught the string and spoiled the shot. This was annoying, but some one suggested that they might trim his claws, which was accordingly done, and on a second trial it was found that the arrow went straight to the mark. But here the chief, the old White Bear, objected, saying it was necessary that they should have long claws in order to be able to climb trees. "One of us has already died to furnish the bowstring, and if we now cut off our claws we must all starve together. It is better to trust to the teeth and claws that nature gave us, for it is plain that man's weapons were not intended for us."

No one could think of any better plan, so the old chief dismissed the council and the Bears dispersed to the woods and thickets without having concerted any way to prevent the increase of the human race. Had the result of the council been otherwise, we should now be at war with the Bears, but as it is, the hunter does not even ask the Bear's pardon when he kills one.

The Deer next held a council under their chief, the Little Deer, and after some talk decided to send rheumatism to every hunter who should kill one of them unless he took care to ask their pardon for the offense. They sent notice of their decision to the nearest settlement of Indians and told them at the same time what to do when necessity forced them to kill one of the Deer tribe. Now, whenever the hunter shoots a Deer, the Little Deer, who is swift as the wind and can not be wounded, runs quickly up to the spot and, bending over the blood-stains, asks the spirit of the Deer if it has heard the prayer of the hunter for pardon. If the reply be "Yes," all is well, and the Little Deer goes on his way; but if the reply be "No," he follows on the trail of the hunter, guided by the drops of blood on the ground, until he arrives at his cabin in the settlement, when the Little Deer enters invisibly and strikes the hunter with rheumatism, so that he becomes at once a helpless cripple. No hunter who has regard for his health ever fails to ask pardon of the Deer for killing it, although some hunters who have not learned the prayer may try to turn aside the Little Deer from his pursuit by building a fire behind them in the trail.

Next came the Fishes and Reptiles, who had their own complaints against Man. They held their council together and determined to make their victims dream of snakes twining about them in slimy folds and blowing foul breath in their faces, or to make them dream of eating raw or decaying fish, so that they would lose appetite, sicken, and die. This is why people dream about snakes and fish.

Finally the Birds, Insects, and smaller animals came together for the same purpose, and the Grubworm was chief of the council. It was decided that each in turn should give an opinion, and then they would vote on the question as to whether or not Man was guilty. Seven votes should be enough to condemn him. One after another denounced Man's cruelty and injustice toward the other animals and voted in favor of his death. The Frog spoke first, saying: "We must do something to check the increase of the race, or people will become so numerous that we shall be crowded from off the earth. See how they have kicked me about because I'm ugly, as they say, until my back is covered with sores;" and here he showed the spots on his skin. Next came the Bird—no one remembers now which one it was—who condemned Man "because he burns my feet off," meaning the way in which the hunter barbecues birds by impaling them on a stick set over the fire, so that their feathers and tender feet are singed off. Others followed in the same strain. The Ground-squirrel alone ventured to say a good word for Man, who seldom hurt him because he was so small, but this made the others so angry that they fell upon the Ground-squirrel and tore him with their claws, and the stripes are on his back to this day.

They began then to devise and name so many new diseases, one after another, that had not their invention at last failed them, no one of the human race would have been able to survive. The Grubworm grew constantly more pleased as the name of each disease was called off, until at last they reached the end of the list, when some one proposed to make menstruation sometimes fatal to women. On this he rose-up in his place and cried: "*Wadâñ'!* (Thanks!) I'm glad some more of them will die, for they are getting so thick that they tread on me." The thought fairly made him shake with joy, so that he fell over backward and could not get on his feet again, but had to wriggle off on his back, as the Grubworm has done ever since.

When the Plants, who were friendly to Man, heard what had been done by the animals, they determined to defeat the latter's evil designs. Each Tree, Shrub, and Herb, down even to the Grasses and Mosses, agreed to furnish a cure for some one of the diseases named, and each said: "I shall appear to help Man when he calls upon me in his need." Thus came medicine; and the plants, every one of which has its use if we only knew it, furnish the remedy to counteract the evil wrought by the revengeful animals. Even weeds were made for some good purpose, which we must find out for ourselves. When the doctor does not know what medicine to use for a sick man the spirit of the plant tells him.

Source: Mooney, James. "Myths of the Cherokee." *Nineteenth Annual Report of the Bureau of American Ethnology 1897–1898*, part 1 (1900), 250–252.

A PRAYER OF THE FOURTH DAY OF THE NIGHT CHANT (Navajo)

The nine-day healing ritual called the "Night Chant" features complicated sand-paintings and sacred song-chants like the following one praying for physical, psychological, and spiritual health. Origin myths like some of the ones included above would also be recited.

Tse'gíhi.
House made of the dawn.
House made of evening light.
House made of the dark cloud.
House made of male rain.
House made of dark mist.
House made of female rain.
House made of pollen.
House made of grasshoppers.
Dark cloud is at the door.
The trail out of it is dark cloud.
The zigzag lightning stands high up on it.
Male deity!
Your offering I make.
I have prepared a smoke for you.
Restore my feet for me.
Restore my legs for me.

Restore my body for me.
Restore my mind for me.
Restore my voice for me.
This very day take out your spell for me.
Your spell remove for me.
You have taken it away for me.
Far off it has gone.
Happily I recover.
Happily my interior becomes cool.
Happily I go forth.
My interior feeling cold, may I walk.
No longer sore, may I walk.
Impervious to pain, may I walk.
With lively feelings, may I walk.
As it used to be long ago, may I walk.
Happily may I walk.
Happily with abundant dark clouds, may I walk.

Happily with abundant showers, may I walk.
Happily with abundant plants, may I walk.
Happily on a trail of pollen, may I walk.
Happily may I walk.
Being as it used to be long ago, may I walk.
May it be happy (or beautiful) before me.
May it be beautiful behind me.
May it be beautiful below me.
May it be beautiful above me.
May it be beautiful all around me.
In beauty it is finished.
In beauty it is finished.

Source: Matthews, Washington. "Navaho Myths, Prayers, and Songs." *University of California Publications in American Archaeology and Ethnology* 5, no. 2 (1906).

THE STORY OF SAN´HODE´DI'S MEDICINE (Selection: Navajo)

This myth attributes the origin of the "dreadful sores" diseases, including syphilis, to the spirit San'hode'di who also creates the medicine for curing them.

When San´hode´di arrived at his home the person called Dotso came and whispered to him, saying: "There are two more maidens over here who are calling for suitors. Go try your luck."

Before he went to this village he chewed poison ivy and blew some of the plant over his body. Sores broke out all over him. In this way he went to the home of the two maidens. There was a ladder outside the house. He made one step on the ladder when the mother of the maidens stopped him and said: "What are you doing here?" The young man replied in a mild voice: "I have come to marry your two daughters." But when the woman saw the sores that covered his body she told him to go away.

The next day he chewed another poisonous plant called zen chee'e, which has a blue flower and grows about an inch high. It is found on the mesa near Shiprock, and blooms in the early spring. He blew some of this plant on his body and dreadful sores appeared. Then he returned to the home of the maidens and climbed two rungs of the ladder. The mother came to the top of the ladder and said: "What are you doing here again?" He said: "I have come to marry your two daughters." The woman said: "I say no. With those sores! You go away."

The third day he came with still more dreadful sores. They were called na´kit [Spanish pock, also called syphilis]. The sores covered his hands and his body. He came in this condition to the home of the maidens, and he climbed three rungs of the ladder. The mother stopped him again, and sent him away. He said: "However, I am going to marry your two daughters."

He went away, but the fourth time he blew another kind of sore over himself. This is called des chit [blood poison]. With this disease he returned, and he climbed four rungs of the ladder. This time the mother let him come up and he entered the house.

The maidens had a guessing game, and up to this time no suitor had been able to guess correctly, so the old woman felt safe. The maidens brought out their basket with the guessing game in it and sat down. The young man reached into the basket and took the husk pointing East. He unwrapped the husk as the sun travels; and he wiped the juice that was on it, circling the basket with it. He took the turquoise out and swallowed it with a piece of bread.

The two maidens felt for the stone but found none.

Then the young man unwrapped the husk that had pointed to the South, in the same way, and he took the white bead and swallowed it. The maidens felt for the stone but they could not find it.

He unwrapped the third husk that had pointed to the West, again in the same way, and he took the white shell and swallowed it. The maidens felt for the shell but it was gone. They had tears in their eyes this time, for the young man was covered with dreadful sores, and this did not please them.

Then the young man took the red stone from the center of the basket and swallowed that also. The maidens felt for it but it was not there.

Now all this happened so that medicine might be made known that would cure poison ivy and the other diseases of the skin. Since then the medicine of the young man is known for these sores.

Now they take four leaves from the poison ivy, East, South, West, and North, and they cut a hole through the four leaves. They chew the leaves of the poison ivy mixed with powder of ground chips of stones. Whoever receives this medicine gets it through the holes in these leaves. Afterward he can travel around poison ivy and other poisonous plants. This was San'hode'di's medicine, and with it he cured himself.

After he had won the guessing game he took the two maidens to a new home. Each morning when the sisters returned home to their mother their father asked: "Did he touch you?" And the old man wondered where the young man had gotten the power to guess the game.

After the fourth day San'hode'di was as well as before. Then he lay with the two maidens, and they told their father. They told him also that in the morning they found themselves sleeping under beautiful robes, and in a home filled with everything they could wish for. Their father came over and when he saw all he was pleased with his son-in-law and said: "My daughters have wished for many things. I see that they have them all now".

. . .

There is a peak this side of San Francisco Mountain which is called Tocho whee tso. It is near Tlo chee ko. And that is the place where San'hode'di went with his first two wives. He is there. His home and those of his mother are considered sacred places. . . .

Source: O'Bryan, Aileen. *The Dîné: Origin Myths of the Navaho Indians.* Smithsonian Institution, Bureau of American Ethnology, bulletin 163 (1956).

TSEGU´KSK^U [OR THE FIRST VISITATION OF SMALLPOX]
(Selection: Tsimshian)

The selections from this myth testify to the shocking effects that the first visitation of smallpox had on a coastal British Columbian tribe. The main character Tsegu´ksk^u is a shaman with supernatural powers.
   . . . At this time the Haida [Indians] used to make war upon the villages of Observatory inlet. Tsegu´ksk^u happened to be there with his friends when the Haida made an attack on the village, and he and all his companions were killed. The Haida cut off the heads of the slain to take them along as trophies. Tsegu´ksk^u's head was placed in the bow of the canoe. When the Haida had gone some little distance, his head rolled overboard and swam back to where the body lay. Head and trunk were joined again, and Tsegu´ksk^u rose hale and well. He returned to Nass river. . . .

Once upon a time Tsegu´ksk^u traveled down the river in his canoe. The canoe capsized, and when he was about to be drowned a great number of gulls came to his rescue. They took him on their backs and carried him up the river to his village, singing: . . . "I am taken along on the water, I am taken around the world by gulls."

After a short time an epidemic of smallpox visited the villages. Tsegu´ksk^u placed a pole, which he had painted red, in front of his house to ward off the disease. But, nevertheless, he became sick. He called all the great shamans of his village, and asked them if he would recover. Finally one of them replied that he would not recover. Then he made a bow and four arrows, which he painted red. He ordered one of his friends to shoot the arrows up to the sun. His friend did so, and the arrows did not return; but every time he shot, blood began to flow from Tsegu´ksk^u's forehead and from his cheeks. When Tsegu´ksk^u felt the blood, he said, "I shall not remain dead." He took his rattle and went around the fire twice, following the course of the sun. Then he asked for a coffin box. He crawled into it and died. Then the people took the skin of a mountain-goat, cut ropes out of it, and tied the box tightly. Then they placed it on a large boulder behind the village. On the fourth night after the burial a noise was heard proceeding from the box. When the people went out to see what it was, they saw that Tsegu´ksk^u had broken the thongs, and that he was sitting on the box. He had assumed the shape of a white owl. One man tried to catch him; but as the owl flew away, he became afraid and returned. Then a second man, whose name was Lō-gwisgwấs, tried. He did not succeed. After four men had tried, the owl suddenly fell back into the box, and the thongs were replaced by magic. The staff which Tsɛgu´ksku had raised in front of his house fell to pieces and was seen to be rotten all through.

Before the owl fell back into the box, it said, … "Nobody will be left." The epidemic continued for some time, and all the people died. This was the first visitation of smallpox.

Source: Boas, Franz. *Tsimshian Texts.* Smithsonian Institution, Bureau of American Ethnology, bulletin 27 (1902).

STORY OF THE SHAMAN, G.A´NDOX'S-FATHER
(Selection: Haida)

As told by Abraham of Those-born-at-Q!ā´dʌsgo, this northern British Columbian myth attributes pestilences like smallpox, and their cure, to supernatural forces. The last two spirits who speak through the shaman are vaguely Christianized, attesting to the influence that the arrival of Catholic missionaries had on the evolution of this mythic medicine story. G.A´ndox was the shaman's daughter. Since the excessive use of pronouns and some of the language in this myth can be confusing, a few noun substitutions and short explanatory phrases have been inserted in brackets.

… Pestilence married one of the daughters of the Moon. When he [her brother] heard the news about his sister in some way, Wu´ltc!ixaiya went to get his sister. He put on a steel coat and launched his canoe. His canoe was covered with boards. Then he knocked down the rock front of the house of Pestilence with a bone club. Afterward he went in and got his sister. For that reason there was much sickness [spread around].

Then Wu´ltc!ixaiya had mercy on Sea-grass town and went down there along with DilʌgiÀ´ [Sand-hill crane spirit]. When many people were dying he (DilʌgiÀ´) went in to dance before Pestilence. He held a long cane the surface of which was painted red. He stuck it up slant wise, stood upon it and danced. Then he made him feel good, and the sickness ceased. He [DilʌgiÀ´] spoke through G.A´ndox's-father [the shaman]. Then he told him these things. …

Some time after this, after they had gone to the mainland, a different one [spirit] spoke through him. His name was Bʌlê´la. Then they returned to Sea-grass town with him. Then they sang for G.A´ndox's-father in the canoe. He danced as they came. And when they landed he [Bʌlê´la] asked for a plank in the Tsimshian language. Then they had one rest on the edge of the canoe. He came down upon it to the shore [like a white man descends a gangplank].

And, when he got into the house, the house cover only was open (i.e., it was crowded with people). He danced the way Wu´ltc!ixaiya used to. …

After he had danced for a while he would say: "Stop and throw away the cedar-bark roofing. Destroy also the indoor latrine. Use cedar planks for your houses. When you go to bed leave your smoke holes open. Boxes of property will soon fall upon you. Iron people [white people] will come among you." He said that. He said there would be plenty of property for them.

Then all in the town danced very much again. The Kitkatla people also brought over Bī´ni's songs to Skedans. They sang his also very much as they danced. At this time a schooner was wrecked (in Cumshewa inlet). Then blankets were gradually distributed in quantities. This went on for a long time. Then, according to his word, they used cedar planks for house roofs. They also stopped using indoor latrines. …

Afterward Sʌqaiyū´ɫ [an earlier spirit] again spoke through him [G.A´ndox's-father]. And, after the dancing had gone on awhile longer, he [G.A´ndox's-father] wanted to sleep. At that time the Sea-grass town chiefs would not let him. By and by, since they feared the supernatural beings might say something different from what they wanted if they refused, they let him sleep.

When they agreed they made a sail house for him [G.A´ndox's-father] in the corner. And just at evening he went in and lay down. Next day, very early, before the raven cried he awoke (lit., departed). After that they again came in dancing. When they stopped dancing he had me sit near him. Then he began to tell me quietly (what had happened).

At that time he (Sᴀqaiyūⱡ) stood on top of the mountain on Q!ᴀ′ñga with him. Then he took a handkerchief out of his pocket [he is dressed like a white man], put it over his face, and wept. His clothes were all white. But he had no coat. Something with [bicycle-like] wheels stood near him, and presently he put him [G.ᴀ′ndox's-father] into his pocket on the right side. Then he got into this [thing with wheels], and he struck it. It went right along. After he had gone along slowly he came to a city [an oblique reference to the Christian concept of heaven?] with him and took him out of his pocket. And he stood up.

A big being with a black skin stood there. He also had a big gun. He stood pointing it downward at the earth. Sᴀqaiyūⱡ handed something to him out of his pocket. After a while he took it without looking at him and put it into his mouth. He [G.ᴀ′ndox's-father] did not know what it was. He thought it was Indian tobacco.

Then Sᴀqaiyūⱡ said to him: "Do not be afraid, master. Even the supernatural beings die. Where my three sets of clothing hang up, I have lived a long time. I died three times, but my body never dies" [an oblique reference to the Christian concept of the trinity?].

When he went thither with him, he saw a large kettle boiling out of doors. He said he did not see what made it boil. Near it was a long thing, the lower end of which was square, on which the Kwakiutl who had killed a certain one along with a Haida were nailed. They had put them into the kettle. There they remained [an oblique reference to the Christian story of the crucifixion?].

There he [G.ᴀ′ndox's-father] saw his uncle [another shaman]. Then his uncle asked him: "Did you see the one standing there with the black skin? He shoots down on those people below who treat each other badly. Then the land below is full of smoke, and there is sickness everywhere."

Then his uncle spoke to him through the doorway. "Why are you here?" "Sᴀqaiyūⱡ brought me around in that thing." "Be watchful. If one always watches, he, too, will live here. The black man always keeps watch on those who are foolish."

At that time his uncle said to him: "Some time ago one came down through me. And he lived in this town. Now he lives far inland. They fear to mention his name" [Wu′ltc!ixaiya, vaguely identified with the Christian deity?]. His uncle talked with him for a while. Again he said to him: "Do not let his name be mentioned again below. You can not mention his name (for it is too great.) If a child mentions his name tell him to stop."

Then he went down again with him in the thing with wheels. At that time he [G.ᴀ′ndox's-father] awoke in the sail house. Not a long time afterward he died.

This is the end of it.

Source: Swanton, John. *Haida Texts and Myths.* Smithsonian Institution, Bureau of American Ethnology, bulletin 29 (1905).

FIRST SHIP SEEN BY THE CLATSOP *(Chinook)*

This northwestern myth compactly but vividly records initial reactions to a first encounter with the Europeans and the emergence of copper, brass, and iron as sources of wealth.

The son of an old woman had died. She wailed for him a whole year and then she stopped. Now one day she went to Seaside. There she used to stop, and she returned. She returned walking along the beach. She nearly reached Clatsop; now she saw something. She thought it was a whale. When she came near it she saw two spruce trees standing upright on it. She thought, "Behold! it is no whale. It is a monster." She reached the thing that lay there. Now she saw that its outer side was all covered with copper. Ropes were tied to those spruce trees and it was full of iron. Then a bear came out of it. He stood on the thing that lay there. He looked just like a bear, but his face was that of a human being. Then she went home. Now she thought of her son, and cried, saying, "Oh, my son is dead and the thing about which we heard in tales is on shore." When she nearly reached the town she continued to cry. (The people said,) "Oh, a person comes crying. Perhaps somebody struck her." The people made themselves ready. They took their arrows. An old man said, "Listen!" Then the people listened. Now she said all the time, "Oh, my son is dead, and the thing about which we heard in tales is on shore." The people said, "What may it be?" They went running to meet her. They said, "What is it?" "Ah, something lies there and it is thus. There are two bears on it, or maybe they are people." Then the people ran. They reached the thing that lay there. Now the people, or what else they might be, held two copper kettles in their hands. Now the first one reached there. Another one arrived. Now the persons took their hands to their mouths and gave the people their kettles. They had lids. The men pointed inland and asked for water. Then two people ran inland. They hid themselves behind a log. They returned again and ran to the beach. One man climbed up and entered the thing. He went down into the ship. He looked about in the interior of the ship; it was full of boxes. He found brass buttons in strings half a fathom long. He went out again to call his relatives, but they had already set fire to the ship. He jumped down. Those two persons had also gone down. It burnt just like fat. Then the Clatsop gathered the iron, the copper, and the brass. Then all the people learned about it. The two persons were taken to the chief of the Clatsop. Then the chief of the one town said, "I want to keep one of the men with me." The people almost began to fight. Now one of them was taken to one town. Then the chief was satisfied. Now the Quenaiult, the Chehalis, the Cascades, the Cowlitz, and the Klickatat learned about it and they all went to Clatsop. The Quenaiult, the Chehalis, and the Willapa went. The people of all the towns went there. The Cascades, the Cowlitz, and the Klickatat came down the river. All those of the upper part of the river came down to Clatsop. Strips of copper two fingers wide and going around the arm were exchanged for one slave each. A piece of iron as long as one-half the forearm was exchanged for one slave. A piece of brass two fingers wide was exchanged for one slave. A nail was sold for a good curried deerskin. Several nails were given for long dentalia. The people bought this and the Clatsop became rich. Then iron and brass were seen for the first time. Now they kept these two persons. One was kept by each chief; one was at the Clatsop town at the cape.

Source: Boas, Franz. *Chinook Texts.* Smithsonian Institution, Bureau of American Ethnology, bulletin 20 (1894).

HOW THE SPANIARDS CAME TO SHUNG-OPOVI, HOW THEY BUILT A MISSION, AND HOW THE HOPI DESTROYED THE MISSION *(Hopi)*

In 1540, the first Spanish expedition arrived in Hopi country where the belief in a returning white god or "Bahana" was fairly common. The soldiers also frightened the Hopi into submission by destroying the first Hopi village that resisted them. The "kachinas" were nature spirits who played important roles in the Hopi religious ceremonies that were forbidden by the Spanish priests. The final events in this story refer to the famous Pueblo Revolt on August 13, 1680.

It may have taken quite a long time for these villages to be established. Anyway, every place was pretty well settled down when the Spanish came. The Spanish were first heard of at Zuni and then at Awatovi. They came on to Shung-opovi, passing Walpi. At First Mesa, Si-kyatki was the largest village then, and they were called Si-kyatki, not Walpi. The Walpi people were living below the present village on the west side. When the Spaniards came, the Hopi thought that they were the ones they were looking for—their white brother, the Bahana, their savior.

The Spaniards visited Shung-opovi several times before the missions were established. The people of Mishongovi welcomed them so the priest who was with the white men built the first Hopi mission at Mishongovi. The people of Shung-opovi were at first afraid of the priests but later they decided he was really the Bahana, the savior, and let him build a mission at Shung-opovi.

Well, about this time the Strap Clan were ruling at Shung-opovi and they were the ones that gave permission to establish the mission. The Spaniards, whom they called Castilla, told the people that they had much more power than all their chiefs and a whole lot more power than the witches. The people were very much afraid of them, particularly if they had much more power than the witches. They were so scared that they could do nothing but allow themselves to be made slaves. Whatever they wanted done must be done. Any man in power that was in this position the Hopi called *Tota-achi*, which means a grouchy person that will not do anything himself, like a child. They couldn't refuse, or they would be slashed to death or punished in some way. There were two *Tota-achi*.

The missionary did not like the [Native] ceremonies. He did not like the Kachinas and he destroyed the altars and the customs. He called it idol worship and burned up all the ceremonial things in the plaza.

When the Priests started to build the mission, the men were sent away over near the San Francisco peaks to get the pine or spruce beams. These beams were cut and put into shape roughly and were then left till the next year when they had dried out. Beams of that size were hard to carry and the first few times they tried to carry these beams on their backs, twenty to thirty men walking side by side under the beam. But this was rather hard in rough places and one end had to swing around. So finally they figured out a way of carrying the beam in between them. They lined up two by two with the beam between the lines. In doing this, some of the Hopis were given authority by the missionary to look after these men and to see if they all did their duty. If any man gave out on the way he was simply left to die. There was great suffering. Some died for lack of food and water, while others developed scabs and sores on their bodies.

It took a good many years for them to get enough beams to Shung-opovi to build the mission. When this mission was finally built, all the people in the village had to come there to worship, and those that did not come were punished severely. In that way their own religion was altogether wiped out, because they were not allowed to worship in their own way. All this trouble was a heavy burden on them and they thought it was on account of this that they were having a heavy drought at this time. They thought their gods had given them up because they weren't worshiping the way they should.

Now during this time the men would go out pretending they were going on a hunting trip and they would go to some hiding place, to make their prayer offerings. So today, a good many of these places are still to be found where they left their little stone bowls in which they ground their copper ore to paint the prayer sticks. These places are called *Puwa-kiki*, cave places. If these men were caught they were severely punished.

Now this man, Tota-achi (the Priest) was going from bad to worse. He was not doing the people any good and he was always figuring what he could do to harm them. So he thought out how the water from different springs or rivers would taste and he was always sending some man to these springs to get water for him to drink, but it was noticed that he always chose the men who had pretty wives. He

tried to send them far away so that they would be gone two or three days, so it was not very long until they began to see what he was doing. The men were even sent to the Little Colorado River to get water for him, or to Moencopi. Finally, when a man was sent out he'd go out into the rocks and hide, and when the night came he would come home. Then, the priest, thinking the man was away, would come to visit his wife, but instead the man would be there when he came. Many men were punished for this.

All this time the priest, who had great power, wanted all the young girls to be brought to him when they were about thirteen or fourteen years old. They had to live with the priest. He told the people they would become better women if they lived with him for about three years. Now one of these girls told what the Tota-achi were doing and a brother of the girl heard of this and he asked his sister about it, and he was very angry. This brother went to the mission and wanted to kill the priest that very day, but the priest scared him and he did nothing. So the Shung-opovi people sent this boy, who was a good runner, to Awatovi to see if they were doing the same thing over there, which they were. So that was how they got all the evidence against the priest.

Then the chief at Awatovi sent word by this boy that all the priests would be killed on the fourth day after the full moon. They had no calendar and that was the best way they had of setting the date. In order to make sure that everyone would rise up and do this thing on the fourth day the boy was given a cotton string with knots in it and each day he was to untie one of these knots until they were all out and that would be the day for the attack.

Things were getting worse and worse so the chief of Shung-opovi went over to Mishongnovi and the two chiefs discussed their troubles. "He is not the savior and it is your duty to kill him," said the chief of Shung-opovi. The chief of Mishongnovi replied, "If I end his life, my own life is ended."

Now the priest would not let the people manufacture prayer offerings, so they had to make them among the rocks in the cliffs out of sight, so again one day the chief of Shung-opovi went to Mishongnovi with tobacco and materials to make prayer offerings. He was joined by the chief of Mishongnovi and the two went a mile north to a cave. For four days they lived there heartbroken in the cave, making pahos. Then the chief of Mishongnovi took the prayer offerings and climbed to the top of the Corn Rock and deposited them in the shrine, for according to the ancient agreement with the Mishongnovi people it was their duty to do away with the enemy.

He then, with some of his best men, went to Shung-opovi, but he carried no weapons. He placed his men at every door of the priest's house. Then he knocked on the door and walked in. He asked the priest to come out but the priest was suspicious and would not come out. The chief asked the priest four times and each time the priest refused. Finally, the priest said, "I think you are up to something."

The chief said, "I have come to kill you." "You can't kill me," cried the priest, "you have no power to kill me. If you do, I will come to life and wipe out your whole tribe."

The chief returned, "If you have this power, then blow me out into the air; my gods have more power than you have. My gods have put a heart into me to enter your home. I have no weapons. You have your weapons handy, hanging on the wall. My gods have prevented you from getting your weapons."

The old priest made a rush and grabbed his sword from the wall. The chief of Mishongnovi yelled and the doors were broken open. The priest cut down the chief and fought right and left but was soon overpowered, and his sword taken from him.

They tied his hands behind his back. Out of the big beams outside they made a tripod. They hung him on the beams, kindled a fire and burned him.

Source: Nequatewa, Edmund. *Truth of a Hopi* (1936; Flagstaff, AZ: Northland Press, 1967).

[LEGEND OF THE PEACEMAKERS] *(Selections: Iroquois)*

Here is an example of history in the process of being converted into myth. The Iroquois Confederacy (the "Great Peace") was created in the fifteenth century (or much earlier, according to Native sources), but the historical founders, the prophet Deganawida and his compatriot Ayonhwatha, quickly acquired supernatural auras in the repeated retellings of their stories. Ayonhwatha is also remembered as the creator of wampum and of the important Condolence Ceremony of the Iroquois. In the nineteenth century, the popular white poet Henry Wadsworth Longfellow created a version of the story that misleadingly merged several different traditional characters into one ideal hero named Hiawatha.

The following text is based on selections from one source supplemented by excerpts from a second source, which is indicated by italics. Given the inconsistent spellings of the founders' names, even within one source, I have substituted one set of spellings for the founders' names, in the interests of clarity.

[Part I. The Birth and Mission of Deganawida]

... [The] birthplace of Deganawida was called Kah-ha-nah-yenh, somewhere in the neighborhood of the Bay of Quinte.

According to tradition, a woman was living in that neighborhood who had one daughter of stainless character.... In the course of time, notwithstanding, she showed signs of conception....

It so happened that as the time approached when the daughter would deliver the child, that the mother dreamed that she saw a man whom she did not know, and that he said that he appeared as a messenger to her....

"I will tell you what has happened. It is the wish of the Creator that she should bear a child, and when you will see the male child you shall call him Deganawida. The reason you shall give him that name is because this child will reveal to men-beings ... the Good Tidings of Peace...."

Then the daughter was also made glad, and when she was delivered of the child, it was as had been predicted....

The child grew up rapidly, and when he had become a young man he said: "The time has come when I should begin to perform my duty in this world...."

Then he began to build his canoe out of a white rock, and ... Deganawida said, "This will be the first sign of wonder that man will behold; a canoe made out of stone will float."

... It happened at that time a party of hunters had a camp on the south side of the lake now known as Ontario and one of the party went toward the lake and stood on the bank of the lake, and beheld the object coming toward him at a distance, and the man could not understand what it was that was approaching him; shortly afterwards he understood that it was a canoe, and saw a man in it, and the moving object was coming directly toward where he stood, and when the man (it was Deganawida) reached the shore he came out of his boat and climbed up the bank.

Then Deganawida asked the man what had caused them to be where they were, and the man answered and said: "We are here for a double object. We are here hunting game for our living and also because there is a great strife in our settlement."

Then Deganawida said, "You will now return to the place from whence you came. . . . And I want you to tell your chief that the Ka-rih-wi-yoh (Good Tidings of Peace and Power) have come and if he asks you from whence came the Good Tidings of Peace and Power, you will say that the Messenger of the Good Tidings of Peace and Power will come in a few days."

Then the man said: "Who are you now speaking to me?"

Deganawida answered: "It is I who came from the west and am going eastward and am called Deganawida in the world."

Then the man wondered and beheld his canoe and saw that his canoe was made out of white stone. . . .

Then after saying these words Deganawida went on his way and arrived at the house of Ji-kon-sah-seh and said to her that he had come on this path which passed her home and which led from the east to the west, and on which traveled the men of blood-thirsty and destructive nature.

Then he said unto her, "It is your custom to feed these men when they are traveling on this path on their war expeditions." He then told her that she must desist from practicing this custom. He then told her that the reason she was to stop this custom was that the Karihwiyoh or Good Tidings of Peace and Power had come. He then said: "I shall, therefore, now change your disposition and practice." Then also, "I now charge you that you shall be the custodian of the Good Tidings of Peace and Power, so that the human race may live in peace in the future." Then Deganawida also said, "You shall therefore now go east where I shall meet you at the place of danger (to Onondaga), where all matters shall be finally settled and you must not fail to be there on the third day. I shall now pass on in my journey."

Then he journeyed on a great way and went to another settlement. . . .

[Part II. The Condolence of Ayonhwatha]

In those same days the Onondagas had no peace. A man's life was valued as nothing. For any

slight offence a man or woman was killed by his enemy and in this manner feuds started between families and clans. At night none dared leave their doorways lest they be struck down by an enemy's war club. Such was the condition when there was no Great Law.

South of the Onondaga town lived an evil-minded man. . . . His body was distorted by seven crooks and his long tangled locks were adorned by writhing living serpents. Moreover, this monster was a devourer of raw meat, even of human flesh. He was also a master of wizardry and by his magic he destroyed men but he could not be destroyed. Adodarhoh was the name of the evil man. . . .

The time came, however, when the Onondaga people could endure him no longer. . . . Ayonhwatha called the council for he had many times sought to clear the mind of Adodarhoh and straighten his crooked body. . . . It was decided that half the people should go by boat across the creek where it widens and that others should skirt the shore. Adodarhoh was not in his nest in the swale but in a new spot across the wide place in the creek.

The boats started and the people walked. From the bushes that overhung the shore a loud voice sounded. "Stand quickly and look behind you for a storm will overwhelm you."

In dismay the people arose in their canoes and turned about. As they did so the canoes overturned and the men were plunged into the water and many were drowned. A few escaped and then all survivors returned to the village. So had Adodarhoh frustrated the attempt to meet with him. . . .

Another council was held in the lodge of a certain great dreamer. He said, "I have dreamed that another shall prevail. He shall come from the north and pass to the east. Ayonhwatha shall meet him there in the Mohawk country and the two together shall prevail. Ayonhwatha must not remain with us but must go from us to the Flint land people." . . . Then the dreamer held two councils and those who believed in him conspired to employ Osinoh, a famous shaman. . . .

At night Osinoh climbed a tree overlooking his lodge and sat on a large limb. Filling his mouth with clay he imitated the sound of a screech owl. Calling the name of the youngest daughter [of Ayonhwatha] he sang:

"Unless you marry Osinoh
You will surely die, -whoo-hoo!"
Then he came down and went to his own home.
In three days the maiden strangely died. . . .

Shortly afterwards the second daughter [of Ayonhwatha] took sick and in a short time died. . . . Then the people assembled at the home of the Ayonhwatha and they spoke unto him words of condolence that he might forget his grief and bereavement.

But [he] did not answer them. So then the warriors decided that they would play a game of lacrosse in order to cheer him and during the time that they were playing, the last daughter of Ayonhwatha came out of the family abode to go after some water and when she had gone half way to the spring she saw flying high up in the air above a beautiful bird. She paused in her journey and the bird flew downwards toward her. She cried out aloud, being frightened, and said, "O, see this bird!" after which she ran away.

Then the warriors saw it and as it was then flying low, the warriors followed it, and as they were looking at the bird they did not notice the daughter of Ayonhwatha before them and in their haste they ran over and trampled her to death, and it transpired that the daughter of Ayonhwatha was with child. . . .

The grief of Ayonhwatha was terrible. He threw himself about as if tortured and yielding to the pain. No one came near him so awful was his sorrow. Nothing would console him and his mind was shadowed with the thoughts of his heavy sorrow.

"I shall cast myself away, I shall bury myself in the forest, I shall become a woodland wanderer," he said. . . . Ayonhwatha "split the heavens," Watanwhakacia, when he departed and his skies were rent asunder.

Toward the south he went. . . . [He] came to a group of small lakes and upon one he saw a flock of ducks. So many were there and so closely together did they swim that they seemed like a raft.

"If I am to be truly royaneh (noble)," he said aloud to himself, "I shall here discover my power." So then he spoke aloud and said: "Oh you who are 'floats' lift up the water and permit me to pass over the bottom of the lake dryshod."

In a compact body the ducks flew upward suddenly and swiftly, lifting the water with them. Thus did he walk down the shore and upon the bottom of the lake. There he noticed lying in layers the empty shells of the water snail, some shells white, and other purple. Stooping down he filled a pouch of deer skin with them, and then passed on to the other shore. Then did the ducks descend and replace the water. . . .

On the tenth day of his journey . . . [late] in the evening he came to the edge of another settlement and as was his custom he kindled a fire and erected a horizontal pole on two upright poles. On this he placed three strings of the wampum shells. Then he sat down and repeated his saying: "Men boast what they would do in extremity but they do not do what they promise. If I should see any one in deep grief I would remove these shells from this pole and console him. The shells would become words and lift away the darkness with which they are covered. Moreover, I truly would do as I say." This he repeated.

The chief man of the village saw the smoke at the edge of the forest and sent a messenger to discover who the stranger might be. . . . [He] returned and reported what he had seen and heard.

Then said the chief man, "The person whom you describe must truly be Ayonhwatha whom we have heard left his home at Onondaga. He it is who shall meet the great man foretold by the dreamer. We have heard that this man should work with the man who talks of the establishment of peace."

. . . So the chiefs of the town . . . chose five men as an escort for Ayonhwatha . . . [to] the town where Deganawida was staying. . . . When Ayonhwatha had entered the house . . . Deganawida arose . . . and he said: "My younger brother I perceive that you have suffered from some deep grief. . . . I shall now undertake to remove your sorrow so that your mind may be rested. Have you no more shell strings on your pole?"

Ayonhwatha replied, "I have no more strings but I have many shells in a tanned deer's skin." So he opened his bundle and a great quantity of shells fell out. So then Deganawida said, "My younger brother, I shall string eight more strands because there must be eight parts to my address to you." . . . So then he took one bunch off the pole and held it in his hand while he talked. While he talked one after another he took them down and gave one to Ayonhwatha after each part of his address. . . . When the eight ceremonial addresses had been made by Deganawida the mind of Ayonhwatha was made clear. He was then satisfied and once more saw things rightly. . . .

Deganawida then said, "My junior brother, your mind being cleared and you being competent to judge, we now shall make our laws and when all are made we shall call the organization we have formed the Great Peace. It shall be the power to abolish war and robbery between brothers and bring peace and quietness. . . .

Ayonhwatha then said, "What you have said is good, I do agree."

[Part III. The Peacemakers Confront Adodarhoh]

…Then Ayonhwatha announced to his colleagues and people that they assemble to hear Deganawida….He then turned and asked his colleagues and all the people what answer they should give….

Then the chief warrior answered and said: "I am still in doubt and I would propose (as a test of power) that this man (Deganawida) climb up a big tree by the edge of a high cliff and that we then cut the tree down and let it fall with him over the cliff, and then if he does not die I shall truly believe the message which he has brought us…."

Then Deganawida said, "This shall truly be done and carried out." He then climbed the tree and when he had reached the top of the tree he sat down on a branch, after which the tree was cut down, and it fell over the cliff with him….

Now when the new day dawned one of the warriors arose before sunrise and…at once returned to the Ayonhwatha and when he arrived there he said that he had seen the man sitting by the fire, and that it was he who was on the tree which was cut the evening before….

The chief warrior then said, "…Deganawida, you may now listen to the answer we have concluded to give you. We have received the message which you brought us, and we have jointly concluded to accept the message of Good News of Peace and Power…."

Then Ayonhwatha said … : "The time is now come when we should go to the conference…." After they had all assembled in conference, Deganawida stood up and said:

"This conference met here composed of four nations being now assembled, you will therefore now first consider what we shall do with reference to a certain woman, our mother [Ji-kon-sah-seh], who has not yet arrived." They then considered the matter and they decided that they would proceed with the business on hand and the matter would be in progress when she arrived….

They then entered the boat and he (Deganawida) stood in front of the boat and Ayonhwatha sat in the stern and the rest of the [men] then noticed that the boat was made of white marble. Then they embarked in this boat from the shore and they had not proceeded far on their journey when they heard a voice [Adodarhoh's] calling out, "A-soh-kek-ne————eh," and as soon as this voice had called out a strong wind arose and caused the lake to become very rough and troubled and great billows formed upon its surface

and more especially around the boat. Then those in the boat became frightened and said: "We are now going to die," but Deganawida spoke and … said to the wind and lake, "Be thou quiet, Gä-hä", and rest." Then the wind and the roughness of the lake ceased…. [They] had only gone a short distance when they beheld [Adodarhoh] sitting on a high, round knoll and when they arrived where he was sitting they stood all around him and Deganawida stood directly in front of him, then he spoke and said: "We have now arrived, we representing the four nations. You will therefore now answer the message which we have left here with you…."

Then the man looked around and saw these men …standing all around him, but he did not answer but kept silent. Then … they saw his hair moving as if it were all alive and they saw that the movements of the hair greatly resembled that of serpents, and they looked at his hands and saw that his fingers were twisting and contorting continually in all directions and in all manner of shapes, and they became impatient because he would not answer the message.

Then Deganawida said to Ayonhwatha: "You shall now recross the lake and the chief warrior and De-ha-riho-ho-ken and Dyon-yonho-koh and our mother Ji-kon-sah-seh, shall accompany you back in the boat (when you return here)."

… [When] he had come to shore on the other side of the lake, they asked what had occurred. Ayonhwatha answered and said: "It is not yet complete, I have therefore come after the chief warrior[s] … and our mother Ji-kon-sah-seh," and they answered him and said: "She has now arrived."

Then … when they had returned to where the man was sitting, Ayonhwatha said, "Everything is completed, we are now all assembled here…."

When Deganawida started to address this man [Adodarhoh], the man became troubled and after all of the [men] finished addressing the man his sympathy was affected and he shed tears. Then Deganawida said: " … The [men] and all the chief warriors and this great woman, our mother [Ji-kon-sah-seh], have all agreed to submit the Good Tidings of Peace and Power to you, and thus if you approve and confirm the message, you will have the power and be the Fire-Keeper of our Confederate Council, and the smoke from it will arise and pierce the sky, and all the nations shall be subject to you."

Then the twisting movements of the fingers and the snakelike movements of the hair of Adodarhoh ceased….

Then Deganawida said: "We have now accomplished our work and completed everything that was required with the exception of shaping and transforming him (by rubbing him down), removing the snake-like hair from him and circumcising him."

The [men] therefore all took part in doing this and Ohdahtshedeh was the first to rub down Adodarhoh and the others followed his example so that the appearance of Adodarhoh might be like that of other men.

When this had been done then Deganawida again said: "You, the chief warrior, and you, our mother [Ji-kon-sah-seh], you have the control of the power (the authority), and we will now put upon him a sign, by placing upon his head the horns of a buck deer. The reason why we do this is because all people live upon the flesh of the deer, and the reason that we take the emblem of the deer horns is that this institution, the Great Peace, shall be the means of protecting our children hereafter."

Source: Selections from the text compiled by the Chiefs of the Six Nations Council, "The Traditional Narrative of the Origin of the Confederation of the Five Nations;" and by Seth Newhouse, "The Dekanawida Legend," in Arthur C. Parker, *The Constitution of the Five Nations or The Iroquois Book of the Great Law.* New York State Museum, bulletin 184. (1916).

CORNPLANTER AND WASHINGTON *(Iroquois)*

This anecdote was related by Emily Tallchief, the great-great-granddaughter of Cornplanter (1740?–1836), a Seneca war chief and statesman. It illustrates the role that the Iroquois League of the Five Nations played in the late eighteenth century during the American Revolutionary War and immediately thereafter.

"Now during the war of the thirteen fires against the king of Great Britain, we, the Iroquois, were loyal to our old allies, the British. We fought for them, but, alas for us they were beaten. Now Washington, the great leader of the thirteen fires, was determined to punish us for our part in the war, for he did not realize that we were but keeping our treaties with the British when we fought. So Washington said, 'Depart from among us and go to the west far from the white people.' But Cornplanter said, 'Not so. We are determined not to move. We have long lived here and intend to continue in our own territory as long as we are able to hold it.' 'Not so,' answered Washington, 'you fought against us and therefore you must move on to the west and if you refuse we shall compel you.' 'Then,' answered Cornplanter, 'we will resist you by force of arms. If you win we will have to go, otherwise we will remain where we now are.'

"Cornplanter returned from Washington to his people and spread the news. Quickly it traveled among all the Indians to the south, the east and the west. All were very angry and said, 'We will fight. When the white man tries to move us as they please it is time that we moved a few white men.' Then the western Indians began to massacre the settlers. The news came to Washington. 'It is a mistake to encourage another Indian war,' he said and then sent for Cornplanter. 'I want to settle our difficulties,' said he, 'and I wish peace. I do not wish war, therefore you, Cornplanter, must pacify your people.' 'I care not to meddle further with matters,' said Cornplanter. 'But you must go,' insisted Washington, 'you are the only man who can restore peace and good will.' Thus it was that Cornplanter accepted the commission. He returned home and collecting a party of chiefs sent abroad declarations of peace. The delegation went through Sandusky into the farther west. There Cornplanter called a council and said, 'We must be peaceful with the white men and cease tormenting them.' Now the tribe was a very fierce one and was very angry that Cornplanter advised peace. They mixed poison with the food which they served the delegation and a number died. Cornplanter also was made severely ill. Then Cornplanter became very angry and calling a council said, 'You have acted with treachery. Now I cease to plead. I now command that you let the white people live in peace. Do not kill another one. If you do I will bring the whole Five Nations against you and with a great army of white men will kill every one of you. The Senecas are the greatest nation of all nations and whatever they plan they do. We are always successful and always victorious in sport, debate or battle. So beware.' Now the western Indians councilled among themselves and said, 'We must hastily agree for if the Senecas come against us we surely will be defeated.'"

Source: Parker, Arthur C. *The Code of Handsome Lake, the Seneca Prophet.* New York State Museum, bulletin 163 (1912).

HOW THE WHITE RACE CAME TO AMERICA AND WHY THE GAI'WIIO' BECAME A NECESSITY *(Iroquois)*

This satire of the Columbus legend was related by Edward Cornplanter (So-Son-Do-Wa). The Gai´wiio' ["Good Message"] refers to the teachings of the prophet Handsome Lake (1735–1815) who preached temperance and self-discipline as a corrective to what he saw as the excesses and corrupting influences of the European intruders.

Now this happened a long time ago and across the great salt sea, odji´´ke'dāgi´ga, that stretches east. There is, so it seems, a world there and soil like ours. There in the great queen's country where swarmed many people—so many that they crowded upon one another and had no place for hunting—there lived a great queen. Among her servants was a young preacher of the queen's religion, so it is said.

Now this happened. The great queen requested the preacher to clean some old volumes which she had concealed in a hidden chest. So he obeyed and when he had cleaned the last book, which was at the bottom of the chest, he opened it and looked about and listened, for truly he had no right to read the book and wanted no one to detect him. He read. It was a great book and told him many things which he never knew before. Therefore he was greatly worried. He read of a great man who had been a prophet and the son of the Great Ruler. He had been born on the earth and the white men to whom he preached killed him. Now moreover the prophet had promised to return and become the King. In three days he was to come and then in forty to start his kingdom. This did not happen as his followers had expected and so they despaired. Then said one chief follower, "Surely he will come again sometime, we must watch for him."

Then the young preacher became worried for he had discovered that his god was not on earth to see. He was angry moreover because his teachers had deceived him. So then he went to the chief of preachers and asked him how it was that he had deceived him. Then the chief preacher said, "Seek him out and you will find him for indeed we think he does live on earth." Even so, his heart was angry but he resolved to seek.

On the morning of the next day he looked out from the opening of his room and saw out in the river a beautiful island and he marveled that he had never seen it before. He continued to gaze and as he did he saw among the trees a castle of gold and he marveled that he had not seen the castle of gold before. Then he said, "So beautiful a castle on so beautiful an isle must indeed be the abode of him whom I seek." Immediately he put on his clothes and went to the men who had taught him and they wondered and said, "Indeed it must be as you say." So then together they went to the river and when they came to the shore they saw that it was spanned by a bridge of shining gold. Then one of the great preachers fell down and read from his book a long prayer and arising he turned his back upon the island and fled for he was afraid to meet the lord. Then with the young man the other crossed the bridge and he knelt on the grass and he cried loud and groaned his prayer but when he arose to his feet he too fled and would not look again at the house—the castle of gold.

Then was the young man disgusted, and boldly he strode toward the house to attend to the business which he had in mind. He did not cry or pray and neither did he fall to his knees for he was not afraid. He knocked at the door and a handsome smiling man welcomed him in and said, "Do not be afraid of me." Then the smiling man in the castle of gold said, "I have wanted a young man such as you for some time. You are wise and afraid of nobody. Those older men were fools and would not have listened to me (direct) though they might listen to some one whom I had instructed. Listen to me and most truly you shall be rich. Across the ocean that lies toward the sunset is another world and a great country and a people whom you have never seen. Those people are virtuous, they have no unnatural evil habits and they are honest. A great reward is yours if you will help me. Here are five things that men and women enjoy; take them to these people and make them as white men are. Then shall you be rich and powerful and you may become the chief of all great preachers here."

So then the young man took the bundle containing the *five things* and made the bargain. He left the island and looking back saw that the bridge had disappeared and before he had turned his head the castle had gone and then as he looked the island itself vanished.

Now then the young man wondered if indeed he had seen his lord for his mind had been so full of business that he had forgotten to ask. So he opened his bundle of five things and found a flask of rum, a pack of playing cards, a handful of coins, a violin and a decayed leg bone. Then he thought the things very strange and he wondered if indeed his lord would send such gifts to the people across the water of the salt lake; but he remembered his promise.

The young man looked about for a suitable man in whom to confide his secret and after some searching he found a man named Columbus and to him he confided the story. Then did Columbus secure some big canoes and raise up wings and he sailed away. He sailed many days and his warriors became angry and cried that the chief who led them was a deceiver. They planned to behead him but he heard of the plan and promised that on the next day he would discover the new country. The next morning came and then did Columbus discover America. Then the boats turned back and reported their find to the whole world. Then did great ships come, a good many. Then did they bring many bundles of the five things and spread the gifts to all the men of the great earth island.

Then did the invisible man of the river island laugh and then did he say, "These cards will make them gamble away their wealth and idle their time; this money will make them dishonest and covetous and they will forget their old laws; this fiddle will make them dance with their arms about their wives and bring about a time of tattling and idle gossip; this rum will turn their minds to foolishness and they will barter their country for baubles; then will this secret poison eat the life from their blood and crumble their bones." So said the invisible man and he was Hanïsse'ono, the evil one.

Now all this was done and when afterward he saw the havoc and the misery his work had done he said, "I think I have made an enormous mistake for I did not dream that these people would suffer so." Then did even the devil himself lament that his evil had been so great.

So after the swarms of white men came and misery was thrust upon the Ongwe-oweh the Creator was sorry for his own people whom he had molded from the soil of the earth of this Great Island, and he spoke to his four messengers and many times they tried to tell right men the revelations of the Creator but none would listen. Then they found our head man sick. Then they heard him speak to the sun and to the moon and they saw his sickness. Then they knew that he suffered because of the cunning evils that Hanïsse'ono had given the Ongwe-oweh. So then they knew that he was the one. He was the one who should hear and tell Gai'wiio'. But when Ganio'dai'io' spoke the evil being ceased his lament and sought to obstruct Gai'wiio', for he claimed to be master....

Source: Parker, Arthur C. *The Code of Handsome Lake, the Seneca Prophet.* New York State Museum, bulletin 163 (1912).

FIRST IMPRESSIONS OF CIVILIZATION (Sioux)

In this selection from his autobiography, Ohiyesa or Charles Alexander Eastman (1858–1939) describes growing up to be a Sioux warrior and his early encounters with white civilization. As a child, he believed his father had been killed in the 1862 Minnesota Sioux uprising. Later, in 1890, Eastman received a medical degree from Boston University School of Medicine. He was a physician at the Pine Ridge Reservation Agency and witnessed some of the after-events connected with the Wounded Knee Massacre on December 29, 1890.

I was scarcely old enough to know anything definite about the "Big Knives," as we called the white men, when the terrible Minnesota massacre broke up our home and I was carried into exile. I have already told how I was adopted into the family of my father's younger brother, when my father was betrayed and imprisoned. We all supposed that he had shared the fate of those who were executed at Mankato, Minnesota.

Now the savage philosophers looked upon vengeance in the field of battle as a lofty virtue. To avenge the death of a relative or of a dear friend was considered a great deed. My uncle, accordingly, had spared no pains to instill into my young mind the obligation to avenge the death of my father and my older brothers. Already I looked eagerly forward to the day when I should find an opportunity to carry out his teachings. Meanwhile, he himself went upon the warpath and returned with scalps every summer. So it may be imagined how I felt toward the Big Knives!

On the other hand, I had heard marvelous things of this people. In some things we despised them; in others we regarded them as *wakán* (mysterious), a race whose power bordered upon the supernatural. I learned that they had made a "fire-boat." I could not understand how they could unite two elements which cannot exist together. I thought the water would put out the fire, and the fire would consume the boat if it had the shadow of a chance. This was to me a preposterous thing! But when I was told that the Big Knives had created a "fire-boat-walks-on-mountains" (a locomotive) it was too much to believe.

"Why," declared my informant, "those who saw this monster move said that it flew from mountain to mountain when it seemed to be excited. They said also that they believed it carried a thunder-bird, for they frequently heard his usual war-whoop as the creature sped along!"

Several warriors had observed from a distance one of the first trains on the Northern Pacific, and had gained an exaggerated impression of the wonders of the pale-face. They had seen it go over a bridge that spanned a deep ravine and it seemed to them that it jumped from one bank to the other. I confess that the story almost quenched my ardor and bravery.

Two or three young men were talking together about this fearful invention.

"However," said one, "I understand that this fire-boat-walks-on-mountains cannot move except on the track made for it."

Although a boy is not expected to join in the conversation of his elders, I ventured to ask: "Then it cannot chase us into any rough country?"

"No, it cannot do that," was the reply, which I heard with a great deal of relief.

I had seen guns and various other things brought to us by the French Canadians, so that I had already some notion of the supernatural gifts of the white man; but I had never before heard such tales as I listened to that morning. It was said that they had bridged the Missouri and Mississippi rivers, and that they made immense houses of stone and brick, piled on top of one another until they were as high as high hills. My brain was puzzled with these things for many a day. Finally I asked my uncle why the Great Mystery gave such power to the Washechu (the rich)—sometimes we called them by this name—and not to us Dakotas.

"For the same reason," he answered, "that he gave to Duta the skill to make fine bows and arrows, and to Wachesne no skill to make anything."

"And why do the Big Knives increase so much more in number than the Dakotas?" I continued.

"It has been said, and I think it must be true, that they have larger families than we do. I went into the house of an Eashecha (a German), and I counted no less than nine children. The eldest of them could not have been over fifteen. When my grandfather first visited them, down at the mouth of the Mississippi, they were comparatively few; later my father visited their Great Father at Washington, and they had already spread over the whole country."

"Certainly they are a heartless nation. They have made some of their people servants—yes, slaves! We have never believed in keeping slaves, but it seems that these Washechu do! It is our belief that they painted their servants black a long time ago, to tell them from the rest, and now the slaves have children born to them of the same color!

"The greatest object of their lives seems to be to acquire possessions—to be rich. They desire to possess the whole world. For thirty years they were trying to entice us to sell them our land. Finally the outbreak gave them all, and we have been driven away from our beautiful country.

"They are a wonderful people. They have divided the day into hours, like the moons of the year. In fact, they measure everything. Not one of them would let so much as a turnip go from his field unless he received full value for it. I understand that their great men make a feast and invite many, but when the feast is over the guests are required to pay for what they have eaten before leaving the house. I myself saw at White Cliff (the name given to St. Paul, Minnesota) a man who kept a brass drum and a bell to call people to his table; but when he got them in he would make them pay for the food!

"I am also informed," said my uncle, "but this I hardly believe, that their Great Chief (President) compels every man to pay him for the land he lives upon and all his personal goods—even for his own existence—every year!" (This was his idea of taxation.) "I am sure we could not live under such a law.

"When the outbreak occurred, we thought that our opportunity had come, for we had learned that the Big Knives were fighting among themselves, on account of a dispute over their slaves. It was said that the Great Chief had allowed slaves in one part of the country and not in another, so there was jealousy, and they had to fight it out. We don't know how true this was.

"There were some praying-men who came to us some time before the trouble arose. They observed every seventh day as a holy day. On that day they met in a house that they had built for that purpose, to sing, pray, and speak of their Great Mystery. I was never in one of these meetings. I understand that they had a large book from which they read. By all accounts they were very different from all other white men we have known, for these never observed any such day, and we never knew them to pray, neither did they ever tell us of their Great Mystery.

"In war they have leaders and war-chiefs of different grades. The common warriors are driven forward like a herd of antelopes to face the foe. It is on account of this manner of fighting—from compulsion and not from personal bravery—that we count no *coup* on them. A lone warrior can do much harm to a large army of them in a bad country."

It was this talk with my uncle that gave me my first clear idea of the white man.

I was almost fifteen years old when my uncle presented me with a flint-lock gun. The possession of the "mysterious iron," and the explosive dirt, or "pulverized coal," as it is called, filled me with new thoughts. All the war-songs that I had ever heard from childhood came back to me with their heroes. It seemed as if I were an entirely new being—the boy had become a man!

"I am now old enough," said I to myself, "and I must beg my uncle to take me with him on his next war-path. I shall soon be able to go among the whites whenever I wish, and to avenge the blood of my father and my brothers."

I had already begun to invoke the blessing of the Great Mystery. Scarcely a day passed that I did not offer up some of my game, so that he might not be displeased with me. My people saw very little of me during the day, for in solitude I found the strength I needed. I groped about in the wilderness, and determined to assume my position as a man. My boyish ways were departing, and a sullen dignity and composure was taking their place.

The thought of love did not hinder my ambitions. I had a vague dream of some day courting a pretty maiden, after I had made my reputation, and won the eagle feathers.

One day, when I was away on the daily hunt, two strangers from the United States visited our camp. They had boldly ventured across the northern border. They were Indians, but clad in the white man's garments. It was as well that I was absent with my gun.

My father, accompanied by an Indian guide, after many days' searching had found us at last. He had been imprisoned at Davenport, Iowa, with those who took part in the massacre or in the battles following, and he was taught in prison and converted by the pioneer missionaries, Drs. Williamson and Riggs. He was under sentence of death, but was among the number against whom no direct evidence was found, and who were finally pardoned by President Lincoln.

When he was released, and returned to the new reservation upon the Missouri river, he soon became convinced that life on a government reservation meant physical and moral degradation. Therefore he determined, with several others, to try the white man's way of gaining a livelihood. They accordingly left the agency against the persuasions of the agent, renounced all government assistance, and took land under the United States Homestead law, on the Big Sioux river. After he had made his home there, he desired to seek his lost child. It was then a dangerous undertaking to cross the line, but his Christian love prompted him to do it. He secured a good guide, and found his way in time through the vast wilderness.

As for me, I little dreamed of anything unusual to happen on my return. As I approached our camp with my game on my shoulder, I had not the slightest premonition that I was suddenly to be hurled from my savage life into a life unknown to me hitherto.

When I appeared in sight my father, who had patiently listened to my uncle's long account of my early life and training, became very much excited. He was eager to embrace the child who, as he had just been informed, made it already the object of his life to avenge his father's blood. The loving father could not remain in the teepee and watch the boy coming, so he started to meet him. My uncle arose to go with his brother to insure his safety.

My face burned with the unusual excitement caused by the sight of a man wearing the Big Knives' clothing and coming toward me with my uncle.

"What does this mean, uncle?"

"My boy, this is your father, my brother, whom we mourned as dead. He has come for you."

My father added: "I am glad that my son is strong and brave. Your brothers have adopted the white man's way; I came for you to learn this new way, too; and I want you to grow up a good man."

He had brought me some civilized clothing. At first, I disliked very much to wear garments made by the people I had hated so bitterly. But the thought that, after all, they had not killed my father and brothers, reconciled me, and I put on the clothes.

In a few days we started for the States. I felt as if I were dead and traveling to the Spirit Land; for now all my old ideas were to give place to new ones, and my life was to be entirely different from that of the past.

Still, I was eager to see some of the wonderful inventions of the white people. When we reached Fort Totten, I gazed about me with lively interest and a quick imagination.

My father had forgotten to tell me that the fire-boat-walks-on-mountains had its track at Jamestown, and might appear at any moment. As I was watering the ponies, a peculiar shrilling noise pealed forth from just beyond the hills. The ponies threw back their heads and listened; then they ran snorting over the prairie. Meanwhile, I too had taken alarm. I leaped on the back of one of the ponies, and dashed off at full speed. It was a clear day; I could not imagine what had caused such an unearthly noise. It seemed as if the world were about to burst in two!

I got upon a hill as the train appeared. "O!" I said to myself, "that is the fire-boat-walks-on-mountains that I have heard about!" Then I drove back the ponies.

My father was accustomed every morning to read from his Bible, and sing a stanza of a hymn. I was about very early with my gun for several mornings; but at last he stopped me as I was preparing to go out, and bade me wait.

I listened with much astonishment. The hymn contained the word *Jesus*. I did not comprehend what this meant; and my father then told me that Jesus was the Son of God who came on earth to save sinners, and that it was because of him that he had sought me. This conversation made a deep impression upon my mind.

Late in the fall we reached the citizen settlement at Flandreau, South Dakota, where my father and some others dwelt among the whites. Here my wild life came to an end, and my school days began.

Source: Eastman, Charles Alexander. *Indian Boyhood.* New York: McClure, Phillips (1902).

SONGS OF THE GHOST DANCE *(Selections: Arapaho, Sioux, Paiute, Kiowa)*

Nearly defeated by 1890, many western and plains tribes desperately embraced a new messianic religion called the "Ghost Dance," which promised, among other things, an all-Indian future and the return of the buffalo. Many more verses could be added to these sequences, and most of the lines would be repeated one or more times.

Ghost Dance Songs *(Arapaho)*

My children, when at first I liked the whites,
I gave them fruits.
Father, have pity on me;
I am crying for thirst;
All is gone—I have nothing to eat.

Ghost Dance Song *(Sioux)*

The whole world is coming,
A nation is coming, a nation is coming,
The Eagle has brought the message to the tribe.
The father says so, the father says so.

Over the whole earth they are coming.
The buffalo are coming, the buffalo are coming,
The Crow has brought the message to the tribe,
The father says so, the father says so.

Ghost Dance Songs: Songs of Life Returning *(Paiute)*

A slender antelope, a slender antelope,
He is wallowing upon the ground.
The wind stirs the willows,
The wind stirs the grasses.
Fog! Fog!
Lightning! Lightning!
Whirlwind! Whirlwind!
There is dust from the whirlwind,
The whirlwind on the mountain.
The rocks are ringing,
They are ringing in the mountains.
The cottonwoods are growing tall,
They are growing tall and verdant.

Ghost Dance Songs *(Kiowa)*

The Father will descend.
The earth will tremble.
Everybody will arise.
Stretch out your hands.
The spirit host is advancing, they say.
They are coming with the buffalo, they say.
They are coming with the (new) earth, they say.

That wind, that wind
Shakes my tipi, shakes my tipi,
And sings a song for me.

Source: Mooney, James. "The Ghost-Dance Religion and the Sioux Outbreak of 1890." *Fourteenth Annual Report of the Bureau of American Ethnology 1892–1893*, part 2 (1896; Chicago: University of Chicago Press, 1965).

Chronology of Native America

c. 50,000–10,000 B.C.E.	According to the most commonly accepted theories, ancestors of Native Americans migrate into western North America by crossing a land bridge from Siberia across the Bering Strait. These people are often called Paleo-Indians and this era is referred to as the Lithic period.
25,000–10,000 B.C.E.	The Sandia people flourish. Their remains are the earliest evidence of humans in what became New Mexico.
15,000–8000 B.C.E.	Paleo-Indian hunters move through the North American plains. Evidence of their unique projective points are found in the American Southwest. They will be called the Clovis people after the town in New Mexico where artifacts were first discovered. They hunted large game, especially the mammoths.
11,000 B.C.E.	Hunter-gatherers settle in southern Mexico and northern Central America.
9000–7000 B.C.E.	Archaic cultures develop in the Eastern Woodlands area of the United States. They subsist on hunting, gathering, and fishing.
9000–7000 B.C.E.	The Folsom people expand throughout the Southwest. They developed the atlatl, which extended the range of their spears.
8000–6000 B.C.E.	The Plano culture develops. These people were known for specialized spear points and developing the cliff-jump technique of hunting bison.
7000–2000 B.C.E.	Central American cultures develop serious agricultural efforts. Pottery will also be developed.
6500 B.C.E.	Northwest coastal cultures develop. These people lived primarily by harvesting marine creatures.
5500 B.C.E.–1000 C.E.	Cultures develop along the southern California coast.
5000 B.C.E.	Mound dweller cultures develop along the Ohio River valley.
7000–500 B.C.E.	The Cochise culture appears in the American Southwest. They develop the staple foods of the era: corn, beans, and squash.
4000–1500 B.C.E.	Small conical burial mounds are the earliest earthworks along the Mississippi.
4000 B.C.E.	Shell-mound sites are occupied in the coastal estuaries of the Soconusco region of the Pacific coastal plain of Mexico and Guatemala.

5000–1000 B.C.E.	The Old Copper culture develops in the vicinity of the Great Lakes. These people mined the local copper to produce tools.
3440–3000 B.C.E.	Mound builders flourish near modern-day Watson Brake, Louisiana.
3114 B.C.E., August 12	According to the Maya calendar, the present creation of the world happened on this day. The same calendar says the world will end in December 2012.
3000 B.C.E.	An early form of maize is developed in the southern part of the state of Puebla, Mexico.
3000–1000 B.C.E.	Aleuts and Inuits migrate from Siberia into North America.
2600 B.C.E.–1850 C.E.	Lovelock Cave is occupied in western Nevada. It will be one of the first major archaeological excavations in the great Basin area. It is known for its variety of artifacts.
2000 B.C.E.	Pottery is made in the Savannah River valley of Georgia and South Carolina. The Olmec civilization is at its peak. Agriculture and pottery spread into much of North America.
1500 B.C.E.–1000 C.E.	The "Formative period" is in evidence across North America. There is now widespread use of agriculture, trade, carvings, and religious or ceremonial structures.
1500 B.C.E.	Mound builders flourish near Poverty Point, Louisiana.
1200–800 B.C.E.	The Na-Dené tribal group arrive in Alaska from Siberia. They are made up of four major groups: Athabascan, Eyak, Haida, and Tlingit.
1100 B.C.E.	The canoe is now being used by many groups in the Great Lakes and northeastern area of what would become the United States.
1000 B.C.E.–1600 C.E.	The Woodland Tradition flourishes between the Mississippi River and the Appalachian Mountains.
800 B.C.E.–100 C.E.	The Adena culture expands in the Eastern Woodlands.
300 B.C.E.–1300 C.E.	The Anasazi develop in the Four Corners of the Southwestern United States. They were known for their adobe structures, basketwork, and complex society.
300 B.C.E.–1300 C.E.	The Mogollon culture exists in the American Southwest.
200 B.C.E.–200 C.E.	The Tlingit and Athabascan separate into their own separate tribes.
200 B.C.E.	The Hopewell period begins in the Mississippi and Ohio River valleys.
200 B.C.E.–1450 C.E.	The Hohokam people thrive in Arizona. They are known for their use of irrigation.
100 B.C.E.	The city of Teotihuacan is founded in what would become Mexico City. At times, it would be the largest city in North America.
1–1000 C.E.	Yuman-speaking peoples move from the area of the Colorado River into the southern California coastal region.
378, January 15	Mayan King Chak Tok Ich'aak I (Great Burning Claw) of Tikal, Guatemala, dies. His death is one of the earliest recorded dates for a Mayan ruler.
426, September 9	Yax K'uk Mo establishes a Maya dynasty at Copán, Honduras.
500	The bow and arrow is now extensively used throughout North America.
679, May 3	Mayan forces from Dos Pilas, Guatemala, attack and defeat the forces at Tikal. Tikal King Nun Bak Chak is killed in the fighting.

700–1500	The Mississippi culture spreads throughout the areas along the Mississippi River and as far as Florida. Members of this group are known for their large mound structures and hierarchical society. Cahokia is its largest city.
700–1100	The Anasazi culture moves into its Pueblo period. This is marked by the use of adobe for structure building.
755, May 7	According to a sculptured lintel in the ruins at Yaxchilan in Mexico, a battle takes place. The sculpting shows Mayan warriors Jeweled Skull and Bird Jaguar taking captives. The date is established by the Mayan glyphs also on the sculpture.
900	End of the Classic Period of Mayan history. Many southern cities are abandoned, including Tikal.
1100	Hopis establish themselves with permanent villages in the American southwest. Chaco Canyon is at its peak.
1150	The Pueblo of Oraibi is established. The Pueblo of Acoma (Sky City) is also founded. It and Oraibi are the oldest continuously occupied towns in the United States.
1200	Northern Mayan cities begin to be abandoned.
1200–1400	Middle Mississippian Period. Cahokia is at its peak in 1200.
1200–1500	The Aztec begin their domination of central Mexico.
1200–1400	Ancestral Apache and Navajo bands break from northern Athapascan groups and migrate into the Southwest.
1244	The Itzá abandon Chichén Itzá.
1275–1325	Many pueblos are abandoned in the American Southwest because of raids by Athapascans and a drought. The Kachina (Katsina) cult develops in the same area. It is known for its supernatural beings and doll manifestations.
1325–1350	Tuzigoot pueblo, in northern Arizona, is abandoned.
1350–1398	Archaeological evidence today shows Navajo structures in New Mexico during this period.
1398	The Hohokan pueblo of Casa Grande is destroyed by Navajo and Apache raiders.
1390	The Great Binding Law establishes the Five Nations of the Iroquois Confederacy. It was comprised of the Cayuga, Mohawk, Oneida, Onondaga, and Seneca. The Tuscarora would become the sixth nation at a future date.
1400–1500	Late Mississippian Period.
1492, August 3	Columbus sailed for the New World from Palos, Spain.
1492, October 12,	According to some sources, Columbus landed in the New World. According to the Taino (Arawak), they were the first Native Americans to greet Columbus on the island of Guanahani (San Salvador).
1493, May 20	A civil war battle among the Cakchiquel (Kaqchikel) Maya takes place in Guatemala.
1493, November 3	Columbus lands on Dominica.
1493, November 4	Columbus lands on Guadeloupe in the Caribbean region.

1494, June 7	The New World is divided between Spain and Portugal by the Catholic church.
1495, March	Europeans forces engage a group of Tainos on Hispaniola. The Tainos are led by Manicaotex.
1497, June 24	Explorer John Cabot claims Newfoundland.
1500	The Algonquin, Ojibwa, Ottawa, and Potawatomi begin to develop as separate tribes. The Ojibwa, also known as the Chippewa, begin a relocation from the East Coast toward the Great Lakes.
1500	The Comanches split off from the Eastern Shoshone in Wyoming.
1503, April 6	Columbus has established a garrison in western Panama at the mouth of the Belen River. Indians attack the Spaniards on this date. Most of Columbus's crew survives the attack, but they soon abandon the outpost.
1506	Vasco Núñez de Balboa "discovers" the Pacific Ocean while standing on a mountain in Panama.
1511	The Spanish Valdivia expedition is shipwrecked off Jamaica. Approximately twenty survivors manage to get into a lifeboat. The lifeboat washes up on the eastern shore of Yucatán, near Cozumel. The local Mayas take the survivors as captives. Gonzalo Guerrero and Jeronimo de Aguilar are the only two people who survive the trip and captivity. Guerrero eventually joins his captors and marries into a Maya leader's family. When explorer Hernan Cortés arrives in the area in 1519, he arranges freedom for Guerrero and Aguilar. Guerrero decides to stay with his adopted family. In the future, Guerrero will help the Maya resist Spanish invasions in the Yucatán.
1512	The King of Spain authors the "Laws of Burgos." This law codifies the treatment of the indigenous people the Spaniards encounter as a part of their colonization of the New World.
1513, April 2	According to some sources, Ponce de Leon "discovers" Florida. He lands south of the St. John's River and claims Florida for Spain. There is considerable debate as to the exact date of this event.
1513, May 24	While exploring the Gulf Coast of Florida, Ponce de Leon encounters Calusa natives near Charlotte harbor. In a fight with the Calusa, de Leon captures four warriors.
1514, August 15	Spanish Bishop Bartoleme de las Casas releases the Indians he holds as serfs in Hispaniola.
1517	The first organized Spanish expedition arrives on the shores of Yucatán under Hernandez de Cordoba. He will be the person to apply the name Yucatán to this area. Cordoba will die in 1524 from wounds received in battle against the Maya.
1519	Spaniard Alonso Alvarez de Piñeda enters a densely populated Mississippi River estuary as a part of his expedition to explore the upper Gulf of Mexico.
1519, April	Shortly after arriving in Mexico, Hernan Cortés meets with a representative of Montezuma, in the Yucatan. The representative, Teudile, delivers Montezuma's best wishes and some gifts. Cortés says he represents the ruler of most of the world (the king of Spain). He demonstrates the might of his soldiers. Teudile is impressed by the power of the conquistadors. It is from

here that Cortés and his army start their travels toward Tenochtitlán (modern Mexico City).

1519, November 8 — According to some sources, Cortés and his soldiers first enter Tenochtitlán (modern Mexico City) by way of one of the three causeways.

1520, April 23 — An expedition under Panfilo de Navarez lands at what would eventually become Vera Cruz, Mexico. Navarez represents a Spanish faction that hopes to arrest Cortés and remove him from Mexico.

1520, June 30 — According to some sources, Montezuma dies. Some say he is killed by other Aztecs. Others say he is stabbed to death by Spaniards under Hernan Cortés.

1520, July 1 — According to many sources, Hernan Cortés and his followers attempt to escape from Tenochtitlán (modern Mexico City) by way of one of the causeways. They have to fight their way through large numbers of Aztec warriors. Thousands of people are killed on both sides. Many of the Spanish soldiers carried so much looted gold that when they fell in the lake, they drowned. This event is often called Noche Triste (Night of Tears or Sorrows).

1520, December 28 — According to some sources, Hernan Cortés and his army start their second excursion to Tenochtitlán (modern Mexico City) from Tlascala, Mexico. This time they have made and bring a group of small boats to use on the lake surrounding the city.

1521, June 30 — Spanish captains Francisco Gordillo and Pedro de Quexos land in and claim Florida for the king of Spain.

1521, August 13 — Montezuma's nephew, and successor, Cuahtemoc surrenders to Cortés. His name is spelled Guatimozin in some sources.

1524, April 14 — Spaniards under Pedro de Alvarado are welcomed as they enter the Cakchiquel (Kaqchikel) Maya town of Iximche, Guatemala.

1524, March 7 — Giovanni da Verrazano, sailing for France, anchors near Wilmington, North Carolina, in the Dauphine. He kidnaps a child they encounter to bring back to Europe. Some sources report this happening on March 1. Verrazzano goes on to explore the East Coast of North America.

1524 — Cortés encounters the Itzá in Honduras. The Itzá will be the last of the Mayan people to be conquered by the Spanish.

1526 — Spaniard Lucas Vasquez de Ayllon establishes a colony on the South Carolina or Virginia coast.

1528, April 14 — Panfilo de Narvaez, with four or five ships, and approximately four hundred to five hundred men, including Cabeza de Vaca, sight land on the western coast of Florida. This is the first significant exploration of Florida. On April 16, Narvaez sights Native houses near today's Tampa Bay, Florida. He anchors his boats in the area. Seeing Narvaez, the Native peoples abandon their village. Narvaez holds Spanish royal title to the land between the Rio de Las Palmas and the cape of Florida.

1528, April 17 — Narvaez visits a Native house that is big enough to hold three hundred people. He also finds a "rattle" made of gold in the abandoned house. The discovery of gold spurs Narvaez onward across Florida.

1528, November 6 — Cabeza de Vaca and eighty men of a Spanish expedition wash up on today's Galveston Island in Texas. Most of his men eventually die or become captives. Cabeza de Vaca marches across the continent to California, before he reaches a Spanish outpost. He is the first "white man" many Native Americans see.

1528   The Spanish under Francisco de Montejo begin their conquest of the Maya of the Yucatan. After twelve years of fighting, Montejo will have defeated most of the Maya in the area. He will establish settlements at Campeche, Salamanca, and Valladolid.

1531, December 9   According to most sources, Juan Diego (Cuauhtlatoatzin), a Nahua, first sees the apparition of the Virgin Mary on a hill called Tepeyacac in Mexico. Many Aztec and Nahua considered Tepeyacac to be a sacred site. Juan Diego sees her several times. On this date, according to Juan Diego, the Virgin Mary instructs him to carry some roses in his macehualli (a cloak) to the local bishop as proof of her appearance. When the macehualli is opened before the bishop, an image of the Virgin Mary appears on the cloak among the rose petals. The macehualli is still on display in the church (Our Lady of Guadalupe) built to honor the event.

1534   Jacques Cartier explores the St. Lawrence River with help of some Hurons. He will meet Micmacs in Chaleur Bay, Canada.

1535, September 8   Cartier reaches Stadacone, where the modern city Quebec is located. The next month, he arrives in the area of what eventually becomes Montreal. He encounters the Wyandot there.

1537, April 20   Hernando de Soto receives royal permission to "conquer, pacify, and people" the land from Rio de la Palmas to Cape Fear (Florida) on the Atlantic.

1539, May 24   Mexican Viceroy Don Antonio de Mendoza has decided to send an expedition to search for wealthy cities north of Mexico. On March 7, 1539, Friar Marcos de Niza started the expedition from Culiacan. According to Niza's journal, he finally sees Cibola, although he never sets foot in the pueblo. His report will lead to future expeditions looking for the "Seven Cities of Gold."

1539, May   Hernando de Soto's Spanish expedition arrives off the shore of western Florida. Their mission is to explore Florida, and the surrounding countryside. Having been in Florida for only a few days, Hernando de Soto formally claims Florida for the King of Spain.

1540, May 25   Hernando de Soto's army enters Cherokee lands. They spend the night near modern Highlands in North Carolina.

1540, May 30   Hernando de Soto's army arrives in the Cherokee village of Guasili, modern Murphy, in western North Carolina. This is the first recorded meeting between Cherokees and Europeans. The Cherokees give de Soto three hundred dogs to be used as food. De Soto's chroniclers describe the village as having three hundred homes and wide streets.

1540   Francisco Vasquez de Coronado begins his expedition to find the Seven Lost Cities. In the process, he explores the American southwest.

1540, October 18   Hernando de Soto arrives at the Mobile Native American village of Mabila, in present-day Clark County, Alabama. The Mobile Natives, under Chief Tuscaloosa (Tascaluca), attack de Soto's invading army. In the bloody conflict, as many as 3,000 Native Americans are killed by the armored Spaniards. Approximately 20 Spaniards are killed, and 150 wounded, including de Soto, according to their chroniclers.

1541, June 18	Hernando de Soto's expedition reached the Mississippi River on May 8, 1541, near the village of Quizquiz, in northwestern Mississippi. After exploring the near side, they finally cross to the west side of the river on June 18.
1542, June 29	Coronado reaches the Arkansas River, in Kansas. He is only three hundred miles from Hernando de Soto's expedition, which is in Arkansas, near the Oklahoma border.
1550, April 16	King Charles V orders a stop to Native American land conquests.
1559, August 14	Tristan de Luna y Arellano has been appointed to establish Spanish settlements on Pensacola Bay by the Spanish Viceroy in Mexico. His expedition of thirteen ships, several priests, five hundred soldiers, and one thousand settlers arrive in Pensacola Bay, in Florida. Much of the expedition is killed or starves because of a hurricane that strikes the area a few days later.
1560–1570	Leaders of the Cayuga, Mohawk, Oneida, Onondago, and Seneca tribes establish the Iroquois Confederacy.
1565, September 8	Pedro Menendez de Aviles, accompanied by 1,500 soldiers and colonists, establishes the town of St. Augustine, Florida. St. Augustine is the oldest constantly occupied European town in the United States. To secure his foothold in the area, de Aviles attacks the French settlements on the nearby St. Johns River.
1570, August 5	A Spanish colony expedition sails up the Chesapeake in Virginia, when they reach the area they will call Axaca somewhere near the Rappahannock. The locals will force the Spanish to abandon the effort.
1579, June 17	Sir Francis Drake lands north of San Francisco, probably at what is today called Drake's Bay, in California. He reports the Native peoples to be "people of a tractable, free and loving nature, without guile or treachery."
1585	Squanto (Tisquantum) is believed to have been born. Later in his life, he will be kidnapped and taken to Europe as a slave. When he finally makes his way back to North America, most of his tribe, the Patuxet, will have been killed by disease or conflict.
1585, July 16	After the first encounter between the Roanoke colony and the Algonquins in the village of Aquascogoc, in Hyde County North Carolina, colonists discover one of their silver cups is missing. On this date, led by colony Governor Ralph Lane, the colonists return to the Native village, and demand the return of the cup. When the cup is not returned, "we burned and spoiled all their corn" according to the governor's journal. This is one of the first significant conflicts in the area between the Europeans and the native inhabitants.
1598, December 3	Juan de Zaldivar "discovers" the Acoma pueblo. On December 4, the Spanish convince the Acoma to give them some flour. The Acoma are short of food themselves, but they decide to accommodate the Spaniards. One of the soldiers steals two turkeys and a fight breaks out. Thirteen of the nineteen Spaniards, including de Zaldivar, are killed.
1599, January	After some fighting, the Acoma surrender to Spanish forces seeking revenge for the killing of Juan de Zaldivar. Approximately five hundred are taken prisoner. Seventy Acoma will be tried by Juan de Oñate, Zaldivar's uncle.

1600	Franciscans establish missions in areas occupied by the Hopi (Arizona and New Mexico).
1600	Spanish kidnap Apaches, Navajos, and Utes in New Mexico to work as slaves in their fields and households. On many occasions, the Spaniards used Pueblo men to help them capture people from other tribes.
1600s	The Hurons (Wendat) begin to establish trade with the French. European men establish the settlement of Tadoussac (Quebec). They begin to inter-marry with the Native women. Most people believe this marks the begin-ning of the Metis culture in Canada.
1600s	Smallpox, carried by Europeans, continues to strike the Native people of North America.
1602	The Spanish Viceroy (Mexico City) names Sebastian Vizcaino as expedi-tion leader to seek out ports along the northern Pacific coast for the Spanish ships coming from the Philippines to Acapulco. Vizcaino leaves Acapulco on May 5 with three ships: the San Diego, the San Tomas, and the Tres Reyes. In mid-November he discovers a large bay that he names for his ship and the feast day of San Diego de Alcala. The first recognized Christian religious service in California will be held in what becomes San Diego. On December 1, he lands in what would become Los Angeles. On December 13, he enters Monterey Bay.
1607, February 9	There has been a long period of fighting between the tribes of the Powhatan Confederacy and the English colonists in Virginia. While lead-ing a Paspahegh war party near Jamestown, Chief Wochinchopunck is seen by the colonists. A fight ensues, and the chief is killed.
1609	Spanish land grants are given for the areas around Santa Fe, New Mexico.
1609	English settler John Smith is captured by the Powhatans. It is this episode that leads to the famed stories of Pocahontas' intercession for his life.
1609	Samuel de Champlain and a Wyandot (Huron) war party attack a larger group of Mohawks near Ticonderoga. Champlain has firearms, which make his small group more than a match for the Iroquois.
1616–1620	A massive pandemic spreads among the Native groups of New England. Smallpox, cholera, measles, and whooping cough are the most destructive of the diseases. Some entire tribal groups will die off. It is often called the Great Dying.
1620	Pilgrims on the Mayflower land at Plymouth Rock on December 21, 1620.
1621	Wampanoag Chief Massasoit signs a treaty with John Carver and gives lands to the Pilgrims.
1622	The first of a series of conflicts between the English settlers and the Powhatan Confederacy takes place. Opechancanough leads thirty-two of the Powhatans against the colonists at Jamestown, Virginia.
1622	Jesuits begin missionary work among the Hurons.
1626	An arrangement between New Netherlands Governor Peter Minuit and the Canarsees is reached to share land on Manhattan island. Mahicans and their Dutch allies battle the Iroquois Confederacy. The Iroquois win. The Dutch will all but abandon Fort Orange (Albany).
1633	Smallpox kills hundreds of Narragansett in New England.

1637   The Pequot War intensifies. European colonists join with other tribes to attack the main Pequot town near the Connecticut River. Almost five hundred Pequots are killed. Many of those who survive become slaves.

1640   First recorded contact with the Dakota Sioux by Jesuits occurs in the area of southern Minnesota and Wisconsin.

1644   Opechancanough, chief of the Powhatan Confederacy, stages his last attack on English settlers of Virginia. His eventual defeat leads to an end to the Powhatan Wars.

1653   During a series of battles over the next few years, the Iroquois overwhelm the Erie tribe.

1660   The Ojibwa (Chippewa) begin a migration into the Mississippi Valley. Having firearms from traders forces other tribes to move out of their way.

1675–1678   King Philip's (Metacomet) War against the English colonists takes place in Massachusetts and Rhode Island. Many people will be killed on both sides. The colonists will win the war.

1680   Led by Popé (Tewa), the Pueblo rebel against the Spanish in New Mexico and parts of Arizona. Most of the Spanish will flee the area until 1692.

1682   William Penn signs a treaty with the Delawares, giving the settlers land. Penn and the Quakers will have one of the few truly beneficial relationships with the indigenous people.

1687   La Salle meets some Comanches near Trinity River. This will be one of the first encounters between the French and the Comanche.

1688   Colonists and the Wabanaki battle in Maine as a part of King William's War.

1692–1696   The Spanish, under Diego de Vargas, begin their successful return to the American Southwest.

1700s   Many Native American tribes acquire horses. This leads many of them, especially the Comanche and the Lakota, to move into the Great Plains.

1700   Traditional Hopis attack and kill the male inhabitants of the Hopi village of Awatovi. The leaders of this village were friendly with the Spanish and developed a new system of leadership.

1701   In order to deal with the British colonists more effectively, the Passamaquoddy, Penobscot, Maliseet, and Micmac start taking steps to form a council known as the Wabanaki Confederacy.

1715   South Carolina settlers battle the Yamasee and several other groups of Native peoples. Many settlers are killed over the next several years and the natives regain some control over the area.

1721–1726   Lovewell's War takes place between the British colonists of Norridgewock, Kennebec, and Old Town, and the Wabanaki.

1724   Comanches fight a major battle with the Apache. The Comanches are victorious.

1730   Shoshonis on horseback attack a group of Blackfeet. This is the first time the Blackfeet have seen horses. The Blackfeet call horses "elk dogs."

1738   A smallpox epidemic strikes the Cherokee Nation. A large percentage of the Cherokees will die. Cherokee "Beloved Woman" Nancy Ward is born.

1744–1748	As part of King George's War, the English declare war on the Maliseets and Micmacs.
1754–1763	The French and Indian War takes place. It was the North American version of Europe's Seven Years' War. It pitted the British and their Native American allies against the French and their Native allies. A major battle took place at Fort Oswego, Fort Ticonderoga, and Fort William Henry. A large number of people were killed on both sides.
1763	Delaware Native leader Teedyuscung is killed when his cabin burns to the ground. There is considerable supposition as to whether it was other natives or the British who set the cabin on fire.
1766	A large conference is held in Oswego, New York. Ottawa Chief Pontiac is one of the major participants. He will eventually agree to a peace, which will end the uprising he initiated several years ago.
1769	The mission San Diego de Alcala is established by Franciscan friar Junipero Serra. It is be the first of twenty-one California missions.
1774	In the southern Ohio River Valley, a conflict breaks out between the local Shawnee and Mingo Natives and settlers and traders who have moved into the area. Lord Dunmore, governor of Virginia, leads a large group of soldiers into the area and deals a deadly blow to the Native forces.
1775	The Continental Congress establishes a Committee on Indian Affairs. Commissioners are appointed to negotiate peace treaties with the Native Americans.
1776–1778	James Cook of England explores the Pacific Northwest.
1778	The first treaty is signed between the U.S. federal government and a Native American nation, the Delaware.
1778	The Iroquois under Joseph Brandt (also spelled Brant) and British soldiers attack American settlers in the Cherry Valley and Wyoming Valley of New York and Pennsylvania.
1780–1800	Smallpox and measles epidemics break out among the Native peoples of Texas and New Mexico.
1781	A smallpox epidemic hits Blackfeet country, killing hundreds.
1782	Smallpox spreads among the Sanpoils tribe of Washington.
1782	The massacre at Gnadenhutten, Pennsylvania, takes place. Settlers attack a peaceful group of Christian Delaware Native Americans.
1786	The Cherokees sign the Treaty of Hopewell. This gives away a large percentage of their traditional homelands.
1786	The secretary of war takes over responsibility for Native matters for the U.S. federal government.
1787	The Northwest Ordinance is passed. Some of its provisions are for the establishment of dedicated Native lands. It also accelerates the settlement of the area by Europeans.
1790	Congress passes the Indian Trade and Intercourse Act. This act placed most interactions with Natives by non-Natives under federal control. It set some boundaries to Native land and regulated trade and the sale of alcohol.

1790–1794   Little Turtle's War takes place. Little Turtle is the primary leader of a group of Chipewa, Miami, Potawatomi, and Shawnee Indians. The war culminates in the Battle of Fallen Timbers in Ohio, where forces under Mad Anthony Wayne defeat the natives.

1791   The Cherokees sign the Treaty of Holston. It is their understanding that by ceding land in eastern Tennessee, the government will keep settlers out of their remaining lands.

1794   The Mohawk Native Americans sign a treaty that, among other things, allows them unrestricted rights to cross the United States-Canadian border.

1795   The Treaty of Greenville is signed by U.S. authorities and several tribal groups in Ohio. The Shawnee, and several other tribes, had been trying to maintain their tribal lands against the encroachment of European settlers. The Native Americans' defeat led them to sign this treaty that ceded much of their lands.

1796   The Penobscots sign a treaty with Massachusetts, giving up land. The federal government never ratified this agreement for jurisdictional reasons.

1802   Congress appropriates funds to "civilize and educate" Native Americans. Another law prohibits the sale of liquor to Native peoples.

1803   The Louisiana Purchase is acquired by Thomas Jefferson from France, adding vast lands to the United States. It also adds a large Native population.

1803–1806   Meriwether Lewis and William Clark explore large sections of the Louisiana Purchase. One of their jobs is to explain to the Native peoples they encounter that Washington, D.C., is the home of their "Great White Father."

1805–1820   Simon Fraser explores the river that now bears his name in British Columbia in Canada. He is the first white man to visit the Carrier tribe.

1809–1811   Shawnee Chief Tecumseh organizes a large confederacy of tribes to oppose the efforts of non-Native peoples to take over their land. In 1811, the natives are defeated by William Henry Harrison's forces at the Battle of Tippicanoe, which brings an end to many of Tecumseh's efforts.

1809   The Treaty of Fort Wayne is signed by William Henry Harrison and members of the Delaware, Potawatomi, and Miami tribes. The Native Americans cede almost 3 million acres of land in Ohio and Indiana.

1809–1821   Sequoyah single-handedly creates an eighty-five-character syllabic alphabet for the Cherokee language. He is the first illiterate person in recorded history to create an alphabet for his Native language. Sequoia trees are named for him.

1812–1841   Russians build and occupy Fort Ross in northwestern California. This is Pomo Indian country.

1813–1814   Members of the Creek Nation engage in a war with European settlers. Several other tribes join Andrew Jackson's forces in opposition to the "Red Stick" Creeks.

1816–1818   Andrew Jackson's forces attack groups of Seminoles in and around northern Florida. His efforts will have limited success, but they will lead the

Spanish to relinquish control of the area. This campaign is often called the First Seminole War.

1819–1824	Several skirmishes and meetings take place in an effort to get the Kickapoo to leave Illinois.
1823	In the *Johnson v. McIntosh* case, the Supreme Court decides that Native American tribes cannot sell land to anyone other than the federal government. The Court also decides that the U.S. government has rights to all Native lands by "rights of conquest."
1823, February	A Treaty between the Navajos and the Republic of Mexico is signed at Paguate.
1824	The Bureau of Indian Affairs is organized as part of the War Department. In 1832, it will be formally organized by an act of Congress.
1824	A constitution is enacted in Mexico. It guarantees equal citizenship to everyone under Mexican jurisdiction, including Native Americans in California.
1830	Congress passes the Indian Removal Act. This act requires the removal of southeastern Natives to native territory west of the Mississippi River.
1831–1839	The relocation begins of the southeastern tribes, as called for in the Indian Removal Act.
1831	The Cherokees resist removal to west of the Mississippi River by bringing a case before the Supreme Court based on previous treaties. The Supreme Court will rule for the Cherokees, but President Andrew Jackson will ignore the decision.
1832	Black Hawk, a Sauk chief, has attempted to get white settlers off his tribe's land. The settlers call up the Illinois and Wisconsin militia to support them. What will be called the Black Hawk War develops. The Sauk will eventually lose the war and their lands.
1833–1834	Prince Maximilian and the painter Karl Bodmer explore the upper Missouri River territory. Bodmer paints many pictures of the Native Americans they encounter.
1835, December 29	A small group of Cherokees sign the Treaty of New Echota. They agree to give up their lands in the east for money and lands west of the Mississippi River. A vast majority of Cherokees repudiate the treaty as not representing the tribe's true wishes. Despite a petition signed by the majority of the tribe stating they do not agree to the treaty, the U.S. Senate endorses the treaty.
1835–1842	The Second Seminole War takes place. The U.S. Army actively seeks to remove the Seminoles from their lands in Florida. The Seminoles resist. Great numbers of people are killed on both sides. On a percentage basis, this will be one of the most expensive wars in U.S. history.
1837	The Chickasaw sign the Treaty of Doaksville. This requires their removal to Native territory.
1837	A major smallpox epidemic strikes the tribes along the upper Missouri River. The Arikara, Blackfeet, and Hidatsa tribes are severely affected by the disease. Almost 99 percent of the Mandan are killed during this outbreak.

1838	The bulk of the Cherokees are finally forced to emigrate to Native territory. During the "Trail of Tears," as many as a quarter of the Cherokees will die.
1842	Seneca Natives, members of the Iroquois Confederation, move to the Allegheny and Cattaraugus Indian Reservations.
1843	The Russian-Greek Orthodox Church establishes the first mission school for Eskimos in Alaska.
1847–1850	The Cayuse Indian War takes place in Oregon. As was the case in many conflicts between indigenous people and settlers, this conflict was over land and the treatment of Native Americans by European settlers.
1847	The Yucatán Maya rise up against the Mexican government in the War of the Castes. For a few years, the Maya will regain control over much of the Yucatán.
1848, February 2	Mexico and the United States sign the Treaty of Guadalupe Hidalgo, which ends the Mexican War. Many southwestern tribes now come under the jurisdiction of the United States.
1849	The Courthouse Rebellion takes place in Canada. The Metis of the Red River will take part.
1850	The first of a series of treaties between Canada and Canadian tribes is signed. This process of trying to establish peace with all of the western tribes lasts until 1923.
1850–1851	The Mariposa War takes place in California primarily between gold rush miners and Miwoks and Yokuts.
1851	Many of the Plains Natives sign the Treaty of Fort Laramie. Large sections of land are set aside as reservations for these tribes.
1855–1856	The Yakima War takes place in Washington State. The Cayuse, Umatillas, Walla Walls, and the Yakama (as it is spelled now) take part in the fighting against government forces.
1855–1856	The Rogue River War takes place among settlers and local tribes in southern Oregon and northern California.
1855–1858	The third, and final, major conflict between the United States and the Seminole tribe takes place in the Florida Everglades. Seminoles under Chief Billy Bowlegs will eventually lose to the U.S. Army and be transported to Native territory.
1858	At Coeur d'Alene in Washington State, northern Paiute, Palouse, Spokane, and Yakima tribes battle settlers and the military in what will be called the Coeur d'Alene War or Spokane War.
1859	Native Americans on reservations in Texas are forced to leave the state.
1860–1864	A series of conflicts breakout between the U.S. military and the Navajo in what is now Arizona and New Mexico. The Navajos will lose the overall conflict.
1861–1865	During the Civil War, the Confederacy will actively recruit tribes in the South and in Native territory to join their cause. As inducements, the Confederacy offers possible concession on tribes' former lands and allows them to have representatives in the Confederate Congress. Many tribes

fight on both sides of the conflict. Cherokee Stand Watie will be the last Confederate general to surrender. Tribes that support the South will suffer great losses at the hands of the northern forces after the war ends.

1861–1863   There is a series of battles between Apaches and soldiers and settlers in the American southwest. The Apaches are led by Chiefs Cochise and Mangas Colorado.

1862   The Homestead Act opens up vast sections of Native land in Kansas and Nebraska to settlers. The average plot will cover 160 acres.

1862–1863   After a series of misunderstandings and disagreements over treaty provisions, the Santee Sioux revolt in Minnesota. Led by Chief Little Crow, they seize undistributed food supplies, and engage in several skirmishes with soldiers and settlers. On December 26, 1862, thirty-eight Sioux are hanged at Mankato, Minnesota. This will be the largest mass execution in U.S. history.

1863, January 29   California volunteers under Colonel Patrick E. Connor attack a camp of Shoshoni along the Bear River in Utah. The cause of the fighting was settlers on Shoshoni lands and Shoshonis raiding settlers. Almost three hundred Shoshonis are killed in the fighting. The soldiers lose twenty-three men. This is alternately called the Bear River Campaign, or the Bear River Massacre.

1864   After losing their battle with the U.S. Army, the Navajos are forced to give up their homelands along the Arizona-New Mexico border. Eight thousand Navajo men, women, and children are forced to march three hundred miles to the stark Bosque Redondo, near Fort Sumner in central New Mexico. Mescalero Apache are also moved to this reservation. The Navajos call the march the Long Walk. After signing a new treaty in 1868, the Navajos are allowed to return to their land.

1864–1865   A series of battles develop in Kansas and Colorado between the U.S. Army and the Cheyenne and Arapaho. These culminate in the massacre at Sand Creek on November 29, 1864. Black Kettle and his followers had been trying to avoid the fighting. They had sought the help of the Colorado government. At the government's request, they camped along Sand Creek. Soldiers under Colonel Chivington's Colorado Volunteers attack the camp at dawn and kill more than three hundred Native Americans. Black Kettle survives the fighting.

1866–1868   Despite treaty provisions to the contrary, the Bozeman Trail is developed through Native lands in Wyoming and Montana. Arapaho, Cheyenne, and Sioux warriors under Chief Red Cloud attack various locations and forts along the trail. Several forts will eventually be abandoned by the army.

1867   Arapahos and Cheyennes sign the Treaty of Medicine Lodge. They will receive lands in Native territory that was taken from those tribes who supported the South during the Civil War.

1868   The Sioux sign the second Treaty of Fort Laramie. Among other things, they are guaranteed the Black Hills region.

1868, November 27   Looking for a few Native Americans who had attacked settlements in Kansas, George Armstong Custer and the 7th Cavalry attack Black Kettle's camp of southern Cheyenne at dawn on the Washita River in Native territory. Custer will claim to have killed one hundred Native Americans, while losing only twenty-one soldiers.

1868–1869	The Southern Plains War takes place. This is an extended series of battles between the U.S. Army and Native Americans of the southern Great Plains. These tribes were primarily the Arapaho, Cheyenne, Comanche, Kiowa, and Sioux.
1869	Brigadier General Ely Parker (Donehogawa) served under Ulysses Grant during the Civil War. He wrote the final surrender papers signed by Grant and Robert E. Lee at Appomattox. In 1869, he becomes the first Native American to serve as the Commissioner of Indian Affairs.
1869	The First Riel Rebellion takes place in Canada. The Red River Metis are active participants.
1871	The Indian Appropriation Act is enacted. One of its provisions states that there will no longer be any treaties signed between Native tribes and the federal government.
1872–1873	In northern California and southern Oregon, the Modocs fight with settlers and the U.S. Army over land. One of their leaders, Captain Jack, is hanged for his actions during the war.
1874–1875	The Red River War takes place on the Southern Plains. General William T. Sherman's forces battle the Arapaho, Comanche, Cheyenne, and Kiowa tribes.
1876–1877	With the discovery of gold in the Black Hills (South Dakota) in 1874, prospectors and settlers have been pouring into lands set aside for the Cheyenne and Sioux. The Native peoples fight back. Many battles take place between the tribes and the U.S. Army. Some of the more notable battles are Battle of the Rosebud (June 17, 1876), Battle of the Little Big Horn (June 25, 1876), and Battle of Wolf Mountain (January 8, 1877).
1877, September 5	Crazy Horse is shot and killed while in U.S. custody at Fort Robinson, Nebraska.
1877	The Flight of the Nez Perce takes place under Chief Joseph. A series of events takes the Nez Perce from their traditional homelands in Idaho on a 1,500-mile trek through Idaho, Wyoming, and Montana. Their goal was to get away from soldiers who wanted to take them to a reservation. They fought a series of battles with the army and, while trying to make it to Canada, they finally lose a major battle and surrender at Bear Paw, Montana. They are just fifty miles from Canada.
1879	The Carlisle Indian School is founded in Pennsylvania. Its purpose is to assimilate Native peoples into white culture.
1881–1886	Geronimo and his Apache followers seek to elude the army in the American southwest. Geronimo eventually surrenders in 1886.
1885	The Second Riel Rebellion takes place along the Saskatchewan River in Canada. Metis and Cree Natives participate.
1887	Congress passes the General Allotment Act (the Dawes Act), in which reservation lands are given to individual Native Americans in parcels. The end result is that Native tribes lose millions of acres of land.
1890	The Ghost Dance movement sweeps across the tribes of the Great Plains. Paiute prophet Wovoka tells his followers the dance will help return Native Americans to the traditional ways and will make the white man disappear.

1890, December 29	Fearing the influence of the Ghost Dance, the army orders Native Americans to cease their participation and to return to their reservations. At Wounded Knee, on the Pine Ridge reservation, soldiers attack Big Foot's Sioux; 350 natives are killed.
1898	The Curtis Act is passed by Congress. Among other things, it will require the breakup of tribal lands in Native territory into small individual plots. This will have a staggering effect on the Cherokee, Creek, Choctaw, Chickasaw, and Seminole nations.
1900	The total Native American population in California drops to about 16,500 (11,800 of this number are considered "landless").
1901	Congress confers citizenship on all Native Americans in Native territories.
1903	In the *Lone Wolf v. Hickcock* case, the Supreme Court decides that Congress could override certain provisions of treaties.
1903	In southern California, the Cupenos are forcibly transported to the Pala reservation by Native agents in a three-day Trail of Tears. The Cupenos will eventually intermingle with the local Luiseño people.
1905	Comanche Chief Quanah Parker rides in President Theodore Roosevelt's Inaugural Parade in Washington, D.C.
1908	A Supreme Court decision in the *Winters v. United States* case determines that Native Americans have federally protected water rights.
1909	Red Cloud dies at Pine Ridge Agency.
1910	The U.S. Census reports that 2,268 Native Americans are living on the Blackfeet reservation, about the same number that lived there in 1885.
1910	The U.S. government forbids the Sun Dance of Plains Natives for reasons of self-torture.
1913	The "buffalo head" nickel is issued with Cheyenne, Seneca, and Sioux chiefs on one side of the coin.
1914–1918	During World War I, approximately 17,000 Native Americans enlist and fight for the United States. Some Indians resisted the draft because they were not citizens. In 1919, Native American veterans of the war were granted citizenship.
1917	For the first time in fifty years, Native American births exceed deaths.
1918	The Native American Church is organized in Oklahoma. It combines some traditional Christian beliefs with the Native practice of using the hallucinatory plant peyote. Many states will ban the use of peyote.
1924	Citizenship is granted to all remaining Native Americans who had not received it through prior treaties or legislation.
1930s	The Bureau of Indian Affairs (BIA) starts a process that will close many of the mandatory Native boarding schools. This allows Native children to attend nearby regular schools. The BIA also appropriates funding to teach Native languages at tribal schools.
1934	The Indian Reorganization Act (IRA) is passed by Congress, encouraging Native Americans to "recover" their cultural heritage. It allows the teaching of art in government Native schools and ends an allotment policy. In order to take advantage of funding under the IRA, tribes are required to

adopt a U.S.-style constitution. Some 174 tribes accept the act, 135 of which draft tribal constitutions. Seventy-eight tribes reject the IRA because of concerns of further federal mandates.

1937   The state of Maine offers free hunting and fishing licenses to the Passamaquoddy and Penobscot tribal members in recognition of their ancestral right to hunt and fish.

1941   During World War II, approximately 25,000 Native Americans serve in the armed forces. Many more worked in war-related industrial positions. Although several tribes participated in similar roles, the Comanche and Navajos took special roles as "Code Talkers." The Navajo Code Talkers saw service in the Pacific. The Comanche Code Talkers were in the D-Day Invasion and George S. Patton's tank battalions. Code Talkers developed sophisticated codes based on Native languages that withstood enemy efforts to decipher them.

1944   The National Congress of American Indians (NCAI) is organized. It is the nation's first large-scale national organization designed to monitor federal policies.

1946   The Indian Claims Commission Act is passed. The Commission was created to settle tribal grievances over treaty enforcement, resource management, and disputes between tribes and the U.S. government. Until the Commission ended operations in 1978, it settled 285 cases and paid more than $800 million in settlements.

1948   In the *Trujillo v. Garley* case, the Supreme Court decides that states are required to grant Native Americans the right to vote.

1953   The U.S. government begins a policy of tribal termination by withdrawing all federal support and recognition to several dozen tribes. This also involved the closing of some reservations and the relocation of Native peoples to urban areas. Over one hundred tribes were "terminated."

1953   Public Law 280 is passed. This congressional law transferred jurisdiction over most tribal lands to state governments in California, Oregon, Nebraska, Minnesota, and Wisconsin. Alaska was added in 1958. Additionally, it provided that any other state could assume such jurisdiction by passing a law or amending the state's constitution.

1954   As the last state to do so, Maine finally allows members of its two recognized tribes (Passamaquoddy and Penobscot) to vote in national elections.

1961   Over five hundred Native Americans gathered for the American Indian Chicago Conference to promote tribal sovereignty and survival. Later that year, a more militant organization called the National Indian Youth Council is formed. Many other Native organizations are formed throughout the 1960s, and they all sought an end to termination and relocation policies and demanded self-determination for Native peoples.

1968   N. Scott Momaday's *House Made of Dawn* wins the Pulitzer Prize. He is the first Native American to be so honored.

1968   The Civil Rights Act extends the Bill of Rights to reservation Natives; the decree says states cannot assume law-and-order jurisdiction without tribes' consent. Project Own is established so that Indians can open small businesses on the reservations.

1969   "Indians of All Tribes" occupy Alcatraz Island in San Francisco Bay. The jail had been abandoned. Their effort to bring light to the problems of Native Americans would last for two years.

1969   The American Indian Movement (AIM) is organized. It will act as a civil rights organization for Native Americans.

1969   Vine Deloria writes *Custer Died for Your Sins*.

1970   In a Special Message to Congress on Indian Affairs, President Richard M. Nixon called for the United States to break decisively with the past and create conditions for a new era in which the future of Native Americans would be determined by Native acts and decisions. He formally ends the termination policy.

1970   After sixty years of protest, the Sacred Blue Lake is returned to the Taos Pueblo.

1970   Dee Brown publishes the best-selling history *Bury My Heart at Wounded Knee*.

1972   A march to Washington, D.C., called The Trail of Broken Treaties, is organized by Native American activists. Its purpose is to air grievances and to get the U.S. government to allow tribal self-determination. Some marchers occupy the Bureau of Indian Affairs building.

1972   The Indian Education Act provides educational programs for Native Americans.

1972   The Passamaquoddy tribe and the Penobscot Nation file a lawsuit claiming 12.5 million acres of land had been taken from them in treaties that violated federal law (because they were not ratified by Congress). The land in question comprises more than two-thirds of the state of Maine.

1973   The occupation of Wounded Knee starts. Local Lakotas and American Indian Movement members stage a protest about political changes and economic problems on the Pine Ridge Reservation in South Dakota. The confrontation lasts seventy-one days.

1975   Two Federal Bureau of Investigation agents are killed while investigating a crime on the Pine Ridge reservation. American Indian Movement member Leonard Peltier is later convicted of the killings and sent to federal prison.

1975   The Indian Self-Determination Act is passed by Congress. Among its provisions are "the Congress hereby recognizes the obligation of the United States to respond to the strong expression of the Indian people for self-determination by assuring maximum Indian participation in the direction of educational as well as other Federal services to Indian communities so as to render such services more responsive to the needs and desires of those communities."

1978   The American Indian Freedom of Religion Act is passed by Congress. It promises to "protect and preserve for American Indians their inherent right of freedom to believe, express, and exercise" traditional religions, "including but not limited to access to sites, use and possession of sacred objects, and the freedom to worship through ceremonial and traditional rites."

1978   The Indian Child Welfare Act takes effect to address the practice of transferring the care and custody of Native children to non-Natives. Tribal courts have authority to hear the adoption and guardianship cases of Native children.

1979   All Montana public school teachers on or near Native reservations are required to have a background in Native American studies.

1980   The U.S. Census reports that the Native American population in the United States exceeds 1 million (1,418,195).

1980   President Jimmy Carter signs the Maine Indian Land Claims Settlement Act, which acknowledges that Congress never ratified treaties with Maine tribes.

1980   In the *United States v. Sioux Nation of Indians* case, the Supreme Court ruled that the Sioux were entitled to an award of $17.5 million, plus 5 percent interest per year since 1877. This amounts to $106 million for the illegal appropriation of the Black Hills. Sioux tribal councils have refused to accept the money, opting to hold out for the return of the land itself.

1983   The Barona Band of Kumeyaay Native Americans establishes the first tribal bingo hall in California.

1985   Wilma Mankiller, a Cherokee, becomes the first modern woman leader of the Cherokee Nation. Mankiller will serve in this position through 1995.

1988   Congress passes the Indian Gaming Regulatory Act (IGRA). This act affirmed the right of tribes to conduct gaming on Indian lands. Certain types of gaming require a compact between state and tribal authorities.

1990   Congress passes Public Law 101–644 to prevent the selling of "authentic" Native American art created by non-Natives.

1990   The Native American Languages Act is passed. This congressional act made it U.S. policy to "preserve, protect, and promote the rights and freedom of Native Americans to use, practice, and develop Native American languages."

1990   The Native American Grave Protection and Repatriation Act (NAGPRA) is passed by Congress. The act requires all institutions that receive federal funds to inventory their collections of Native human remains and artifacts, make their lists available to Native tribes, and return any items requested by the tribes.

1990   President George H.W. Bush approves a joint resolution designating November 1990 as National American Indian Heritage Month.

1992   The Mashantucket Pequots open the first large casino (Foxwood Casino) in the United States in Connecticut.

1992   Ben Nighthorse Campbell of Colorado becomes the first Native American elected to the U.S. Senate.

1994   The first of three planned facilities of the National Museum of the American Indian opens in New York City at the George Gustav Heye Center.

1996, July 28   Human skeletal remains are found in Kennewick, Washington. These ancient bones are often called the Kennewick Man, or the Ancient One. A controversy will ensue as to whom the remains should be given to—local tribal groups or archaeologists.

1997   The Corporation for Public Broadcasting establishes Native American Public Telecommunications, Inc. (NAPT), to promote, produce, and distribute Native American television and radio programming.

1998   The National Museum of the American Indian's Cultural Resources Center opens in Suitland, Maryland. It houses an extensive collection of Native American artifacts.

2000   California voters enact Proposition 1A. This constitutional amendment removes the legal blocks to expanded gaming facilities owned and operated by Native American tribes.

2004, September 21   The Smithsonian opens the main National Museum of the American Indian on the mall in Washington, D.C.

Phil Konstantin

This resource guide focuses on recent scholarly publications in the fields of Native American history, culture, and the prehistory of North America, with the addition of a few important classic works published since the 1970s. Included are a number of useful encyclopedias, biographical dictionaries, and other reference works as well as those works listed in the suggested readings following each chapter.

Abrams, Elliot M., and AnnCorinne Freter, eds. *The Emergence of the Moundbuilders: The Archaeology of Tribal Societies in Southeastern Ohio*. Athens, OH: Ohio University Press, 2005.

Akers, Donna. *Living in the Land of Death: The Choctaw Nation, 1830–1860*. East Lansing, MI: Michigan State University Press, 2004.

Ambler, Richard J. *Anasazi: Prehistoric Peoples of the Four Corners Region*. Flagstaff, AZ: Museum of Northern Arizona, 1989.

Axtell, James, ed. *The Indian Peoples of Eastern America: A Documentary History of the Sexes*. New York: Oxford University Press, 1981.

Barnes, Celia. *Native American Power in the United States, 1783–1795*. Madison, NJ: Fairleigh Dickinson University Press; London: Associated University Presses, 2003.

Bataille, Gretchen M., ed. *Native American Women: A Biographical Dictionary*. New York: Garland, 1993.

Biographical Dictionary of Indians of the Americas. Newport Beach, CA: American Indian Publishers, 1983.

Blanton, Dennis B., and Julia A. King, eds. *Indian and European Contact in Context: The Mid-Atlantic Region*. Gainesville, FL: University Press of Florida, 2004.

Bray, Tamara, ed. *The Future of the Past: Archaeologists, Native Americans, and Repatriation*. New York: Garland, 2001.

Brose, David S., C. Wesley Cowan, and Robert C. Mainfort, Jr., eds. *Societies in Eclipse: Archaeology of the Eastern Woodlands Indians, A.D. 1400–1700*. Washington, DC: Smithsonian Institution Press, 2001.

Bruchac, Joseph. *Return of the Sun: Native American Tales from the Northeast Woodlands* (illustrations by Gary Carpenter). Freedom, CA: Crossing Press, 1989.

Bruchac, Joseph, ed. *Returning the Gift: Poetry and Prose from the First North American Native Writer's Festival*. Tucson, AZ: University of Arizona Press, 1994.

Bruchac, Joseph, and Janet Witalec, eds. *Smoke Rising: The Native North American Literary Companion*. Detroit, MI: Visible Ink Press, 1995.

Brumble, H. David, III. *An Annotated Bibliography of American Indian and Eskimo Autobiographies*. Lincoln, NE: University of Nebraska Press, 1981.

Brumble, H. David, III. *American Indian Autobiography*. Berkeley, CA: University of California Press, 1988.

Champagne, Duane. *Native America: Portrait of the Peoples*. Detroit, MI: Visible Ink Press, 1994.

Chapman, Abraham, ed. *Literature of the American Indians: Views and Interpretations. A Gathering of Indian Memories, Symbolic Contexts, and Literary Criticism*. New York: New American Library, 1975.

Chet, Guy. *Conquering the American Wilderness: The Triumph of European Warfare in Colonial Northeast.* Amherst, MA: University of Massachusetts Press, 2003.

Clark, Ella Elizabeth. *Indian Legends of the Pacific Northwest* (illustrated by Robert Bruce Inverarity). Berkeley, CA: University of California Press, 1953 (2003 printing).

Cordell, Linda S. *Ancient Pueblo Peoples.* Washington, DC: Smithsonian Books, 1994.

Cordell, Linda S. *Archaeology of the Southwest.* New York: Academic Press, 1997.

Crown, Patricia L., and W. James Judge, eds. *Chaco and Hohokam: Prehistoric Regional Systems in the American Southwest.* Santa Fe, NM: School of American Research Press; Seattle, WA: Distributed by the University of Washington Press, 1991.

Deloria, Vine, Jr., *Red Earth, White Lie.* Golden, CO: Fulcrum, 1997.

Diamond, Jared, *Guns, Germs, and Steel.* New York: W.W. Norton, 1997.

Diaz-Granados, Carol, and James R. Duncan, eds. *The Rock-Art of Eastern North America: Capturing Images and Insight.* Tuscaloosa, AL: University of Alabama Press, 2004.

Dictionary of Indians of North America. St. Clair Shores, MI: Scholarly Press, 1978.

Dumond, Don E. *The Eskimos and Aleuts.* London: Thames and Hudson, 1987.

Dunmire, William W. *Gardens of New Spain: How Mediterranean Plants and Foods Changed America* (illustrated by Evangeline L. Dunmire). Austin, TX: University of Texas Press, 2004.

Dutton, Bertha Pauline. *Navahos and Apaches: The Athabascan Peoples.* Englewood Cliffs, NJ: Prentice-Hall, 1976.

Evers, Larry, and Ofelia Zepeda, eds. *Home Places: Contemporary Native American Writings from Sun Tracks.* Tucson, AZ: University of Arizona Press, 1995.

Feest, Christian F. *Indians of Northeastern North America.* Leiden, Netherlands: E.J. Brill, 1986.

Ferguson, William M. *Anasazi of Mesa Verde and the Four Corners.* Boulder, CO: University of Colorado Press, 1996.

Ferguson, William M., and Arthur H. Rohn. *Anasazi Ruins of the Southwest in Color.* Albuquerque, NM: University of New Mexico Press, 1987.

Fowler, Loretta. *The Columbia Guide to American Indians of the Great Plains.* New York: Columbia University Press, 2003.

Frazier, Kendrick. *People of Chaco: A Canyon and Its Culture.* New York: W.W. Norton, 1986.

Garroutte, Eva Marie. *Real Indians: Identity and the Survival of Native America.* Berkeley, CA: University of California Press, 2003.

Gibson, Jon L., and Philip J. Carr, eds. *Signs of Power: The Rise of Cultural Complexity in the Southeast.* Tuscaloosa, AL: University of Alabama Press, 2004.

Grande, Sandy. *Red Pedagogy: Native American Social and Political Thought.* Lanham, MD: Rowman and Littlefield, 2004.

Green, Rayna. *Native American Women: A Contextual Bibliography.* Bloomington, IN: Indiana University Press, 1983.

Grenier, John. *The First Way of War: American War Making on the Frontier, 1607–1814.* New York: Cambridge University Press, 2005.

Grounds, Richard A., George E. Tinker, and David E. Wilkins, eds. *Native Voices: American Indian Identity and Resistance.* Lawrence, KS: University Press of Kansas, 2003.

Grumet, Robert S., ed. *Northeastern Indian Lives, 1632–1816.* Amherst, MA: University of Massachusetts Press, 1996.

Gulliford, Andrew. *Sacred Objects and Sacred Places: Preserving Tribal Traditions.* Niwot, CO: University Press of Colorado, 2000.

Gumerman, George J. *The Anasazi in a Changing Environment.* New York: Cambridge University Press, 1988.

Gumerman, George J., ed. *Exploring the Hohokam: Prehistoric Desert Peoples of the American Southwest.* Dragoon, AZ: Amerind Foundation; Albuquerque, NM: University of New Mexico Press, 1991.

Gumerman, George J., and Dean, J. S. "Prehistoric Cooperation and Competition in the Western Anasazi Area." In Linda S. Cordell and George J. Gumerman, eds., *Dynamics of Southwest Prehistory* (pp. 99–137).Washington, DC: Smithsonian Press, 1989.

Hann, John H. *Indians of Central and South Florida, 1513–1763.* Gainesville, FL: University Press of Florida, 2003.

Hays, Hoffman Reynolds. *Children of the Raven: The Seven Indian Nations of the Northwest Coast.* New York: McGraw-Hill, 1975.

Hoxie, Frederick E., ed. *Encyclopedia of North American Indians.* New York: Houghton Mifflin, 1996.

Jones, David Shumway. *Rationalizing Epidemics: Meanings and Uses of American Indian Mortality since 1600.* Cambridge, MA: Harvard University Press, 2004.

Kennett, Douglas J. *The Island Chumash: Behavioral Ecology of a Maritime Society.* Berkeley, CA: University of California Press, 2005.

Kirk, Ruth. *Hunters of the Whale: An Adventure of Northwest Coast Archaeology* [with Richard D. Daugherty. Photos by Ruth and Louis Kirk]. New York: Morrow, 1974.

Klein, Barry T. *Reference Encyclopedia of the American Indian.* West Nyack, NY: Todd, 1995.

Kooyman, Brian, and Jane H. Kelley, eds. *Archaeology on the Edge: New Perspectives from the Northern Plains.* Calgary: University of Calgary Press, 2004.

Krech, Shepard. *The Ecological Indian: Myth and History.* New York: W.W. Norton, 1999

Krupat, Arnold, ed. *Native American Autobiography: An Anthology.* Madison, WI: University of Wisconsin Press, 1994.

Lenik, Edward J. *Picture Rocks: American Indian Rock Art in the Northeast Woodlands.* Hanover, NH: University Press of New England, 2002.

Lentz, David L., ed. *Imperfect Balance: Landscape Transformations in the Precolumbian Americas.* New York: Columbia University Press, 2000

Lister, Florence Cline. *Troweling through Time: The First Century of Mesa Verdean Archaeology.* Albuquerque, NM: University of New Mexico Press, 2004.

Lister, Robert Hill. *Those Who Came Before: Southwestern Archeology in the National Park System: Featuring Photographs from the George A. Grant Collection and a Portfolio by David Muench* (with Florence C. Lister; foreword by Emil W. Haury). Albuquerque, NM: University of New Mexico Press; Tucson, AZ: Southwest Parks and Monuments Association, 1994.

Littlefield, Daniel F., Jr., and James W. Parins. *A Bibliography of Native American Writers 1772–1924: A Supplement.* Metuchen, NJ: Scarecrow Press, 1985.

Loewen, James. *Lies My Teacher Told Me.* New York: Touchstone, 1996.

Mainfort, Robert C., and Lynne P. Sullivan, eds. *Ancient Earthen Enclosures of the Eastern Woodlands.* Gainesville, FL: University Press of Florida, 1998.

Mann, Barbara A. *Native Americans, Archaeologists and the Mounds* [foreword by Ward Churchill]. New York: P. Lang, 2003.

Matlock, Gary. *Enemy Ancestors: The Anasazi World with a Guide to Sites.* Flagstaff, AZ: Northland, 1988.

Matson, R. G., Gary Coupland, and Quentin Mackie, eds. *Emerging from the Mist: Studies in Northwest Coast Culture History.* Vancouver: UBC Press, 2003.

McHugh, Paul G. *Aboriginal Societies and the Common Law: A History of Sovereignty, Status, and Self-determination.* New York: Oxford University Press, 2004.

McNitt, Frank, and Richard Wetherill. *Anasazi.* Albuquerque, NM: University of New Mexico Press, 1957.

Morgan, William N. *Ancient Architecture of the Southwest* (foreword by Rina Swentzell). Austin, TX: University of Texas Press, 1994.

Morris, Theodore. *Florida's Lost Tribes* (with commentary by Jerald T. Milanich). Gainesville, FL: University Press of Florida, 2004.

Morrow, Baker H., and Price, V. B., eds. *Anasazi Architecture and American Design.* Albuquerque, NM: University of New Mexico Press, 1997.

Nassaney, Michael S., and Kenneth E. Sassaman, eds. *Native American Interactions: Multiscalar Analyses and Interpretations in the Eastern Woodlands.* Knoxville, TN: University of Tennessee Press, 1995.

Niatum, Duane, ed. *Harper's Anthology of 20th Century Native American Poetry.* San Francisco, CA: Harper andand Row, 1988.

Noble, David Grant. *In Search of Chaco: New Approaches to an Archaeological Enigma.* Santa Fe, NM: School of American Research Press, 2004.

Núñez Cabeza de Vaca, Alvar. *The Narrative of Cabeza de Vaca.* Edited, translated, and with an introduction by Rolena Adorno and Patrick Charles Pautz. Lincoln, NE: University of Nebraska Press, 2003.

O'Brien, Sean Michael. *In Bitterness and in Tears: Andrew Jackson's Destruction of the Creeks and Seminoles.* Westport, CT: Praeger, 2003.

O'Rourke, David K. *How America's First Settlers Invented Chattel Slavery Dehumanizing Native Americans and Africans with Language, Laws, Guns, and Religion.* New York: Peter Lang, 2005.

Owsley, Douglas W., and Rihard L. Jantz, eds. *Skeletal Biology in the Great Plains: Migration, Warfare, Health, and Subsistence.* Washington, DC: Smithsonian Institution Press, 1994.

Page, Jake. *Apacheria.* New York: Del Rey, 1998.

Page, Jake. *In the Hands of the Great Spirit: The 20,000 Year History of American Indians.* New York: Free Press, 2003.

Parker, Kay. *The Only True People: A History of the Native Americans of the Colorado Plateau.* Denver, CO: Thunder Mesa, 1991.

Pauketat, Timothy R. *Ancient Cahokia and the Mississippians.* New York: Cambridge University Press, 2004.

Plog, Stephen. *Ancient Peoples of the American Southwest.* London: Thames and Hudson, 1997.

Porter, Frank W., III, ed. *Strategies for Survival: American Indians in the Eastern United States* (foreword by Eugene Crawford). Westport, CT: Greenwood Press, 1986.

Riley, Patricia, ed. *Growing Up Native American: An Anthology.* New York: William Morrow, 1993.

Ritzenthaler, Robert Eugene. *The Woodland Indians of the Western Great Lakes* (with Pat Ritzenthaler). Milwaukee, WI: Milwaukee Public Museum, 1983.

Rothschild, Nan A. *Prehistoric Dimensions of Status: Gender and Age in Eastern North America.* New York: Garland, 1990.

Rothschild, Nan A. *Colonial Encounters in a Native American Landscape: The Spanish and Dutch in North America.* Washington, DC: Smithsonian Books, 2003.

Schobinger, Juan. *The Ancient Americans: A Reference Guide to the Art, Culture, and History of Pre-Columbian North and South America.* Armonk, NY: M.E. Sharpe, 2000.

Shoemaker, Nancy. *A Strange Likeness: Becoming Red and White in Eighteenth-Century North America.* New York: Oxford University Press, 2004.

Shutler, Richard, ed. *Early Man in the New World.* Thousand Oaks, CA: Sage Publications, 1983.

Silverberg, Robert. *Mound Builders of Ancient America: The Archaeology of a Myth.* Athens: Ohio University Press, 1986.

Stannard, David. *American Holocaust.* New York: Oxford University Press, 1993.

Stensland, Anna Lee. *Literature By and About the American Indian: An Annotated Bibliography.* Urbana, IL: National Council of Teachers of English, 1979.

Stuart, David E. *Anasazi America: Seventeen Centuries on the Road from Center Place.* Albuquerque, NM: University of New Mexico Press, 2000.

Stuart, Gene S. *America's Ancient Cities.* Washington, DC: National Geographic Society, 1988.

Swanton, John Reed. *The Indian Tribes of North America.* Baltimore, MD: Genealogical Publishing, 2003.

Tooker, Elisabeth, ed. *Native North American Spirituality of the Eastern Woodlands: Sacred Myths, Dreams, Visions, Speeches, Healing Formulas, Rituals, and Ceremonials.* New York: Paulist Press, 1979.

Trafzer, Clifford, ed. *Blue Dawn, Red Earth: New Native American Storytellers.* New York: Doubleday, 1996.

Underhill, Ruth M. *The Navajos.* Norman, OK: University of Oklahoma Press, 1989.

Vellie, Alan R, ed. *American Indian Literature: An Anthology.* Norman, OK: University of Oklahoma Press, 1991.

Vizenor, Gerald. *Native American Literature: A Brief Introduction and Anthology.* New York: HarperCollins, 1995.

Waldman, Carl. *Who Was Who in Native American History: Indians and Non-Indians from Early Contacts through 1900.* New York: Facts on File, 1990.

Walthall, John A. *Prehistoric Indians of the Southeast: Archaeology of Alabama and the Middle South.* Tuscaloosa, AL: University of Alabama Press, 1980.

Wesson, Cameron B. *Historical Dictionary of Early North America.* Lanham, MD: Scarecrow Press, 2005.

White, Phillip M., compiler. *Bibliography of Native American Bibliographies.* Westport, CT: Praeger, 2004.

Wiget, Andrew. *Native American Literature.* Boston: Twayne, 1985.

Wiget, Andrew, ed. *Dictionary of Native American Literature.* New York: Garland Publishing, 1994.

Wilkinson, Charles F. *Blood Struggle: The Rise of Modern Indian Nations.* New York: W.W. Norton, 2005.

Wills, W., H. *Early Prehistoric Agriculture in the American Southwest.* Santa Fe, NM: School of American Research Press, 1988.

Woodward, Susan L. with Jerry N. McDonald. *Indian Mounds of the Middle Ohio Valley: A Guide to Adena and Ohio Hopewell Sites.* Newark, OH: McDonald and Woodward, 1986.

Wright, Amos J. *Historic Indian Towns in Alabama, 1540–1838* (foreword by Vernon J. Knight, Jr.). Tuscaloosa, AL: University of Alabama Press, 2003.

Young, Biloine W. with Melvin L. Fowler. *Cahokia: The Great Native American Metropolis.* Urbana, IL: University of Illinois Press, 2000.

Index